The Troubled
Money Business

THE TROUBLED MONEY BUSINESS

The Death of an Old Order and the Rise of a New Order

Richard D. Crawford

William W. Sihler

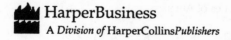

HarperBusiness
A Division of HarperCollinsPublishers

To Our Families

International Standard Book Number: 0–88730–515–6

Printed in the United States of America

91 92 93 94 SWD/HC 9 8 7 6 5 4 3 2 1

Contents

Exhibits

Preface

One way to judge the validity of an interpretation of history is to evaluate its consistency with information that subsequently comes to light. The same evaluative methodology applies to interpretations of current events, except that the corroborative evidence comes along much faster. It came along particularly rapidly as this book was being written with the newspaper containing at least one supportive item each day. The stream of relevant information continued and perhaps even increased in volume during the few weeks that this book was at the compositor.

We think our insights are withstanding this brief but vigorous test of time. For instance, the speed Congress was making earlier this year in dealing constructively with reforms of the financial system has slowed to a crawl. For reasons we discuss in Chapter 12, this was not a surprise; the surprise was that the initial progress was so constructive and so rapid. Unfortunately, no movement was made to address the questions we raise in Chapter 13 about fundamental revisions to the financial-services industry.

While Congress dallied, continuing to act as though the banking system were a natural monopoly, three major bank mergers were announced. NCNB Bank acquired C&S/Sovran with the intention of operating under the name NationsBank. This combination would have been the second-largest bank in the United States, but it was quickly eclipsed by Manufacturers Hanover Trust's merger with Chemical Bank under Chemical's name and by Security Pacific's agreement to merger with Bank of America.

These events confirm our interpretation in Chapter 3 of the

power of the marketplace and the need for bank consolidation to survive the demise of the increasingly weak, unnatural monopoly of the banking system. The announced reduction-in-force as a result of these three mergers is a big start toward the number of positions we expect to be squeezed out of the banking system over the next decade.

The scandals surrounding the Bank of Credit and Commerce International, which have stretched around the globe, reinforce our suggestion in Chapter 13 that the present regulatory structure weakens rather than strengthens regulatory ability and power. Perhaps the Salomon situation, a violation of the rules in bidding in the Treasury-bill auction, also fits this explanation. The effort of the Securities and Exchange Commission to assume an expanded role in regulating financial-services organizations, as it did when it began to regulate the assets of money-market mutual funds, may be enhanced in the fallout of the Salomon problem. Without a thorough reformulation of the regulatory structure, however, this will be another short-term solution of little long-term benefit, doing more harm than good.

The financial scandals in Japan illustrate a different problem–the increasing difficulty of using profits from a market in which a financial firm has a strong position to subsidize activities in a market in which competition is stronger. The rapid drop in Nomura Securities's share of Japanese stock market transactions from 33 percent to 8 percent dramatically demonstrates that the Japanese consumer does not like to be the source of a subsidy any more than investors elsewhere like it.

The U.S. insurance industry suffered its first "run" in memory on an insurance company during the summer of 1991, a more dramatic event than we had anticipated for this business. Rumors regarding the solvency of Mutual Benefit Life Insurance Company, which had conservatively avoided putting its #13 billion in assents into junk bonds but had been aggressive in real estate lending, panicked holders into cashing in their policies. An insurance company can no more pay off its policy holders all at once that a commercial bank can pay off all its depositors instantaneously. Mutual Benefit's directors therefore turned the company over to the New Jersey insurance regulators, who had the power to prohibit policy redemptions while the company's true situation was evaluated.

Insurance truly is not quite as sure, as we discuss in Chapter 4, although there was the good news that the policyholders of First Executive (which had been taken over by California authorities earlier in the year) may receive 85 percent of what they are due. The recovery depends in part on a French insurance company's buying in. Another French insurance firm is advancing its efforts to secure a controlling block of Equitable when Equitable converts from a mutual to a stock insurance company. We don't know enough about the insurance industry in France to understand why these investments appear attractive. The new infusion of capital is welcome and may postpone for a time greater federal regulation and support of the industry, which we think demographics make inevitable.

On the mutual fund scene, low short-term rates and an unusually step yield-curve are causing investors to move their funds out of money-market mutual funds. Declining rates have helped ensure that the funds have no trouble meeting the redemptions, but the cash is not returning to banks. Instead, it is moving to bond mutual funds as investors, particularly retired individuals (an increasing factor in the financial markets), seek out higher interest rates. This development is consistent with our interpretation of the fenceless financial markets and the continued erosion of the banks' special status. According to an article in *Forbes*, the Fidelity mutual fund group is now managing $137 billion in assets, up from the $100 billion figure when Chapter 6 was written.

One of our "case studies" in the news was Citicorp's residential mortgage program, described in Chapter 2. The strategy achieved its volume targets, but speculation exists about whether the quality of the portfolio has met expectations. The problem is said to result in part from applicants falsifying their financial information. It may also stem from the recession and the secular decline in the real value of real estate. The first problem in an administrative matter. The second will be corrected by the passage of time. The final element we identify as causing problems that may last a decade or more for the entire financial-services industry.

We do not deal with foreign capital markets, although they are clearly undergoing structural changes similar to those taking place in the United States. The consolidation in Japan has

perhaps been accelerated by rapid management changes occa-
sioned by recent scandals, but it has its foundation in doubtful
credit standards and a decline in real-estate values. The
Scandinavian financial-services industry, although not suffering
from scandal or fraud, had also been consolidating in the face of
freer competition, credit problems, and a real-estate collapse.

So far, therefore, events have been kind enough to reinforce
rather than to upset our insights. This gives us proof-of-the-
pudding confidence that our arguments will still be valid by the
time you, the reader, encounter them and should help you interpret money-business developments as they unfold in a period
of dramatic change.

Richard D. Crawford
William W. Sihler

Charlottesville, Virginia
September 7, 1991

Acknowledgments

This book grew out of the material developed for two new second-year MBA elective courses offered at the Darden Graduate Business School of the University of Virginia. Thanks are due to Dean John W. Rosenblum and to the Darden Graduate Business School Foundation for providing the released time from teaching and the funding to support the research for those courses. Thanks are also due to the many institutions and their officers who assisted in developing the material; where possible, these institutions have been indicated in the text, but the need to protect the confidentiality of sources has prevented explicit acknowledgment in some instances. Subsequent research assistance was provided by Brian D. L. Aaron and the trade associations of many components of the financial-services industry. Thomas C. Bomar, Anthony T. Enders, Richard B. Fisher, Robert J. Harrity, Jr., Paul H. Hunn, Garnett L. Keith, Robert A. G. Monks, P. Henry Mueller and S. Waite Rawls, III, read part or all of the manuscript and made many helpful suggestions. William E. Albrecht provided the information needed to construct Figure 12.1. Martha Jewett and James Childs, editors at HarperBusiness, nurtured the project throughout its gestation. Jon Ewing and Rosemary Winfield managed the editorial process. We acknowledge that despite the efforts of this distinguished group to correct our errors of fact and presentation, errors and infelicities will remain, for which we accept full responsibility.

I
THE DEATH OF THE OLD FINANCIAL SYSTEM

1

The Financial System in Crisis

Headlines in the 1980s told tales of change, great success, and great failure in the U.S. financial system. Corporate raiders, leveraged buyouts (LBOs), Michael Milken and junk bonds, the savings and loan debacle, the Resolution Trust Corporation (RTC) and the Federal Deposit Insurance Corporation (FDIC), and the failures of major banks were the subjects of recurrent front-page articles in the nation's newspapers. Instead of appearing only in specialized financial newspapers such as the *Wall Street Journal* and *Barrons*, stories about the activities of financial institutions turned up in general-circulation newspapers and magazines. For the first time in fifty years, the general public knew the names of important figures in the world of finance as investment bankers, such as Michael Milken and Ivan Boesky, and regulators, like Danny Wall and William Seidman, were highlighted in the evening news. And for the first time in fifty years, the public saw major financial figures going to jail and worried about the safety of its money.

Like the 1920s, the 1980s were a decade in which great riches were accumulated in the financial markets, and financiers

3

became cult heros. And like the 1920s, the 1980s ended with
financial institutions collapsing in record numbers. The public
was worrying about the future and wondered whether the
United States was about to enter a new depression after record
prosperity. Writers and publishers tried to capitalize on this
fear. Books about the predicted coming debacle had titles such
as *The Great Depression of 1990* and *Day of Reckoning*.

But the 1980s were not the 1920s. Despite the parallels, there
were significant differences in the problems of the financial system in each era. A major crash of the stock market during
October 1987 did not lead to a massively declining economy a
year later, as occurred after the crash of 1929. In fact, in 1990 the
stock market was about where it had been before the crash of
1987. The economy was in a recession, but unemployment was
at only 6 percent, compared to 23 percent at the beginning of
1933.

One parallel between the 1920s and the 1980s is that both
periods preceded massive restructurings of the financial system. In the early 1930s, the collapse of the banking system
under the weight of the Great Depression resulted in the financial legislation of the New Deal. This created an essentially new
financial system for the United States in which the federal government played a central role. In the early 1990s, the massive
problems of the thrift industry, the growing crisis of the commercial banks, and the incipient crisis in the insurance industry
promised that a massive restructuring of the financial system
would again occur.

The Dimensions of the Crisis

In early 1991, the dimensions of the crisis in the financial system
were enormous. Since 1980, the number of savings and loans
doing business had been cut in half, and most of the remaining
institutions were expected to disappear by the year 2000. The
cost to the U.S. Treasury of paying off depositors of defunct savings and loans was estimated to exceed $500 billion, ten times
the cost of the war with Iraq. The number of bank failures was
at its greatest level since the Great Depression, and it was estimated that only one out of six banks in business in 1980 would

still be in existence by the year 2000. The cost to the Treasury of paying off depositors of failed banks was expected to reach $20 billion, and pessimists predicted that it could eventually rival the cost of the savings and loan problems.

For the insurance industry, 40 percent of the companies in existence in 1991 were predicted to be gone by the year 2000. No estimates had been made of the cost to the Treasury of the insurance-industry problems. Although obligations of insurance companies were not covered by federal guarantees, as were the deposits of savings and loans and commercial banks, the Pension Guarantee Corporation might have contingent liabilities should an insurance company fail. There already was growing talk of bringing the insurance business under the umbrella of federal protection, which could result in future costs. In addition, the securities industry had been in its own bear market despite a rising Dow-Jones average, with an overall industry loss recorded of $101 million for 1990, the first loss in eighteen years. Employment in the industry was down 20 percent from three years before. By 1991, as a result of these measures of the economy, profitability rates had recovered to pre-1987 levels.

To address the crisis of the savings and loan industry, in 1989 the Congress passed major legislation—the Financial Institutions Reform, Recovery, and Enforcement Act (FIRREA)—which was expected to stabilize the industry after almost a decade of growing problems. This legislation transferred the responsibility for regulating and insuring the savings and loan industry to the Treasury and the Federal Deposit Insurance Corporation, respectively, from its historical regulator, the Federal Home Loan Bank Board (FLHBB), and its insurer, the Federal Savings and Loan Insurance Corporation (FSLIC). It was expected that the larger staff and more professional qualifications of the Treasury and the FDIC would be able to handle problems that the FHLBB and the FSLIC apparently could not. In addition, the 1989 legislation set up the Resolution Trust Corporation (RTC) to sell the assets of failed savings and loans and recover for the government the money it had spent paying off insured depositors.

By early 1991, it was apparent that the 1989 legislation had not solved the problems of the savings and loan industry.

Losses were still growing. The RTC was continually in need of new funding and was finding it difficult to sell the assets of defunct savings and loans. And after having been specifically directed in the legislation to use the resources of the private sector to the maximum, the RTC had created one of the largest agency staffs in the federal government. Private contractors increasingly complained to Congress that it was almost impossible to do business with the RTC.

The Treasury Reacts to the Growing Crisis: The 1991 Proposals

In February 1991, the probability of massive restructuring of the financial system in the 1990s increased when the Bush administration released a 648-page study of the problems of the thrift industry and the commercial banking system. The report was the product of a three-year study by the Treasury Department under the guidance of Secretary Brady and represented intensive work by some of the best minds of the financial-services industry and academia. An extended discussion of this report appears in Chapter 13. A brief summary is provided here as background for the intervening chapters. The study recommended major changes to the regulatory structure that had been put in place by the New Deal, including the following:

- Abolish the 1933 Glass-Steagall Act's separation of banks from securities firms. Financial holding companies with banking subsidiaries could be owned by nonfinancial corporations.
- Allow banks to operate nationwide branch systems.
- Restrict the coverage of federal deposit insurance. The number of insured accounts that an individual could hold in one bank would be limited, bank-failure standards would be changed to curtail coverage of deposits above $100,000, and coverage of all brokered deposits would end.
- Link regulation more directly to capital, and encourage banks to hold more capital (such as common-stock equity, preferred stock, and loan-loss reserves) as a cushion against failure.

• Simplify bank regulation by establishing a new Federal Banking Agency within the Treasury to regulate all nationally chartered banks and savings and loans. The Federal Reserve would regulate all state-chartered banking organizations, and each banking organization would have only one federal regulator. The FDIC would function solely as an insurer.

The Treasury proposals of February 1991 were both expected and controversial. Many had been debated for several years, but the growing crisis of the financial system created increasing pressure for action. Congressional leaders recognized the need to reform the financial systems' laws but also expressed skepticism of many of the specifics of the Treasury's proposals. Many congressmen worried that enacting the Treasury's proposals would lead to a repeat of the results of deregulating the savings and loan industry in the early 1980s. At that time, the administration and supporters of the legislation in Congress had promised that deregulation would lead to a healthier savings and loan industry as it diversified into real estate development and commercial banking. Instead, losses in the thrift industry increased, with many losses coming from the newly diversified activities.

Congressional skepticism, as well as the expectation of a massive lobbying effort by various segments of the financial-services community, guaranteed that the Treasury's proposals would face a difficult time in Congress and that the financial system's crisis would continue to plague the nation for the foreseeable future.

The Roots of Crisis: A Changing Financial System

What caused this crisis, and where is the financial system headed? The problems that made the financial system newsworthy in the 1980s and early 1990s resulted not from a declining economy but from a changing financial system. This book tells the story of that changing financial system.

Our examination of the roots of the crisis reviews key segments of the financial-services industry and discusses a variety of companies in the industry. We suggest that the crisis was not

Figure 1.1

Financial Assets Held by Depository Institutions as a Percentage of Total
Financial Sector Assets, 1900–2000 (projection)

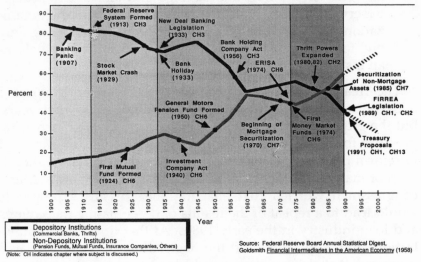

Depository Institutions
(Commercial Banks, Thrifts)
Non-Depository Institutions
(Pension Funds, Mutual Funds, Insurance Companies, Others)
(Note: CH indicates chapter where subject is discussed.)

Source: Federal Reserve Board Annual Statistical Digest,
Goldsmith Financial Intermediaries in the American Economy (1958)

caused by a collapsing underlying economy, as occurred in the 1930s. It was created instead by the passing of an old, now inefficient financial system while a new, more efficient system was growing up. Essentially, the traditional financial system—composed of commercial banks, savings and loans, insurance companies, and investment banks—is being replaced by a new financial system composed of pension funds, mutual funds, the financial subsidiaries of nonfinancial companies, and investment-management companies.

Figure 1.1 shows the changing share of financial assets held by various financial companies in the United States since 1900. As this figure shows, the market share of traditional financial institutions has been eroding steadily in recent years. The problems and losses of thrifts, banks, and insurance companies are the death pangs of the old system. The traditional roles of these institutions are being supplanted by pension funds and mutual funds. Figures 1.2 and 1.3 show how pension funds and mutual funds have expanded relative to depository institutions.

We show that much of the government's effort to contain the financial system crisis only subsidizes the old, inefficient system at a tremendous cost to the taxpayer. In effect, efforts to main-

Figure 1.2
Total Assets of Different Types of
Financial Institutions, 1940–2000 (projected)

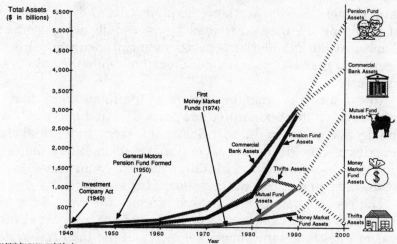

*Includes totals for money market funds

Source: U.S. Department of Commerce, Bureau of Census (commercial bank and thrift data); Office of Thrift Supervision (1990 thrift data); U.S. Department of Labor (pension data); 1990 Mutual Fund Fact Book, Investment Company Institute (Washington, D.C. 1991), authors' projections.

Figure 1.3
Number of Commercial Banks, Thrifts, Mutual Funds, and
Money Market Funds, 1940–2000 (projected)

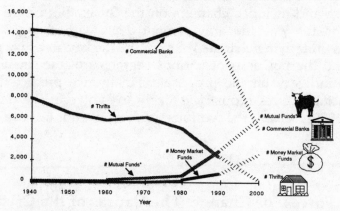

*Includes totals for money market funds

Source: U.S. Department of Commerce, Bureau of Census (commercial bank and thrift data); Office of Thrift Supervision (1990 thrift data); 1990 Mutual Fund Fact Book, Investment Company Institute (Washington, D.C. 1991), authors' projections.

tain the old financial system resemble the efforts of the federal government over the last sixty years to maintain the family farm. Hundreds of billions of dollars in agricultural subsidies have not prevented the demise of the family farm throughout rural America but have massively misallocated the nation's resources without lasting benefit to the farm families and small farm owners. Similarly, the tremendous cost to the government of propping up the old financial system will not prevent the demise of the familiar traditional financial institutions; it will result in a massive resource misallocation while the shift is taking place.

To examine the changing nature of the financial system, we have divided this book into three parts. The first part deals with the decline of the traditional financial system. Individual chapters discuss the decline of several major segments of the financial-services industry, including thrifts, commercial banks, insurance companies, and investment banks.

The second part of the book addresses the rise of the new financial system. Chapters look at the growth of pension funds and mutual funds into major segments of the financial system, the growing securitization of loans of all types and its implications for the financial system, the development of financial futures and options markets, the re-creation of a global capital market, and the rise of the investment-management industry.

The final part of the book looks at the future of the financial system and includes chapters on the forces that create change and on the way that government deals with change and the forces underlying change. We examine the key Treasury proposals and the positions of various segments of the financial-services industry on the proposals. Finally, we predict how the financial-services industry is likely to evolve in the decade of the 1990s, given the various economic and political forces impacting it.

Forces for Change: The Causes of the Crisis

Throughout this book we develop several major themes to explore the forces for change that have weakened the old financial system. Through these themes we present a clear vision of the financial system and how it works. One set of themes is derived from variables external to the financial system—factors such as demography. Another set of themes is related to structural elements—the structure of U.S. domestic financial institutions, the domestic financial system in its international setting, and the government's response to the system's problem.

External Themes

The first external theme is macroeconomic and the easiest to assess—*demographics*. Most of the individuals whose needs will influence the structure of financial institutions over the next quarter century are alive today. Barring a major military catastrophy, population composition over this period can be derived with considerable certainty. In most industrial countries of the world, it is an aging population whose savings and consumption patterns will change considerably. We show how these significant changes will affect the shape of the financial markets.

Related indirectly to demographics is another major macroeconomic theme—*increased use of debt*. Particularly over the last ten years, the use of debt has deviated considerably from the proportions previously maintained by most components of the U.S. economy. In part this change was caused as members of the baby boom moved into the family formation stage, which traditionally is the time of heaviest individual use of debt. Governments, likewise, attempting to provide infrastructure for this population growth, financed it with promises to pay when a more mature stage of development would be reached. The creation of debt at these high levels has had a major impact on the financial markets.

Restoration of a more traditional capital structure will require a series of actions by individuals, corporations, and governmental units, actions with a profound potential impact on the components of the financial markets. We discuss how major elements of the financial-services industry, particularly depository institutions, will be affected as a traditional capital structure is restored. Since the assets of depository institutions are the debts of others, reducing the overall level of the nation's debt will decrease the demand for the services of depository institutions.

It is more difficult to evaluate the third major external theme—*technology*. Technology—especially the high-speed computer—has contributed to creating the strains suffered by the financial system in recent years. A discussion of the financial system as an information system and the revolution in information technology as it affects the financial system is therefore central to an exploration of the crisis of the old system. We look at several issues related to the information-technology revolution and suggest the need for a new structure for the industry reflecting technological reality. For example, the traditional correspondent-banking system can be replaced by an integrated organization built around a computer network. The information-technology revolution makes entry into the financial-services industry easy for information companies (such as AT&T) or companies with a strong information base (such as Sears, General Motors, General Electric, and Ford).

We explain how economies of scale in information gathering increase efficiency while turning financial-services products into commodities. We also show how information technology is stimulating innovation in financial services and is re-creating an integrated global financial system. We analyze how information technology is creating a new electronic money with cash eventually being replaced by a prepaid debit card (such as the one currently issued by the Japanese telephone company). And finally, we explore the ultimate merger of financial and information industries; with products such as the AT&T Universal Card, we will soon be able to access our bank accounts by phone and use private codes to direct payments. Several financial institutions already offer services of this type through the Prodigy network, a joint venture of IBM and Sears.

Structural Themes

Our first structural theme is the effect the *legal structure* of the industry has had on the competitive situation. We discuss how the financial industry, and particularly banking, has historically been a set of legal monopolies, as opposed to natural monopolies, and the implications of that fact. For example, the changing technology of an industry undercuts a legal monopoly as new participants seek a way to tap monopolistic profits. We also suggest that a natural monopoly may be emerging in some areas of the financial-services industry and will require a new type of regulation.

A second structural theme emphasizes the *constructive effects of competition*, the positive (although painful in the short term) side of social Darwinism. Throughout the book, we note how the problems of the financial system reflect Joseph Schumpeter's theory of capitalism's creative destruction as an old, now-inefficient system passes and a new, more-efficient system emerges. We also show how individuals and investment banks, brokerage firms, and commercial banks have profited from this process of transition through loan securitization, commercial paper, credit cards, and money-market funds.

The *effects of international financial markets* on the U.S. system represent a third structural theme. An informative examination of the U.S. financial system cannot be limited to the United States but must integrate the international aspects of the financial system. One significant trend affecting the financial-services industry and the financial system of the United States is that the world's capital markets are moving toward becoming a single, integrated global market. This evolution is of historic significance. National capital markets have been separate for most of the time since 1930, with investment levels and interest rates in individual countries determined by the savings rate, investment activity, and overall governmental policy of each country. The current globalization of finance is a return to the type of structure that existed when the London capital market financed the bulk of international investment and capital in the form of the British pound flowed freely throughout the world.

Today's globalization of finance is different from the global financial system of the British empire, however, because regional markets share data instantaneously, much faster than it used to be shared even between institutions at adjacent addresses in London. This critical fact is shaping the evolution of a global capital market. As modern electronics eliminates cash and checks as primary monetary instruments, it dramatically increases the speed at which information can be moved. With modern communications, it now takes eleven seconds to post a bank transaction from one part of the globe to any other part of the globe. Money is information in motion, and the advent of a global communications network has created a single global capital market in which money is transferred around the world at virtually the speed of light at the touch of a computer button.

As twenty-four-hour trading systems are put in place, the global market is becoming further integrated. Interest rates and stock yields are increasingly moving toward a single global level, and global savings rates determine local interest rates: the cost of a U.S. home mortgage is directly related to the savings rate in Japan.

Along with a single global level of interest rates, a second result of the increasingly interconnected global economy is that new capital markets rival the size and importance of those in the United States. The most important of these are the Euromarkets centered in London and the Japanese market centered in Tokyo. Because of its phenomenal success as an exporter, Japan has become the leading international lender, replacing the role played first by Britain and then by the United States, and Tokyo has become a sophisticated financial center on a par with London and New York.

Major stock markets also exist in Australia, Hong Kong, Singapore, and in several cities in Europe, including Paris, Frankfurt, Milan, and Madrid. Minor stock markets exist in a range of Third World countries, including South Korea, Taiwan, the Philippines, Thailand, Indonesia, India, Brazil, Mexico, Argentina, Chile, Nigeria, and Jordan. Modern communications increasingly tie these individual stock markets into a global system, although the New York, European, and Japanese markets continue to be the central global markets.

Our fourth and final structural theme is that *government typically acts as the guardian of the financial status quo,* responding to crises that result from a changing economy but seldom initiating changes. Furthermore, government's response generally reduces the efficiency of the economy and increases the cost of transforming the financial system. We discuss how the U.S. government's response is generally shaped by a political debate over power—whether power should be centralized or decentralized. Intertwined with the power debate are debates on the benefits of stability versus the benefits of innovation and on the socialization of risk (that is, who pays for uninsurable risks). The conclusion is that government resists change and moves, like the San Andreas fault, only when immense pressures build up.

The Outcome of the Crisis: A New Financial System

In the final part of the book, we discuss the future of the financial system. A natural monopoly is emerging in financial services because of information technology, and we consider its implications, particularly for the depository system. We also discuss issues such as the effect of the new system on costs and innovation and on safety and the role of the traditional intermediary; the role of new-form intermediaries: such as the pension fund and mutual fund; and the "too big to fail" doctrine.

In Chapter 2, we begin our discussion of the changing financial system by looking at the thrift industry—and how America received its first warnings of the crisis in the financial system.

2

It's Not a Wonderful Life: The Demise of the Savings and Loans

By early 1991, the problems of the thrift industry reached crisis proportions. The number of savings and loans (S&Ls) and the level of their deposits had declined, but the industry seemed unable to stem its losses. In addition, the Resolution Trust Corporation (RTC) had been unsuccessful in selling real estate taken over by the government from failed thrifts, and the government's cost to insure the deposits of failed thrifts was estimated to be at least in the $500 billion range. The thrift crisis had become the biggest financial debacle in the history of the United States. For a government that faced growing deficits and increasing pressure to restrain spending, the cost of the thrift bailout represented a massive diversion of resources. The estimated cost of the bailout is equal to two years of the Department of Defense's total budget or fifty years of annual federal aid to education.

Beyond its financial repercussions, the S&L crisis has generated political fallout as well. The Keating Five episode—in which five U.S. Senators allegedly used their influence to reduce the pressure federal regulators were putting on Charles Keating—tarnished the Senate's reputation. Several members of the House Banking Committee lost their reelection bids in 1990. These political problems were compounded by the popular perception that much of the crisis had been caused by criminal activity, although more fundamental forces were actually at work. Front-page news stories, particularly those about Lincoln Savings and Loan's Charles Keating and Vernon Savings and Loan's Don Dixon, inflamed the public. In 1989 and 1990 alone, the Justice Department won convictions of 403 people for savings and loan fraud, including seventy-eight directors or officers, which strengthened the perception of widespread criminal activity. The image of the savings and loan executive had changed dramatically from that of the good guy portrayed by Jimmy Stewart in the movie *It's a Wonderful Life*.

Meanwhile, Congress faced continued requests by the RTC for short-term funds to close insolvent thrifts so their losses and ultimate cost to the government could be contained. In March 1991, the RTC indicated that it had already spent most of the $106 billion appropriated for it in fiscal year 1990 to 1991. It asked for an additional $30 billion to continue operating until October and to handle the 192 institutions it was already responsible for and the additional 225 thrifts expected to fail in 1991. Adding to the pressure on Congress was the administration's estimate that each day of delay in acting on the request added $8 million to the total cost of the bailout. Clearly, the problems of the savings and loans had steadily worsened since 1989, even though they were supposedly under control. They threatened to haunt the president and Congress in the coming 1992 election.

In early 1989, the Federal Savings and Loan Insurance Corporation (FSLIC), which insured the deposits of thrifts, lacked the funds to close all insolvent thrifts and pay off depositors. Many bankrupt thrifts therefore continued to operate and generate losses. Because of these losses (estimated at $15 billion annually) and the fact that one-third of the nation's 3,000 thrifts were either insolvent or on the brink of insolvency, some analysts predicted that the total cost to solve the thrift crisis could exceed $100 billion.

Newly elected President Bush's proposal—a major overhaul of the regulatory environment for thrifts—planned for shifting thrift supervision from the Federal Home Loan Bank Board to the FDIC and for higher capital and higher deposit insurance premiums for thrifts. President Bush's plan was enacted into law in August 1989 as the Financial Institution Recovery, Reform, and Enforcement Act of 1989 (FIRREA), but by early 1991 it was clear that the plan had not stemmed the problems of the thrift industry.

Losses continued to mount, and thrift failures grew. The industry was steadily shrinking in terms of both deposits and operating institutions. There had been a steady withdrawal of deposits from the industry for two and a half years, with the industry losing deposits in every month but one since mid-1988. In 1989 the thrift industry lost $61 billion in deposits, and in 1990 the figure grew to $93 billion. In fact, the growing crisis was a major factor in the comprehensive Treasury proposals in February 1991 for an overhaul of the financial system.

THE THRIFT CRISIS IS A FAMILY MATTER

For the Bush family, the thrift crisis is a family matter. Not only has federal government policy under President Bush earmarked large outlays for the savings and loan bailout, but the President's son Neil is involved in the crisis. Neil served as a director of Silverado Savings and Loan in Denver, Colorado, which was one of the largest thrift failures of the 1980s. When the thrift failed, Neil was charged by the FDIC with conflict of interest in carrying out his responsibilities as a director. Specifically, he was charged with helping two investors in his oil exploration company obtain loans from Silverado. Though he was ultimately given the minimum penalty (being directed to refrain from such conduct in the future), Neil's involvement was a political embarrassment for President Bush and illustrates the hazard of being related to a prominent political figure. He received a lot of negative publicity and was subject to a congressional inquiry into his actions, with hostile questioning from Democratic members, though his actions may have been very minor violations.

The thrift crisis is the most visible symptom of a need to massively overhaul the U.S. financial system. At the beginning of 1991, the outlook for the financial-services industry was mixed. Although the overall demand for financial services was expected to grow in the 1990s and to continue to increase its share of GNP (having already increased its GNP share from 2.3 percent in 1948 to over 5 percent in 1989), profitability of the industry was predicted to be poor because of overcapacity.

Beyond the problem of overcapacity, the financial-services industry was expected to be buffeted by several forces for change in the 1990s: rapidly evolving computer technology was reshaping the economics of financial-services operations, and continuing deregulation and changing regulation of the industry were radically reshaping the external environment in which financial-services companies operated.

In the next sections, we review the history of the thrift industry and explore the role played by a weakening real estate market in its decline. We then examine new competitors for the thrift industry's customers, specifically Citicorp's expansion into the mortgage business. Finally, we study Great Western Bank as a model of a successful savings and loan and offer the case of Ford financial services as a cautionary tale.

The Thrift Industry

Understanding the problems of the thrift industry means understanding its history. The thrift industry traces its origins to the friendly societies of England, which date from the sixteenth century, and to the mutual self-help organizations founded in the first half of the nineteenth century in the United States. The first savings and loan was founded in 1831 in Frankford, Pennsylvania. The Oxford Provident Building Association provided a mechanism for shareholders to pool their savings so they would be able to finance the purchase or construction of a home. These organizations grew and expanded like their cousins, the commercial banks, as industrialization made possible economic growth in the late nineteenth and early twentieth centuries.

At the beginning of the Great Depression, the primary method of home financing was the short-term, rollover mortgage, which was repaid or refinanced every five years. The inability of homeowners to refinance or roll over these mortgages in the 1930s was a major factor in the severity of the Great Depression. After numerous failures in the early years of the Depression, thrifts became the cornerstone of Franklin Roosevelt's New Deal reforms and his effort to revive the economy. The New Deal created a new system of housing finance to achieve three goals: stimulating the overall economy by stimulating home construction, promoting home ownership as a way of increasing social stability and welfare, and eliminating the threat to the financial system posed by short-term, rollover mortgages.

The key legislation of the New Deal was the National Housing Act of 1934, which established the Federal Housing Administration (FHA). Two major goals of the National Housing Act were to revive mortgage lending by private institutions and to develop the long-term mortgage market. The Roosevelt administration sought to achieve these goals by providing two types of federal insurance: mortgage insurance would encourage financial institutions to make more mortgages and lengthen their maturity (thus avoiding the problem of short-term rollover mortgages); and deposit insurance would encourage customers to deposit more funds in financial institutions. These funds would then be used to make mortgages.

Before the Great Depression, mortgage insurance had been provided by private mortgage-insurance companies. The failure of the majority of these companies in the early 1930s led New Deal lawmakers to provide for federal mortgage insurance through the National Housing Act. The FHA established a program of insurance for long-term, thirty-year mortgages that was intended to eliminate the use of short-term, rollover mortgages as the primary means of financing housing.

The number of runs on financial institutions at the beginning of the Depression led to a general consensus that deposit insurance was needed for all financial institutions that took public deposits. The New Deal set up the FSLIC to provide this insurance for savings and loans. Established by the National

Housing Act of 1934 as part of the Federal Home Loan Bank System (which Congress had established in 1932 as a type of Federal Reserve System for thrifts), the FSLIC played the same role for thrifts that the FDIC played for commercial banks.

Until 1979, this system of housing finance accomplished its objectives. After World War II, returning veterans, aided by FHA- and VA-insured mortgages, bought new homes in record numbers. The economy boomed, stimulated by massive home building and the popularity of Detroit's affordable automobile. America moved to new suburbs that sprouted up around the country, and the thirty-year fixed mortgage became a staple of American life. The thrift industry thrived, as providing home mortgages became one of the easiest and most lucrative businesses in the United States.

Occasional problems occurred with the availability of money for home mortgages, but by and large the system worked. To remedy occasional illiquidity in the mortgage system, Congress created the Federal National Mortgage Association (known colloquially as Fannie Mae) as part of the original New Deal Legislation. This institution was to create a secondary market for mortgages originated by thrifts. Thrifts wishing to lighten their portfolios could sell mortgages to Fannie Mae, which would issue its own bonds to the public to raise the money to pay for the mortgages. This set of transactions served to inject additional funds into the housing finance system in times of tight money, and it was so successful that in 1968 the Government National Mortgage Association (Ginnie Mae) and in 1970 the Federal Home Loan Mortgage Corporation (Freddie Mac) were created to accomplish the same purpose. Both Fannie Mae and Freddie Mac are now publicly owned companies but enjoy government-agency status when borrowing. The three agencies have multiplied the methods by which they raise funds to support real estate and have been leaders in creating securitized instruments, as will be outlined in Chapter 7.

In the early 1970s, warnings of potential trouble in the thrift system, because of the thrifts' practice of borrowing short-term deposits and lending them for long-term mortgages, were for the most part ignored. Hearings in Congress on the subject in 1974 produced no action.

AN EARLY WARNING SYSTEM THAT DIDN'T WORK

As in the Pearl Harbor catastrophe at the beginning of World War II, there were early signs of a crisis in the thrift industry. From the late 1960s to the late 1980s, various administrations had received warnings from Congress and from respected experts about flaws in the thrift system and predictions of future problems. These warnings, if properly acted on, could have reduced the scope of the disaster. Like Pearl Harbor, however, the warnings were ignored.

For example, the Commission on Financial Structure & Regulation (the Hunt Commission) in 1971 proposed allowing S&Ls to convert to commercial bank status. At hearings in Congress in 1974, Thomas Bomar, chairman of the Federal Home Loan Bank Board, warned that the thrift industry's practice of taking in short-term deposits to fund long-term mortgages would lead to a future crisis. The Congress took no action, and Bomar's fears came true in the period 1980 to 1982 when very high short-term interest rates caused massive losses for the thrift industry. These losses then led Congress to expand thrift lending powers in legislation passed in 1980 and 1982, which ultimately led to even greater losses for the thrifts from soured real-estate investments and bad loans for commercial properties like office buildings and shopping centers.

In the early 1980s, Burt Ely, a bankruptcy expert, claimed that the entire thrift industry was headed for bankruptcy. These claims, which were printed in the media and included in testimony to Congress (and were increasingly echoed by other experts as the decade passed), went unheeded until Ely's predictions began to prove correct in the late 1980s. Then as losses mounted, the Bush administration and the Congress rushed to pass the Financial Institution Reform and Recovery Enforcement Act of 1989.

In 1990 R. Dan Brumbaugh, an economist who was an early predictor of the thrift crisis, started to predict a similar crisis for the commercial banks.

However, it was clear there would be future problems. Each recession in the 1960s and 1970s brought inverted yield curves in which thrifts lost money borrowing short and lending long. They also saw an overall level of interest rates that was higher each time than the previous recovery, causing losses on their fixed-rate mortgage portfolios. Then in 1979, Paul Volcker and the Federal Reserve System dramatically tightened the money supply to reduce inflation, which was threatening to spiral out of control, and triggered a rapid run up in interest rates to record levels. With most of their assets carrying fixed interest rates but their liabilities carrying the dramatically increasing costs of rising interest rates, thrift institutions experienced record losses.

As a way out of their dilemma, the thrifts sought new powers from Congress. The thrifts saw their salvation in competing with commercial banks for consumer and commercial loans, particularly for commercial mortgages. Congress agreed and overhauled the New Deal legislation to allow the thrifts to operate like commercial banks and real estate developers.

Unfortunately, the thrift-reform legislation of 1980 and 1982 did not solve the industry's basic problems—the effect of a complete maturity mismatch between deposits (borrowings) and loans. Throughout the 1980s, the thrift industry continued to lose money and shrink in size despite support from the Federal Home Loan Bank Board. From 4,000 institutions at the beginning of 1980, the thrift industry had shrunk to less than 2,700 by the end of 1990. Total thrift assets increased over the decade because of inflation, but growth leveled off and was beginning to decline. In 1989, in response to the thrifts' continuing problems, Congress passed FIRREA, the thrift-bailout bill, which forced S&Ls to meet the capital requirements imposed by FIRREA or be subject to closure. Because the industry had no real net worth and continued to experience losses, however, further reduction in the industry was expected to continue throughout the 1990s as bankrupt S&Ls go out of business.

Space for Sale: The Real Estate Debacle of the 1990s

Of particular interest in the thrift-reform legislation of 1980 and 1982 was the new power of thrifts to lend on and invest in commercial real estate. These functions had been very profitable for commercial banks (as construction lenders) and insurance companies (as long-term lenders and investors) during the 1970s. Thrifts believed they could safely compete in the commercial area because of their lending experience in the residential market.

Ultimately, the thrifts' expectations for success in commercial real estate lending were not realized. In fact, a major cause of their decline in the 1980s and 1990s was the weakening of real estate markets in many parts of the United States. Demand for both residential and commercial real estate is expected to continue to fall in the 1990s, resulting in yet a further slide in the markets for developing and financing real estate. By early 1991, the lack of demand in the commercial real estate market had already seriously affected the thrift industry. After being battered by negative interest spreads on their home mortgage portfolios in the early 1980s, the thrifts were hammered by losses in the late 1980s and early 1990s in their loan and investment portfolios in commercial and multifamily real estate.

In seeking to expand their commercial real estate lending, the thrifts failed to recognize two conditions that would thwart their hopes. First, lending to and investing in commercial real estate was significantly more difficult and risky than investing in residential mortgages. (Commercial banks had temporarily learned this lesson in the mid-1970s after they experienced significant losses in commercial real estate loans from overeager lending on new projects and to real estate investment trusts.) Second, the success of commercial real estate in the 1970s was related to unusual market factors that changed in the 1980s.

Beginning in the late 1960s, the U.S. economy was transformed from an industrial to an information-and-service economy. Between 1970 and 1985—as a result of job growth in service sectors such as computers, medicine, accounting, law, education, finance, insurance, real estate, and government— more than 22 million white-collar jobs were added to the economy, a 45 percent increase. Simultaneously, women entered the workforce in unprecedented numbers. The growing information economy and increasing numbers of working women created a tidal wave of demand for new office space and other types of commercial real estate. During this fifteen-year period, the square footage of occupied office space more than doubled, while the U.S. population increased only 17 percent.

In addition, the changing economy and society led to a surge in housing demand. Between 1970 and 1985, the number of individual households increased 40 percent (more than double the rate of growth for the population as a whole), and over 24 million new housing units were constructed, expanding the housing stock by more than one-third. This dramatic growth in households was the result of a variety of social and demographic factors, including an increasing proportion of women working, higher divorce and lower marriage rates, and the aging of the population.

As with commercial real estate, the U.S. housing market was forecasted to decline. By 1988 housing starts had dropped from their 1986 peak of 1.8 million units, and new household formations and real annual growth of residential investment in the 1990s are expected to decline from the levels of the 1970s and 1980s. Residential investment is expected to shrink from 5 percent of GNP in 1988 to 3.9 percent in the year 2000. In fact, the decline in housing demand is expected to be so dramatic in the 1990s and thereafter that a 1989 study for the National Bureau of Economic Research predicted that housing prices would fall 47 percent in real terms by the year 2007.

As the housing market declines, so too will the residential mortgage market. From 1986 to 1988, residential mortgage originations fell from $455 billion to $374 billion. Future reductions in housing starts indicate further declines in residential mortgage originations. After building capacity to meet demand for mortgage refinancings as interest rates dropped, the mortgage-banking industry is expected to have severe overcapacity in the 1990s. Although the mortgage-banking industry consolidated throughout the 1980s as thrifts and commercial banks purchased independent mortgage bankers, further consolidation is expected in the 1990s.

The Big Get Bigger: The Story of Citicorp Mortgage

As the thrift industry encountered difficulties in entering the commercial market and sustaining its position in residential real estate, it also faced strong new competitors in mortgage originations. These included the mortgage operations of major commercial banks and nonfinancial companies such as General Motors. Historically, the thrift industry had been the largest source of mortgage loans in the United States, but by 1989 that situation had changed. Securitization of mortgage loans had transformed the thrifts' basic business, and the industry was in the process of dramatic consolidation, which was expected to be accelerated by legislation proposed to solve the problems of insolvent thrifts. Competition was growing also, however, as illustrated by the story of Citicorp's expansion into the mortgage business.

In 1978 Citicorp was essentially a nonplayer in the national mortgage market (the corporation's mortgage portfolio in the New York branch system totaled less than $100 million). Within ten years it became the largest mortgage lender in the country, originating 35 percent more loans than its next largest competitor. Its $14.8 billion in new mortgages earned it a 3.3 percent share of the $450 billion mortgage market. Furthermore, in 1988 Citicorp's chairman, John Reed, stated a goal of originating 10 percent of all new mortgages in the country by 1992. Clearly, Citicorp posed a major competitive threat to the thrift industry.

At the end of 1988, Citicorp was the largest financial-services organization in the United States and the preeminent global financial institution, with 89,000 employees in ninety countries covering virtually all marketplaces in the world. Citicorp divided its worldwide operations into three core businesses—the Individual Bank, the Institutional Bank, the Investment Bank. The Institutional Bank and the Investment Bank served corporations (ranging from local to multinational businesses), governments, and financial institutions worldwide; the Individual Bank served consumers' financial needs worldwide. Citicorp's U.S. mortgage activities were part of its Individual Bank. From its formation in 1976, the Individual Bank grew rapidly, as staff expanded from 18,000 to 66,000 by 1988. Worldwide assets reached $104 billion, and Citicorp became the largest U.S. MasterCard and VISA-card issuer, with 18.2 million cards in use. Earnings of the Individual Bank grew from nearly zero in 1981 to $667 million in 1988. Citicorp's stated objective for the Individual Bank was to achieve $1 billion in earnings by 1992.

Citicorp's U.S. consumer banking franchise gave it a nationwide presence in thirty-nine states with over 800 offices. Nationally, Citicorp competed with broad, single-product companies, while its local competitors were small banks or thrifts with established customer relationships. Citicorp's consumer banking strategy was to create a special relationship with its customers through superior service, which would create brand loyalty and a large enough franchise to make technological economies of scale feasible. A central element of this strategy was to be close enough to customers to have superior responsiveness compared to the competition. With its eleven banks and S&Ls in nine states and the District of Columbia—markets that represented a third of the total U.S. consumer-deposit base—Citicorp had over 570 branches and 1,500 Citi-owned automatic teller machines (ATMs).

A New Approach to Mortgage Lending

Citicorp's expansion into the mortgage business during the 1980s is a story of aggressive innovation. In 1979, because usury laws in New York limited mortgage rates to a maximum of 8.5 percent, the mortgage business was not attractive to lenders. To find a way to charge market rates for mortgages, Citicorp located an old interpretation of a federal law that permitted a national lender to charge the higher of the state mortgage rate or 5 percent over the federal discount rate. Although it was unclear whether the federal regulation would supersede state usury laws that specifically prohibited an economic mortgage rate, Citicorp implemented a pricing policy based on the more generous interpretation. Despite a penalty for being wrong that was twice the interest paid on every loan plus interest for thirty years, other national lenders quickly followed Citibank's lead. This step essentially provided Citicorp with entrée into the New York mortgage business.

Because Citicorp was new in the mortgage business and had never sold loans to the Federal National Mortgage Association and the Federal Home Loan Mortgage Corporation, it felt no need to conform its process to the existing secondary markets. Instead, it asked the applicant only for the minimal information needed to make a credit decision. The theory behind Citicorp's limited documentation was that individuals who purchased homes for their own occupancy and put significant equity at risk would do a more detailed and cautious analysis than Citicorp could achieve through a simplistic ratio exercise.

This minimum-documentation approach was particularly effective in a new program for financing individual co-op and condominium units under a "bulk liquidity" commitment to builders and converters. The bulk program was an instant success, producing $6 billion of commitments on more than 1,000 projects over a three-year period. Citicorp packaged the features that it developed for simple mortgage processing (low or no documentation) into a commitment format for realtors and mortgage brokers. Its first commitments were for $2 million to $3 million, and realtors paid fees for the funds committed. Like an insurance policy, these were guarantees of availability, but the pricing structure apparently discouraged use of these funds.

A membership approach, introduced in 1981, proved effective in maintaining long-term relationships with customers and in encouraging volume. In addition to the standard features of the program, Citicorp added preappraisal, preapproval, and stretch in lieu of private mortgage insurance. There was minimal budgeting, formal strategic plan, or dedication of resources to the MortgagePower effort. There was simply the mortgage division's vision of how the mortgage business should operate. The program was initially sold through meetings with large numbers of realtors and brokers at corporate headquarters where the program was outlined and participants signed up. It was an instant success.

As volume grew, Citicorp increased staff in the regional centers to support it. The program was self-funding from the start, with account executives added only after membership grew to sustain the cost of additional managers. Citicorp relied on mass meetings with members twice a year to introduce enhancements that provided higher levels of service. The program's range of services quickly outpaced those available from any other single source.

In spring 1982, a special promotion with lower origination fees for MortgagePower clients was introduced to differentiate the program further from Citicorp's walk-in business. The lower origination fee was not purely a marketing tool. It reflected the cost savings associated with the MortgagePower program, which were passed on to the consumer to build business. The program had expanded by then to over 4,000 realtors, mortgage brokers, builders, and major corporations (for their employees), each paying a membership fee. The program was introduced nationally in 1986, and the results were very successful. By 1987, in New York and New Jersey, where the program originated, Citicorp's market share was well in excess of 10 percent.

The service dimensions of this business were extraordinary. In 1988, Citicorp's mortgage sales network was represented in thirty-seven states and had a branch-based presence in thirty-two consumer markets. A national center in St. Louis was used to originate, service, and package mortgage securities for sale to the secondary market. It processed 142,000 mortgage applications with a total volume of $18 billion, and it packaged and sold 56,000 mortgages with a volume of $5 billion. It serviced 564,000 mortgages with a volume of $51 billion, which required 1 million customer-service contacts and 7 million customer statements. In 1988 Citicorp serviced about 3 percent of the country's outstanding mortgages, which the Federal Reserve estimated to be $1,846 billion.

Citicorp also aimed to take full advantage of its internal synergies. For example, although Citicorp used several outside investment banks to sell its securitized mortgage product, it derived substantial benefits from working with its own Investment Bank. In 1988, the Investment Bank sold about a third of Citicorp's mortgage product. The sales force's insights about the appetite and needs of the investor community helped put Citicorp in a position to originate tailored, geographically diverse, or specific mortgages.

Attractions for the Consumer

Citicorp and many other lenders believed that the most efficient and convenient way to originate a mortgage was at point of sale or as close to it as possible. Citicorp therefore interacted with the customer locally. In every Citicorp local marketplace the customer could reach it through several channels—its branch network; a sales network of 5,000 real estate brokers, lawyers, insurance agents, and mortgage banks; its mortgage sales offices; and (increasingly) through its point-of-sale (POS) terminal capability. The POS (MortgagePower Plus) effort, which offered fifteen-minute mortgage approvals, gave realtors on-line access to qualifying the customer. This feature was initially available to network members in only three states but was to be gradually expanded.

To apply for a MortgagePower loan, a home buyer visited one of the brokers or other members of the network, who helped the buyer fill out the short application for the loan. Citicorp guaranteed a response within fifteen business days for standard MortgagePower appliers, about half the industry average. If the network member was equipped to connect to the MortgagePower Plus computer system, the response could be obtained in fifteen minutes. If a buyer used the MortgagePower program, the origination fee would be one point less than the origination fee paid by the buyer going directly to Citicorp.

In addition to the origination fee, homebuyer might have to pay an additional fee (usually 0.5 percent of the loan) to the member of the MortgagePower network who assisted with the application. This fee was paid directly by the consumer to the realtor or mortgage broker for the provision of mortgage-banking services. This fee was not paid or processed by Citicorp. Typically, independent mortgage broker members charged a fee, while less than half of realtor members did. In effect, those members who charged a fee counseled the customer, packaged the supporting material, and followed through to closing.

To protect the consumer, Citicorp required that brokers who charged fees had to disclose up front the services provided and had to have consumers sign a statement acknowledging that Citicorp did not require any fee to be paid. If a fee was being charged, Citicorp would not accept an application without this disclosure and further would not permit the payment of a fee out of closing proceeds. Because Citicorp would close promptly under MortgagePower terms and conditions whether or not any fee was paid by the consumer, it was feasible that a consumer who was not satisfied with a broker's service would simply close the loan and not pay the fee. At that point, the burden of proof was on the member to justify the fee being charged and to reconcile any differences with the consumer.

Citicorp's MortgagePower was not without its critics—primarily from competitors; customers expressed high satisfaction. Although the MortgagePower representative was also the home buyer's real estate agent in only about 15 percent of the cases, critics of the program complained of conflict of interest. They also charged that the representative's fee was an illegal kickback under the 1974 Real Estate Practices Act. Citicorp had apparently successfully protected itself against this complaint by receiving a favorable legal opinion from the U.S. Department of Housing and Urban Development.

Citicorp management further believed that the realtor did not have a conflict of interest in representing the seller for the home and the buyer for the mortgage. The two services were congruent; it was in the interest of all three parties that the financing be obtained with certainty and speed. The three parties essentially wanted the buyer to be in a new home as quickly as possible at a competitive price.

Citicorp's growth in the mortgage market depended more on the speed and quality of its service than on the cost of its mortgages, which were not always the cheapest in the market. This did not mean that it was not competitive on price, however. Pricing varied from market to market and from loan type to loan type. Citicorp was particularly competitive in the nonconforming category with which it did most of its lending. Its jumbo loans were in the lowest 10 to 20 percent of the range of price competition.

Citicorp's success has clearly taken volume from existing channels, compounding the overcapacity problem created by a slumping volume. During the 1990s, Citicorp's mortgage operations should pose an increasing threat to thrifts because of the economies of scale associated with advanced computer technology. Most of the processing of MortgagePower loans in 1988 was still being done manually. Citicorp's new MortgagePower Plus computer technology, which was initially being used in New York, Pennsylvania, and New Jersey, could give Citicorp a significant edge in future mortgage lending. This product was available in the three states that generated about half the system's volume, but it was being expanded at a cost of about $20 million a year. By reducing the cost of processing mortgage loans, the new technology would allow Citicorp to compete as effectively on price as it was competing on service.

COMPUTERS AND MORTGAGES

The mortgage origination business in the United States is increasingly being conducted by computers. After a false start in the early 1980s, when several computerized mortgage origination systems failed, more and more of the mortgage originations in the United States are being handled by computerized loan origination systems (CLOs) that link real estate agents to bankers and mortgage services. A number of large real estate firms have developed such systems, including Century 21 Real Estate, ERA Realty, Coldwell Banker Real Estate Group, and Prudential Real Estate Affiliates (a subsidiary of the Prudential

Insurance Corporation). As these systems give homebuyers access to national mortgage lenders directly through their real estate agents, they will make business more difficult for local mortgage lenders.

The implications to the thrifts of the growth of national mortgage lenders like Citicorp are clear. As Citicorp's expansion is matched by other nonthrift mortgage lenders like Prudential Insurance Company, General Motors Acceptance Corporation, and Sears financial-services activities, there will be less and less business for the thrifts and other traditional players. In a market that is shrinking because of changing demographics, it will be increasingly difficult for the thrifts to compete with national mortgage lenders that enjoy technological economies of scale. Faced with a smaller market and an increasing market share going to other types of lenders, more thrifts will be forced out of business.

John Wayne Rides Again: The Story of Great Western

Savings and loans have adopted a variety of strategies to deal with the growing pressures on their traditional activities. One model for the changing thrift industry is Great Western Bank. As one of the most successful thrifts, Great Western is generally cited as a potential survivor of the industry demise. Its strategy for survival and success calls for its transformation into a specialized commercial bank.

Great Western Bank was the third-largest thrift organization in the United States at the end of 1988, with $33 billion in assets. Its four primary lines of business—real estate finance, mortgage banking, retail banking, and consumer finance—delivered services through a network of over 880 offices in twenty-nine states. This financial strength was unusual among the more than 3,000 thrifts in the country. With substantially more capital than required by regulatory guidelines and continuing profitability, Great Western was highly regarded by the rating agencies and investment-banking community: its bonds were rated A, and its ability to raise significant levels of additional capital in the form of debt or equity was unquestioned.

The financial-services environment that Great Western faced in 1989 was one of rapid change, increasing competition, and growing risk. Forecasts for the 1990s called for dramatic consolidation of the depository industry and the evolution of nationwide banking. Great Western's home state of California, which accounted for over 75 percent of its business, would open to all U.S. depository institutions in 1991. At the same time, accelerating securitization of a wide range of bank loans, including mortgages, auto loans, and credit card receivables, was changing the industry's economics and dynamics. Increasing competition and growing overcapacity in the industry were shrinking margins on most financial-services products. Compounding the dynamic and uncertain nature of the financial-services environment were changing demographics in Great Western's consumer markets: as the population aged, shifts in basic borrowing and savings patterns were occurring.

To be a survivor in the expected consolidation of the industry, Great Western management decided to deliver distinctive competence in selected market niches. Great Western's strategy was to concentrate its corporate resources on selected market segments in which it could be a very strong or the strongest player and in which it could achieve a competitive edge through low costs based on economy-of-scale efficiencies. Great Western's four core businesses—real estate finance, mortgage banking, retail banking, and consumer finance—had been selected because Great Western believed it had or could attain the competitive edge necessary for success. Besides concentrating its resources on core businesses, Great Western also concentrated its corporate resources geographically. Despite the large number of states in which it had offices, over 90 percent of Great Western's activities were located in five key states—California, Arizona, Washington, Florida, and New York.

Industry Becomes Thrifty But Then Thinks Better of It: The Story of Ford Financial Services

The powers given the thrifts to expand into new markets attracted the attention of players from outside the industry, such as the Ford Motor Company. Ford's objective was to position itself in the mass consumer market for financial services as a low-cost, quality-conscious player. Its strategy had three basic components: to invest in businesses that offered middle-income consumers and business firms new options for obtaining financial services; to increase its value to customers by emphasizing excellence and productivity; and to reduce the cost of financial services by applying Ford's experience in running a large, efficient business.

The Ford Financial Services Group's broad strategy called for it to leverage its strengths, which included its large size and existing customer base (4.5 million retail customers), its reputation, its advanced loan-processing capability, its borrowing capabilities, and its nationwide presence. To take advantage of its size and management strength, the Financial Services Group planned to make selective acquisitions in the S&L industry and other financial-services sectors to become the dominant player in the sector, thereby giving it economies of scale. In implementing its acquisition program, the Financial Services Group could utilize Ford's very strong cash position: at the end of 1988, Ford had $11 billion in cash, one of the largest cash positions of any U.S. corporation.

A key component in this strategy was First Nationwide Financial Corporation, the second-largest thrift in the United States at the end of 1988. It had $35 billion in assets, 8,000 employees, and 330 branches in fifteen states. Founded in 1885 in San Francisco, First Nationwide was acquired by Ford Motor Company in August 1985 as the nucleus of its effort to become the largest thrift owner in the country. Various expansion efforts being planned or implemented by First Nationwide at the end of 1988 included the opening of convenience branches in K-Mart stores, the First Nationwide Network (an affiliation of fifty-three independent financial institutions in thirty-eight states sharing common products and services), TranSouth Financial Corporation (a consumer-finance company with 166 offices in eight states in the southeastern United States), and an acquisition program involving both healthy and troubled S&Ls.

At the end of 1988 the Ford Financial Services Group also included the Ford credit and insurance subsidiaries, First Nationwide Financial Corporation, and U.S. Leasing International, Inc. The largest component was Ford Credit, followed by

First Nationwide and U.S. Leasing. Ford Motor Credit was the world's second-largest finance company at the end of 1988. It had $56.3 billion in assets, 8,500 dealer customers, 4.7 million retail customers, 10,000 employees, and 274 offices. Its activities were primarily involved with financing the sale and purchase of Ford Motor vehicles, ranging from direct auto loans and dealer floor plans to insurance. Ford Credit provided 67 percent of the wholesale (i.e., dealer) financing and 39 percent of the retail financing of Ford products in the United States. Ford Credit also financed non–Ford-related business such as leveraged leases of commercial aircraft and electric generating plants. It even provided construction financing for a prison for the state of Alaska. If Ford Motor Credit had been a commercial bank instead of a finance company, it would have ranked among the top ten in the country in terms of asset size. It was also extremely profitable, earning $679 million in net income on revenues of $5.8 billion.

Ford acquired U.S. Leasing in 1987. With assets of $4 billion and 2,000 employees at the end of 1988, U.S. Leasing was the oldest equipment-leasing specialist in the United States. Products leased included business systems and office equipment, automotive fleets, scientific instrumentation, aircraft, railroad rolling stock, and medical equipment.

Implementation of Ford's financial-services strategy in 1988 was not totally successful. After-tax profits for the Financial Services Group declined for the first time since 1974, falling from $858 million in 1987 to $691 million in 1988. Management attributed this decline to lower interest margins and higher credit losses. Of particular significance was the decline in First Nationwide Financial Corporation's net income from $60 million in 1987 to $3 million in 1988. Management attributed this drop to lower net-interest margins as a result of rising rates and the costs associated with rapid expansion (First Nationwide doubled in size in 1988).

While profits were declining, Ford encountered difficulty in making financial acquisitions. It had made a serious but unsuccessful bid to acquire the $30 billion asset American Savings, the second-largest thrift in the country, from the FSLIC. The FSLIC, which had assumed control of the deeply troubled thrift, rejected Ford in favor of the Robert M. Bass Group, Inc., of

Dallas on the grounds of Ford's slow decision-making process and the Bass Group's greater willingness to accept "normal business risk."

The loss of its bid for American Savings marked a turning point in Ford's financial strategy. It started buying consumer and industrial finance businesses, such as The Associates, for which it paid Paramount Communications $3.35 billion in mid-1989. Ford thereby acquired the third-largest independent finance company in the United States, with assets of $14 billion. In June 1991, Ford announced plans to offer MasterCards or VISA credit cards to customers who had bought or leased a Ford vehicle during the previous three years. It planned to offer cardholders purchase rebates 50 percent greater than Sears offered on its Discover card (a product which is discussed in Chapter 3).

Ford's inability to expand into the thrift industry did not entirely liberate it from the problems of that industry. In March 1991, the Office of Thrift Supervision informed First Nationwide that fines would be assessed against it and certain changes in management practices would be required. Meanwhile, profitability problems in the automobile industry drained away Ford's cash surplus.

All in all, Ford's turning from the thrift industry marked the closing of one of the industry's few remaining opportunities for attractive new external capital with deep pockets. Why the regulators allowed the company to escape is not clear, but Ford was undoubtedly lucky to have gotten away so lightly.

"Where Have All the Flowers Gone?" The Future of the Thrift Industry

As the popular song of the 1960s asked, in the future people will ask, "Where have all the thrifts gone?" Like the young men referred to in the song, they will have died. By the year 2000, the thrift industry in the United States will be a memory. Taken over by the federal government and liquidated, merged into commercial banks, or converted into commercial banks, thrifts will no longer exist because a separate thrift industry will no longer serve a useful economic purpose.

A declining demand for housing financing and newer, more efficient ways to provide that financing will eliminate the need for a separate thrift industry. Thousands of jobs will be lost, and the federal government will spend hundreds of billions of dollars to liquidate thousands of thrifts for which it provided deposit insurance. However, before the industry dies, we will go through a national "right to die" debate over whether we should allow the thrifts to die. The question will be, "How much pain and suffering will be endured before the inevitable result?"

3

The Consolidation
of Commercial Banking

A major element of the crisis in the financial service industry is the consolidation of the commercial banking system. For most people, only the symptoms of this consolidation have been apparent. Failures of major banks like the Bank of New England, worries about the soundness of the Federal Deposit Insurance Corporation, and headlines about the real estate problems of banks have alerted consumers to problems in the commercial banking system and led them to question the safety of their own money in the bank. But the underlying forces creating these problems have not been clear. Unlike the thrift industry, the commercial banking system has not lost its economic purpose. Commercial banks are, and will continue to be, a central part of the payment system and of the financing of businesses and consumers. The commercial banking system, however, is now undergoing major consolidation and restructuring to become more efficient and effective in financing the nation's capital requirements.

The Commercial Banking Industry

The modern commercial banking industry has its origins in medieval Europe, when goldsmiths discovered that they could create money by issuing paper IOUs for the gold deposited with them by their customers. By late medieval times, Flemish and Italian bankers, such as Medici, financed wars and trading. With the advent of the Industrial Revolution in England in the eighteenth century, the banking industry grew in scope and complexity. Increased productivity accompanied the Industrial Revolution and generated surplus wealth to invest, while industrialization itself triggered large-scale investment in factories and transportation systems like railroads and canals. In fact, the Industrial Revolution gave rise to much of the technology and services of modern banking, from the checking account to the corporate loan, and to the major banking firms in England and throughout Europe, the most famous of which was owned by the Rothschilds.

No commercial bank existed in the English colonies during the colonial period, although wealthy individuals appeared to have provided some commercial banking functions. The first bank in the United States was established by the Continental Congress in 1781 and until the Civil War, banks principally financed trade and issued bank notes, the main source of currency. The form and shape of the banking system was a major political issue of the early republic. Jefferson and Hamilton squared off over the issue of banking and the role of the first Bank of the United States. In the early nineteenth century, the conflict between the eastern seaboard and western frontier over the role and structure of the banking system was a major factor in the election of Andrew Jackson. In both these situations, the debate focused on centralizing economic power through a strong banking system with a limited number of banks, an issue that is still debated today in discussions of banking reform.

As the United States industrialized in the late nineteenth century, the banking system's development paralleled that of the European system. Industrialization required major financial intermediaries that mobilized savings to be invested in large-scale projects. In the second half of the nineteenth century, banking issues continued to play a major role in politics, with the familiar battlelines drawn between the eastern banker and the western farmer and frontiersman. William Jennings Bryan railed against eastern bankers in several unsuccessful presidential campaigns for the Democratic party.

In the twentieth century, a rising mass consumer society in the United States led to an expanded commercial banking system that financed the needs of ordinary individuals. Checking accounts became a staple of ordinary life for most Americans, not just for a few wealthy individuals, and consumer financial products like home mortgages, automobile loans, and credit cards became standard services offered by most banks. The legal and regulatory structure surrounding the banking system evolved as the economy and banking evolved. In 1913, the Federal Reserve System was created to remedy the ills that resulted in the financial panic of 1907. In the 1930s, major structural changes were enacted in the banking system in response to the banking failures of the Great Depression and to New Deal reforms: commercial banking was separated from investment banking to prevent a recurrence of the abuses of the 1920s, and federal deposit insurance for banks was created to prevent future runs and consequent bank failures.

After World War II, the banking system prospered as the economy grew and New Deal reforms restored confidence in the banking system. Banking assets and offices expanded steadily with few problems until the recession of 1974 to 1975. Then the collapse of Franklin National, the largest bank failure to that time, indicated that the system might have some problems. Few improvements were attempted, however, except to increase the limits on deposit insurance. In 1984, the collapse of the Continental Illinois Bank in Chicago, followed by the wholesale collapse of the banking system in Texas, revealed growing strains on the banking system. By 1990, those strains were painfully evident as the banking system ended the decade with increased bank failures, shrunken bank profits, and a steady decline in the number of banks.

The simultaneous and interrelated occurrence of these strains suggested a permanent change was occurring in the nature and function of commercial banks. This chapter examines the origins of the strains, including the high level of personal and corporate debt in the United States, the erosion of bank capital, the capture of major products by new types of financial services, and the unsuccessful expansion into a new type of business. The other major permanent challenges to the commercial banking industry are discussed elsewhere, such as in Chapters 6 (new institutions) and 7 (securitization). The final section of this chapter outlines an important function that continues to create major opportunities for the small commercial bank.

The New Competitors: Sears Enters Commercial Banking

Compounding the problems of commercial banks is growing competition from nonbank financial-services companies. An example of such a competitor is Sears Roebuck. Sears's initial financial-services strategy was based on two major premises. The first was that the consumer financial-services industry, which in the early 1980s was growing rapidly but was extremely fragmented, was about to enter a period of consolidation. The cause would be high-fixed, low-variable cost automation, which would result in an industry dominated by very large, efficient, low-cost producers. The second major premise was that Sears had a clear opportunity to capitalize on the trends in consumer financial services: it had a large existing customer base, particularly for its credit card and insurance services, a nationwide network of stores and offices, and a massive data processing and credit card processing capability. Sears believed it could cross-sell a wide range of consumer financial services to its existing customer base and that a group of services could be linked by efficient computer systems, giving Sears economies of scale.

Sears's first major step into consumer financial services was to make two major acquisitions. On October 8, 1981, Sears announced the acquisition of Dean Witter Reynolds, a major securities firm, and the acquisition of Coldwell Banker, the largest full-service real estate firm in the United States. The goal was to duplicate and expand its success with Allstate Insurance in the consumer insurance industry. Allstate Insurance booths were located in most Sears stores, and Allstate's profits were the primary source of Sears's earnings during the late 1970s and early 1980s. In addition to insurance services, customers now were to be provided with a full range of financial services including consumer banking, retail securities brokerage, residential real estate brokerage, and mortgage lending.

Sears's first attempt to cross-sell financial services was its Sears Financial Centers, which added sales booths representing the Dean Witter and Coldwell Banker subsidiaries to its existing in-store Allstate booths. Introduced in 1983 and expanded to 312 Sears stores in 1983 and 1984, the Sears Financial Centers failed to generate the business expected and were not profitable. This disappointment led Sears senior management to seek an alternative link for the various elements of the financial-services activities.

After intensive in-house planning, Sears management decided that the integrating element would be a new general-purpose credit card that could be used to finance purchases, make loans, and take deposits and that could also be tied to retail securities accounts. Although travel and entertainment cards, such as American Express, had long existed, and some banks had even developed general-purpose cards for use in a region or locality, the major boost for the credit card industry in the United States occurred in 1961, when Bank of America introduced the BankAmericard (subsequently sold to a bank cooperative and renamed VISA). Once credit cards became a central feature of American life and a major segment of the financial-services industry, acceptance of credit cards by merchants and service establishments became virtually universal. Worldwide, 6.5 million locations accepted VISA and Master-Card, and 2.2 million accepted American Express. Annual charges on credit cards were estimated at approximately $300 billion.

Most credit cards outstanding were bank or bank-related credit cards, and all bank credit cards had several common features. First, the credit card holder had a prearranged line of credit with a bank that issued credit cards. Credit was extended when the credit card holder made a purchase and signed (or approved) a sales draft at a participating retail outlet. The retail merchant presented the sales draft to the bank for the payment in full, less a merchant's discount.

Second, the credit card holder could pay for the draft in full within a grace period (usually twenty to thirty days) and not be charged interest on the outstanding balance—depending on the method used to compute interest charges—or could pay some minimum amount each month on an installment basis. Interest income earned on these credit balances became the major source of income from banks' credit card operations. They also frequently charged an annual fee for the privilege of using a credit card.

The final feature was the plastic credit card itself, which served several purposes: it identified the customer to the merchant; it transferred account information to the sales draft when used with an imprinting machine; and it could be encoded with a magnetic strip or computer chip that provided additional information about the cardholder's financial condition. The cards with the computer chips were called "smart cards."

About 40 percent of outstanding credit card debt was convenience use, where the card holder used the credit card instead of cash or checks and paid the amount owed in full when billed, thereby avoiding interest charges.

Introduced in the fall of 1985, the Discover card was to be the integrating element in Sears's overall consumer financial services network. Through Discover, management planned to avoid both federal restrictions on nationwide deposit taking and the cost of building a nationwide network to take deposits and make loans. By combining traditional credit card features with those of an automatic teller machine card, Sears hoped to convince Sears customers nationally to bank with its subsidiary, Greenwood Trust Company in Greenwood, Delaware. Customers could bank by mail with Greenwood and use automatic teller machines to draw out cash from checking accounts, savings accounts, and lines of credit tied to the Discover card, as well as purchase certificates of deposit and contribute to IRAs. Facilities in 800 Sears stores and a network of 5,428 automatic teller machines provided the physical network to support the Discover initiative.

When Sears rolled out its Discover marketing efforts in fall 1985 and spring 1986, it had ambitious goals. It planned to offer the card to 26 million Sears cardholders. To induce 10 million cardholders to accept and use the Discover card, Sears offered several benefits, including no annual fee (most bank cards charged $15 to $25 per year) and rebates up to 1 percent on the purchase price of an item, to apply to Discover balances or to add to Discover savings accounts (the rebate would be paid annually at a rate that increased with usage; charges of $3,000 annually were required to reach the 1 percent rebate level).

At the same time that Sears was signing up cardholders, it was also signing up merchants and various service providers (such as airlines and restaurants) to accept the card. To encourage their affiliation, Sears offered substantially lower charges for processing credit card invoices (1.5 percent of invoice face amount versus 2 to 3 percent for VISA and MasterCard and up to 5 percent for American Express). Discover also remitted to merchants promptly, often within two days. These were important considerations by early 1991, when a revolt broke out among Boston restauranteurs over the charges they were being assessed by American Express.

In the first two years of marketing Discover cards, Sears made significant progress toward its penetration goals but incurred substantial costs. By February 1988, 22 million Discover cards had been issued, and 16 percent of all households carried Discover cards. In addition, 720,000 merchants, airlines, hotels, and restaurants had signed up to accept the Discovers card for purchases. In the first two years of its launch, however, the Discover card had lost $400 million pretax. Toward the end of its third year of operation (1988), the Discover card appeared to be fulfilling its promise. By November 1988, Discover had shown a small profit for two straight quarters, 26 million cards were outstanding, 19 percent of households in the United States had a Discover card (versus 20 percent with an American Express card), and full 1988 revenue estimates were $1 billion.

The long-term horizon for Discover card is somewhat mixed. On the one hand, Sears management had estimated in 1988 that within five years there would be 40 million Discover cards outstanding generating annual revenues of $2 to $3 billion. Securities analysts estimated that stabilized profits on this level of revenues could reach $200 million to $300 million.

By 1991, these expectations were well within reach. At year-end 1990, Sears had over 33 million Discover cards outstanding and a Discover-card receivables portfolio of $11.5 billion.

Discover was the largest nonbank credit card (and the second largest issuer of credit cards) with a 6.76 percent share of the total credit card market. Its annual credit card billings were third nationally, preceded only by American Express (including its Gold and Green cash travel cards) and Citicorp credit cards. Annual Discover card profits were approaching $150 million. In early 1991, Sears further extended its reach in the credit card market when it received a favorable court ruling in its contest with the Visa organization over Sears's right to issue Visa cards through one of its subsidiaries. Sears announced plans to begin a major campaign and to offer cardholders significant new features.

Sears's success using the Discover card to enter the consumer banking business without having to become a bank or a thrift attracted additional participants, the sincerest form of flattery. First, AT&T began to offer VISA or MasterCards, initially to its telephone credit card customers of good standing. It offered a 10-percent discount on all long-distance telephone charges made to the AT&T-issued VISA and MasterCard cards and promised no annual fees ever provided at least one non-long-distance charge was made each year.

Within three months, AT&T had signed up one million cardholders. By mid-1991, AT&T had some 10 million cards outstanding, but the product was reported not yet to be profitable and was not expected to be profitable until 1992. Industry sources indicated that AT&T's problem was increasing the average usage per cardholder.

Then, to congest the field further, Ford Motor Company announced in June 1991 that it would offer VISA and MasterCards to selected customers who had purchased one of its vehicles within the previous three years. This offer would be made through its finance subsidiary, The Associates, which itself was already one of the top ten credit card issurers. Chrysler reported it was also planning to enter the credit card business to provide "private label" cards for other companies. General Motors had no plans, it said, to issue cards to the public, citing an overly crowded market, but it was issuing them to GM employees. In any event, the VISA organization had placed a moratorium on accepting non-bank issuers of VISA cards, a decision Sears was contesting in the courts.

This additional competition not only exacerbates the loss of the consumer lending business which has affected all banks, but they further undermine the profits of those banks that have selected the credit-card business as their niche. They also make it likely that Sears's Discover card profits will fall short of the high return on investment initially projected.

Competition Pushes Banks Out of Banking: The Story of First Wachovia Corporate Finance

Sometimes banks try to modify their services in response to growing competition. First Wachovia provides an example of such a bank. First Wachovia was one of the largest regional banks in the United States and a dominant bank in its primary market of the Southeast United States. Formed by the merger in 1985 of First Atlanta Corporation of Atlanta, Georgia, and Wachovia Corporation of Winston-Salem, North Carolina, First Wachovia was the twenty-ninth-largest bank holding company in the United States. At the end of 1987, its assets totaled $19.3 billion. Known for its conservative lending practices and high-quality middle-market customer base, First Wachovia was well regarded by Wall Street analysts, enjoying an average price-to-earnings ratio of 12.1 in 1987 and 8.8 in 1988 compared to an industry average of 6.4 for that year.

Because of this favorable view, First Wachovia enjoyed one of the highest market capitalizations of any major bank holding company. First Wachovia's management viewed its favorable reputation and high market capitalization as important assets to be safeguarded. Among First Wachovia's specific strengths that were significant for its corporate finance work were its correspondent bank network, the largest in the Southeast, its position as the largest bond and money-market dealer in the Southeast, and its strong cash-management business. These strengths led First Wachovia to expand the products handled by its Corporate Finance Group.

Formed in the spring of 1987, the mission of the bank's Corporate Finance Group (CFG) was to match the borrowing needs of First Wachovia corporate customers that could not be satisfied directly by the bank with the investment interests of other corporations, institutions, and individuals. First Wachovia had a very strong position at the upper end of the corporate middle market in the Southeast, a highly competitive area because of the other large, aggressive superregional banks in the region. First Wachovia's customers were typically conservatively managed companies with strong financial positions, making them attractive potential customers for competing banks. An additional role of the CFG was thus to develop products for this market segment to tie these customers more tightly to First Wachovia.

The CFG provided a range of services, from making private placements of $10 million and higher for borrowers to arranging short-term loan participations of $500,000 or more for investors. Tax-exempt financing of $1 million to $10 million, Employee Stock Ownership Plan (ESOP) financing, and interest-rate protection were among the other services provided by the CFG. CFG received reimbursement for its expenses, but profits were allocated to line departments.

A long-term goal of the group was to build a securitization system, starting with its new product, which provided loan participations as an alternative to commercial paper. There were several reasons for this objective: to improve the yield on loans despite very competitive pricing in the marketplace, to maintain and improve service to Wachovia's customer base, and to build distribution capacity for future corporate finance products.

COMMERCIAL PAPER: THE NEW SOURCE OF BUSINESS FINANCING

Commercial paper is short-term unsecured debt with maturities ranging from 2 to 270 days issued by financial institutions, such as banks, nonfinancial corporations, and other borrowers, to institutional investors and nonfinancial corporations with temporarily idle cash. Currently, the U.S. commercial paper market is the largest short-term debt market in the world with almost $600 billion in commercial paper outstanding. Approximately two-thirds of outstanding commercial paper is issued by financial institutions and one third by nonfinancial corporations. The principal buyers of commercial paper are institutional investors. Money-market funds are the heaviest investors in commercial paper; approximately half of money-market fund assests are commercial paper. Other major investors include pension funds and insurance companies.

Both Moody's and Standard and Poor's assign ratings to commercial paper. Because commercial paper is issued primarily by high-quality borrowers (such as General Motors and IBM), it carries a rate of interest below bank prime lending rates. However, for investors it offers an interest rate above competitive money-market instruments such as Treasury bills and bank certificates of deposit. Generally, high-quality three-month commercial paper carries an interest rate between one-quarter and three-quarters of 1 percent more than the interest rate for three-month Treasury bills. This characteristic of lower interest costs for borrowers and higher interest income for investors has resulted in commercial paper's increasingly being used by nonfinancial corporations in place of short-term commercial bank loans. Between 1980 and 1990, commercial paper issued by nonfinancial corporations increased almost 500 percent from $35 billion in 1980 to $160 billion in 1990. During this period, the ratio of commercial and industrial loans at commercial banks fell from being 2.3 times the amount of commercial paper outstanding in 1980 to 1.2 in 1990. Needless to say, the loss of this business hurt both banks' income and asset quality.

First Wachovia's loan sale program was established in the summer of 1988. The program was intended to lower the borrowing costs for First Wachovia's most valued corporate customers and provide them with an attractive alternative both to capital market borrowing options, such as commercial paper, and to loan sale programs offered by other commercial (primarily money center) banks. Some of the benefits First Wachovia foresaw for its customers were lower borrowing costs, ease of execution, and a dependable source of financing. The customer's relationship with First Wachovia would be maintained because First Wachovia would always retain a piece of the transaction.

The loan sale program was structured to meet the financial needs of companies that had at least $250 million in sales and were publicly traded so that SEC information filings were available without additional expense to the customer. On the investment side, the program was aimed at investors that needed high-quality, short-term instruments in variable amounts and were willing to take a slightly higher risk to gain a higher return than U.S. government debt provided. These investors included other financial institutions (particularly First Wachovia's correspondent banks), nonfinancial corporations with more than $5 million in assets, and individuals with a net worth of $1 million or annual incomes in excess of $200,000.

The major negative factors for the program were the thin spread Wachovia earned on the loan sales and the possibility that losses on bad loans might far exceed revenues generated by the program. The bank's loan loss provision in 1988 was less than one-half of 1 percent of loans.

Loan losses could fall in two categories. In the first category were loan losses on the portion of a bad loan that Wachovia retained on the initial sale of a loan. This loss would not generate an incremental loss to Wachovia's income statement at the time the loan went bad because a charge against income to increase the bank's loan loss reserve was made when the loan was booked. Actual losses were then charged to the reserve. In the second category were loan losses on the portion of a bad loan that Wachovia sold but might feel obligated to repurchase to protect its reputation. Any repurchase of the sold portion of bad loans would be an incremental loss recorded on Wachovia's income statement at the time of repurchase. In either case, a tax deduction was allowed only when the loss was actually recognized.

Despite these risks, a year later the managers at Wachovia's CFG reported themselves to be highly satisfied with the product. They indicated that it was being expanded according to schedule. The volume had reached a sufficient level that a marginal direct profit was shown. The total returns to the bank were considered much higher because of the bank's ability to retain the business of a number of top-rated customers that it otherwise would have lost.

Put Your Eggs in One Basket—Then Watch the Basket: The Story of Continental Bank

One strategy that banks have pursued in the face of shrinking markets and increasing competition is to focus—to abandon the segments of the business they are weakest in and concentrate on their strengths. Continental Bank has tried to do this.

Continental Bank, N.A., was a premier banking institution in American banking history. Founded in 1857, Continental was one of the ten largest banks in the United States by the early 1970s and, with its archrival, First National Bank of Chicago, one of two major money-center banks located in Chicago, the financial center of the Midwest. Until the mid-1970s, Continental and First Chicago were approximately equal in size, profitability, and status in the Midwest market. Together the banks dominated the Midwest corporate market, but neither dominated the marketplace.

In the mid-1970s, however, First Chicago encountered significant trouble from bad loans as a result of aggressive real estate lending and withdrew from aggressive marketing to the corporate market. Continental responded to First Chicago's problems as an opportunity to establish itself as the leading bank in the Midwest. It aggressively solicited disaffected First Chicago customers and implemented a program of expanded national lending to lock in an increased market share. This aggressive expansion program ultimately created bad loan problems for Continental. In the early 1980s, Continental suffered massive loan losses on energy loans in the Southwest that it had purchased from Penn Square Bank in Oklahoma. In addition, large loans to customers in its natural geographic market turned bad as these "rustbelt" customers suffered the effects of the 1980 to 1982 recession. These losses ultimately caused a panic among institutional and international purchasers of Continental's certificates of deposits, which snowballed into a run on Continental.

To protect the financial system, the Federal Deposit Insurance Corporation took control of Continental in 1984, virtually wiping out the stockholders in the largest bank failure in U.S. history to that time. The FDIC appointed new senior management to restore the bank to health. John Swearingen (former chairman of Standard Oil of Indiana) was named chairman of the board of Continental's holding company, and William Ogden (former vice chairman of Chase Manhattan Bank) was made chairman of the bank. These two men, in conjunction with the FDIC, determined Continental's strategic direction until Thomas Theobald replaced Swearingen as chairman and CEO in 1987. Theobald had spent his career at Citibank, rising to the position of vice chairman with responsibility for the activities collected under the "investment bank" ruberic.

Throughout most of its history, Continental was a "wholesale" bank. Its banking emphasized serving the needs of large corporate and business customers. In the late 1970s, when Continental undertook its aggressive expansion strategy, retail banking accounted for less than 10 percent of Continental's total earnings and was growing slowly. Continental did have a major consumer credit card business, however, with 1.5 million cardholders and $2 billion in credit card receivables, but its other consumer business was limited. The relative unimportance of its consumer banking business was a result of Continental's growth in the major business and financial center of Chicago, the high profitability of corporate banking historically, and Illinois state law, which prohibited banks from having branches (a requirement for large-scale consumer banking).

When Illinois modified its banking laws in 1981 to allow multiple-bank holding companies, but with geographic restrictions on where the banks could be owned, Continental began an acquisition program of community banks in the Chicago area. It acquired two in late 1981, but its energy loan losses, which began in 1982, forced deferral of further community bank acquisitions. Then in 1984, to raise fresh capital, Continental sold its consumer credit card business to Chemical Bankcorp of New York for $176 million. By the time of Swearingen's and Ogden's appointments, Continental's retail business was thus even more limited than it had been in the late 1970s, with no credit card or significant consumer loan business and only $1.2 billion in individual checking and savings accounts.

Because they considered the run on Continental to have been partly caused by Continental's dependence on large certificates of deposit, Swearingen and Ogden agreed soon after their appointments that Continental had to build its core deposit base by expanding its retail activity. To implement this strategy of retail expansion, Continental reactivated the community bank acquisition program it had started in 1981 and then suspended. It also developed a broad-based consumer banking strategy that introduced new consumer banking products and developed centralized consumer banking computer systems. Continental budgeted $175 million to acquire community banks in the Chicago area and $100 million to develop new consumer banking computer systems, to be spent over a five-year period.

By the time of Theobald's appointment as chairman, Continental's retail expansion was well underway. The bank had acquired three community banks, and three acquisitions were in the final stages of negotiations. These community banks were strategically located around the Chicago area to provide hubs for future expansion through branching by the community banks. While Continental expanded its community bank presence, it also developed its consumer banking computer systems and introduced new consumer lending products in the Chicago area.

The implementation of this long-term consumer banking strategic plan was on target in 1987. Core deposits were up to $2.34 billion, Continental had a 10 percent share of the Chicago home equity loan market, significant inroads had been made in the auto leasing market, and new consumer banking computer systems were operational. Of the $275 million budgeted for expansion of Continental's consumer banking area, $35 million had been spent and $240 million remained to be invested.

The Illinois consumer banking environment had changed significantly, however, in the two years since Continental initiated its consumer banking expansion strategy. In 1986, Illinois signed a regional compact with six adjoining states, that allowed banks from the compact states to purchase banks in the state of Illinois on the same basis as banks in Illinois. Numerous out-of-state banks had purchased Illinois banks in 1986 to 1987, particularly in the Chicago area. This increased acquisition activity caused the purchase price for community banks in the Chicago area to rise from 1.5 to 1.7 times book value in 1985 to 2.8 to 2.9 times book value in 1987. Acceleration of acquisition activity was expected in 1990, when Illinois would allow full interstate banking.

In light of these changes, Continental's corporate business was reassessed. Continental's strength lay with midsize corporations with sales between $250 million and $3 billion. It was the strongest money-center bank in this segment, serving national business customers through a network of loan production offices in Los Angeles, Houston, Boston, New York, Philadelphia, Atlanta, and Miami. Continental's services to its corporate customers consisted principally of loans and cash management products (in which Continental was very strong). Its international banking services and its specialized, capital market products, such as private placements, mergers and acquisitions, interest-rate swaps, and Europaper, were limited in scope—limitations that were significant because increasing numbers of Continental's customers were candidates for these types of services.

Surveys conducted by Greenwich Research after Continental's difficulties showed tremendous loyalty to Continental by its corporate customers. Most wished for a rapid and full restoration of Continental's banking capacity and planned to maintain their banking relationship with Continental. The loyalty may not have been entirely voluntary, however, because many of continental's customers lacked easy alternatives. Many had triple B or lower credit ratings, and one-third were privately held companies.

Even though conventional banking wisdom held that a large consumer deposit base was the key to a stable and low-cost liability structure for a bank, some new thinking was emerging in this area. For example, Continental's chief financial officer suggested that because the asset side of a bank's balance sheet looked more and more like the asset side of captive finance companies, the liability side of a bank's balance sheet should change to resemble that of captive finance companies with extensive use of two- to five-year term debt. A second position being advanced was that liquidity problems could be avoided by improving the quality of loans. This was the efficient way to maintain depositors confidence. A third position frequently advanced was that liquidity problems could be avoided by having liquidity in the asset structure through greater holdings of marketable securities and fewer loans through securitization of new loan production. These approaches to asset and liability management differed from conventional wisdom. Reinforcing these arguments were the examples of Morgan Guaranty and Bankers Trust in New York, which were strong and stable despite the lack of a consumer deposit base.

As a result of Continental's weak position in the Illinois retail market, the rapidly increasing cost of the retail strategy, and the new thinking about liability management, Theobald made the decision to withdraw from retail banking. He decided to follow a route pioneered by Bankers Trust and Morgan Guaranty. He did not believe an institution could successfully serve both the coporate and the retail market. Theobald hoped to increase the bank's earnings by increasing its relative level of fee-based services that required no capital. Continental thus withdrew from all retail banking activity and converted into a pure business bank focused on the needs of mid-size and large corporations. Continental's investment banking service was expanded under the direction of S. Waite Rawls III, hired from Chemical Bank as vice chairman to develop enhanced capacity in products such as interest rate caps, currency swaps, and the entire array of derivative securities.

In the middle of 1991, it was not yet clear whether Continental's new strategy of just serving the business market would become a model for other banks seeking to retrench in the face of the industry's overcapacity. Continental's early successes had enhanced the bank's reputation. The bank had fewer employees, having reduced its staff by over 40 percent in three years, but it was still not setting industry records in terms of profitability. The investment banking record was mixed. One subsidiary, First Options of Chicago, purchased by Continental in 1986 for $126 million, lost more than $250 million in its first three years and was then put up for sale. On the other hand, in May 1991, the FDIC had announced it planned to sell to the public its remaining stake in Continental Bank. Returning the bank entirely to public ownership could be viewed as an indication that the FDIC believes its role was complete.

CONSOLIDATION AND BANK EMPLOYMENT

The consolidation of banking will result in fewer banks and fewer bank employees. The excessive number of individual banks in the United States (the source of the current overcapacity in the industry) can be seen from some comparative international statistics. About 12,000 commercial banks currently operate in the United States, compared with 150 in Japan, 550 in the United Kingdom, 65 in Canada, and 900 in Germany. On a per capita basis, the United States has forty times as many banks as Japan, twenty times as many banks as Canada, five times as many banks as England, and four times as many banks as Germany. Currently, the European Common Market (an economy approximately the same size as the United States but with 20 percent more population) has less than 3,000 commercial banks. After 1992, when the European market will achieve an economic structure similar to that of the United States, experts expect a consolidation of the European banking industry, with fewer than 1,500 banks operating in Europe by the year 2000.

Given the experience of other countries, it is not surprising that experts anticipate a massive consolidation of banking in the United States as legal restrictions on interstate banking are removed. Experts vary in their predictions, but most predict that fewer than 5,000 banks will be operating in the United States by the year 2000. This consolidation of banking and reduction in total number of banks will result in a substantial decline in employment in the banking industry. Between 15 and 30 percent of the total jobs currently in the banking industry are estimated to be eliminated over the next ten years. With total employment in the banking industry currently at 1.5 million full-time and part-time employees, this means that between 225,000 and 450,000 bank jobs will be eliminated. That is comparable to eliminating all the U.S. jobs in General Motors.

The Real Estate Debacle and Commercial Banking

Real estate problem loans have not been limited to the thrift industry. Like the thrift industry, the commercial banking industry has suffered from and has been a major contributor to the real estate debacle. As commercial loan volume was increasingly lost to commercial paper and consumer loans lost to credit cards, the commercial banking industry turned to real estate loans to gain assets and enhance profits. Construction loans were particularly attractive to commercial banks because of the large fees booked at the beginning of construction loans. Real estate loans rose dramatically as a share of bank loan portfolios in the 1980s.

The growth in real estate lending by thrifts and commercial banks was the major cause of the real estate debacle of the 1990s. As the thrifts and banks sought easy profits from real estate

Table 3.1
The United States Business Market

Business Category	Market^{a)} Size	Market Character	Financial Sophistication	Commercial Bank Role
Big business:				
Annual sales over $50 million	12,000 firms; $5.2 trillion annual revenue; $220 billion annual profit	Predominantly public companies; no-growth sector and slow-growth firms	Very sophisticated	One of many financial service providers
Small business:				
Annual sales $10 million to $50 million	55,000 firms; $1.1 trillion annual revenue; $30 billion annual profit	Mix of private and public companies; some high-growth, some niche players; growth sector	Sophisticated; level varies with firm	Commercial bank important, but competes with other financial service providers (i.e., investment banks, commercial finance companies, etc.)
Annual sales $1 million to $10 million	500,000 firms; $1.4 trillion annual revenue; $22 billion annual profit	Mostly private, IPOs; mix of high-growth firms and stable-niche companies; growth sector	Some sophistication; depends on firm	Commercial bank dominant; limited use of other financial services
Annual sales under $1 million	17 million firms; $1.5 trillion annual revenue; $71 billion annual profit	Almost all private; mix of startups and "mom & pops"; includes sole proprietors and partnerships; growth sector	Not sophisticated	Almost exclusively commercial bank

^{a)}Source: 1990 Statistical Almanac.

lending to replace their lost business and cover their growing loan losses, they fueled a boom in real estate construction that outpaced demand. Because of the long lead time for most real estate projects, the dramatic overbuilding that resulted became apparent only in the late 1980s as more and more projects were completed without tenants or permanent financing. Both the thrifts and banks have suffered from this overbuilding, even though thrifts tended to fund the more marginal projects and more marginal developers. Furthermore, the overbuilding damaged even good projects. The construction of an unnecessary second shopping center, for example, can result in both the first and second getting into trouble. Commercial banks' real estate problems are, to an extent, a further cost of the thrift calamity.

The Debt Crunch: Overcapacity and Bad Loans

A major factor in the growing problems of the commercial banking industry is the high level of debt in the U.S. economy.

Beginning in the 1970s, total debt in the U.S. economy began to grow rapidly. The historical relationship of total debt in the U.S. economy to GNP changed dramatically as all the major sectors of the U.S. economy accumulated debt. This growth in overall debt is significant for the U.S. banking system. As the U.S. economy deleverages in the 1990s, it will further increase the problems of the commercial banks.

The growing load of debt in the U.S. economy and its prospective decline affects banks in several ways. First, it induced banks to build a lending capacity that is no longer needed. Throughout the 1980s commercial banks increased their capacity to make consumer loans and leverage buyout loans to corporations, but as business and consumers cut their debt in the 1990s much of this lending capacity will no longer be needed. Second, it resulted in reduced rates throughout the 1980s for a specific level of credit quality. As their customers became more leveraged on average, banks reduced rates to keep business away from competitors. Shrinking margins on their basic business forced banks to emphasize fees and the types of loans that generated fees (which were usually the riskier types of loans). And third, the higher overall level of debt in the economy resulted in generally greater risk of business failure and individual bankruptcy, with resulting loan losses for the banks.

Capital and the Banking Industry

A major refrain in the banking crisis today is that banks need more capital: capital is the cushion that protects depositors against bad loans and reduces the risks to the deposit insurance system. There is no question that banks have reduced capital compared to historical levels and that they are highly leveraged compared to many other types of financial service companies. Figure 3.1 traces the decline in the level of bank capital over time and compares bank capital to other types of financial service companies. However, the real problem in the banking industry is not too little capital but too much.

Because of overcapacity in the banking industry, equity capi-

Figure 3.1
Commercial Banks and Capital

Comparative Financial Institution Capital Levels
Median Equity Capital to Total Assets Ratios
(as of December 31, 1989)

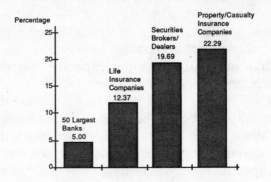

Source: Department of the Treasury, Modernizing the Financial System (Washington, D.C., 1991)

Equity as a Percentage of Assets[a]
for All Insured Commerical Banks
1860–2000 (projected)

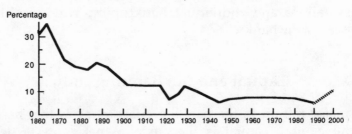

[a] All banks before 1933 and the creation of the FDIC.

Source: Department of the Treasury, Modernizing the Financial System (Washington, D.C., 1991), authors' projections.

tal cannot today earn an adequate return compared to the return available in other industries. As the United States shifts from a debt economy to an equity economy in the 1990s, this problem will increase. Banks that seek to expand in static or shrinking markets will see profits decline due to increasing competition for the available business, and capital will leave the industry as existing capital is depleted through losses and dividends and new investors shun the industry. Banks will go out of business through merger or failure, further reducing the capacity of the industry and bringing it more in line with market needs.

Small Business and Commercial Banks

Even as the competition for consumers intensifies and large corporate customers are lost to commercial paper, one traditional customer of the bank is expanding—American small business. Small business in the United States has always depended on local commercial banks as a primary source of financing and financial advice. As it became apparent in the 1990s that bank financing was less important for large corporations and consumers and that real estate markets needed little new bank financing, the needs of small business were also becoming apparent. Throughout 1990 and 1991, discussions of a credit crunch focused on how more and more small businesses were being denied credit. It is ironic that although small business in the United States is in a period of boom, providing the majority of U.S. employment and new jobs, it is the first market being adversely affected by the problems of the banking and financial system.

Small business can range from a "mom and pop" retail store with $100,000 in sales to a sophisticated manufacturing plant with millions of dollars in sales and hundreds of employees. The most widely accepted definition is that used by the Small Business Administration: a small business has less than $10 million in assets and less than 500 employees. In 1989, 19 million businesses in the United States (corporations, partnerships, and sole proprietorships) qualified under this definition. This number represented an increase of almost 50 percent over the 13 million small businesses enumerated by the SBA at the beginning of the decade. These 19 million small businesses employed 60 percent of the nation's labor force and accounted for half of America's gross national product. America's small business sector represents an economy the size of Japan's.

The 1980s was the decade of the entrepreneur and small business, despite takeovers and LBOs hogging the headlines. In 1950, approximately 93,000 new business corporations were formed annually; by 1987, annual formation of new business corporations increased 750 percent to 684,000. Over the almost forty-year period between 1950 and 1987, the rate of growth in new business incorporations was more than twice the rate of growth of GNP. Including new formation of partnerships and sole proprietorships, total new business starts annually are approximately 1.3 million. One expert on economic change, MIT faculty member David Birch, author of the landmark study *Job Creation in America*, sees a fundamental shift taking place in the United States. Birch contends that U.S. business is being restructured from large-scale enterprises into smaller, more entrepreneurial, and more participatory units and from bureaucratic to entrepreneurial styles of management.

Accompanying the growth of new business formations has been a surge in demand for small business financing. Despite the surge of formal capital sources such as venture capital companies and SBA loans, however, the small business still has problems finding financing. The market for financing of small business is huge. In a June 1988 *Wall Street Journal* article titled "The Hidden Economy," David Birch estimated that 1.8 million small businesses required $82 billion in new financing annually. The 1.3 million in new startups annually needed average startup financing of $25,000, and the 500,000 small, rapidly growing companies required $100,000 annually to sustain their growth.

Birch further estimated that institutional sources (investment banks, commercial banks, and venture capital funds) provide only about 25 percent of the required funds; the balance comes from a diverse assortment of noninstitutional sources—second mortgages on homes, forgone salaries, small investment pools, friends, relatives, and so forth. The 75 percent of new financing raised from noninstitutional sources represents over $60 billion in new financing annually, which makes it the third-largest financial market in the United States in terms of annual financing volume, after the U.S. government debt market and the residential mortgage market.

Despite the size of the small business market, throughout the 1980s many large banks tended to ignore small business in favor of expanding their consumer lending, real estate lending, and financing of investment banking deals like leveraged buy-outs. Small business banking is a labor-intensive, credit-intensive banking market that is not easily automated and hence is a high-cost product. It does not provide the large fees of construction lending and investment banking transactions like LBOs. As the banking system consolidates, therefore, the tendency to ignore small business will grow as the large banks that emerge from mergers concentrate on large loans to large customers.

And yet small business banking is the one market that the banks essentially have to themselves and that is profitable and growing. Most small businesses depend on their commercial banks as their primary source of financing, a reality highlighted in a joint study by the Federal Reserve and the Small Business Administration released in March 1991. The study surveyed over 3,000 small businesses and found that more than 90 percent identified banks located within thirty miles of the business as their primary financial institution, that this local institution was the bank with which they had their principal checking account, and that these small businesses tended to use a cluster of financial services from this primary bank.

Small businesses are dependent on their banks, but they can also be profitable for banks that manage the relationships properly. A study in the late 1980s by the management consulting firm of Booz Allen Hamilton for a major regional bank in the Southeast discovered that the only commercial customers with which the bank was making a profit were its small business customers. Small businesses kept relatively large balances in their checking accounts, which were interest-free funds for the bank. In 1990 the most profitable banks held between $500 million and $2 billion in assets, precisely the size of bank that is most oriented to small business lending.

For commercial banks, small business is an underserved market that could become a primary market in the future, reflecting both difficulties in other bank markets and the dynamism of American small business. As the banking system retrenches and abandons many currently saturated areas of lending, such as real estate, the one market with growth potential will be the small business market. In fact, by 1991, bank consultants were urging banks to price their services aggressively to their smaller business customers because these businesses had now again recognized how important their bank relationships were and were willing to pay to maintain them.

1ST BUSINESS BANK PROFITS FROM SMALL BUSINESS

1st Business Bank of Los Angeles is an excellent example of the profits to be earned by banks that serve small business well. With assets of $566 million and loans of $260 million, 1st Business Bank had loan losses of $23,000 in 1990 or less than one-hundreth of 1 percent compared to the 1 percent or more of loans that many large banks wrote off in 1990. Despite a conservative 52 percent loan-to-deposit ratio, 1st Business Bank's return on equity was over 15 percent, and its return on assets was over 1 percent for 1989 and 1990, figures well above banking industry averages for those two years. In addition to being profitable and financially stable, 1st Business Bank is growing rapidly, with an annual compound growth rate of 13 percent per year and expectations of reaching $1 billion in assets by 1995.

The key to 1st Business Bank's success is its market niche. It concentrates on financing companies with annual sales between $3 million and $100 million, most of which are privately owned. Founded by four former top executives of California's Union Bank, the management of 1st Business Bank knows the market of over 16,000 midsize companies in Los Angeles and Orange County very well. It also is very selective in accepting new customers. It never takes on more than fifteen new customers a month, who are accepted after days of interviews and careful study of business plans, strategies, and financial results. However, once accepted, a customer receives outstanding service. For example, the bank uses couriers to pick up deposits from customers so that they don't have to come into the bank. By serving well the needs of the small business community in Southern California, 1st Business Bank has been able to prosper and grow in a very difficult banking environment also served by many of the largest and most aggressive commercial banks in the country.

As commercial banks face increasing competition from nonbank financial sources and shrinking markets in the areas of large corporate loans and real estate loans, they can expand their lending and services to small business. (Table 3.1, page 56, summarizes the U.S. business market and its sources of financial services.) In fact, many regional banks have prospered while the money-center giants like Chase Manhattan and

Manufacturers Hanover have suffered because regional banks have a strong orientation to small business financing. In the 1990s, banks will increasingly find that small business financing is their ticket to prosperity and longevity.

The Future of Commercial Banking

The commercial banking industry will continue to be a major part of the financial services industry in the years ahead, but it will play a significantly different role than it has in the past. Commercial banks will serve less as holders of financial assets and increasingly as generators of financial assets ultimately held by others and as the heart of the nation's payment system. Commercial banks will continue to play a dominant role in financing small business. And commercial banks will be the most important unit of the diversified organizations that will dominate the financial-services landscape, providing an organizational base to sell a wide array of financial services from asset management to insurance.

4

Insurance Becomes Unsure

One of the big surprises of 1990 was the emergence of a new crisis in the financial-services industry—in the insurance industry. The very name of the industry—insurance—is synonomous with safety. People buy insurance to protect against future risk. Insurance company failure defeats the entire idea of insurance: there is no point in buying insurance if the company might not be there when you need it. And yet, by late 1990 serious problems in the insurance industry (paralleling those of the thrifts and the commercial banks) made widespead insurance company failure a strong possibility.

Highlighting the problem was a report issued by a leading consumer advocate organization, Ralph Nader's Public Citizen, that five of the nation's largest property and casualty insurance companies—including Aetna, the Hartford, and USF&G—would be threatened with insolvency in the event of a severe economic downturn. Congress felt that the potential problem was serious: in December 1990 the Senate Banking Committee asked the Treasury Department to conduct a study of the insurance industry to determine whether the current system of state regulation should be replaced with a system of federal oversight. Also in December 1990 a year-long investigation of the insurance industry was begun by the Senate Antitrust Subcommitee to determine whether federal regulation should be extended to the insurance industry for the first time and whether the industry's forty-five-year-old antitrust exemption should be repealed.

The concern of the Congress was clearly seen in statements by the chairmen of the Senate Banking Committee and the Senate Antitrust Committee. In a letter to Treasury Secretary Brady requesting the Treasury study, Senator Riegle (chairman of the Banking Committee) expressed his concern: "I believe that the recent history of the savings and loan and commercial banking industries makes clear that the Federal government cannot ignore serious problems in any industry that lies close to the heart of the American economy." In an interview about the launching of his subcommittee's investigation, Senator Metzenbaum (chairman of the antitrust subcommittee) expressed his concern more simply: "It's a debacle waiting to happen."

In April 1991, Senator Metzenbaum's prediction of a debacle gained greater urgency when California's insurance regulators tried to mount a rescue for Executive Life Insurance, the largest U.S. life insurance company to fail. With $39 billion of life insurance in force, $3 billion in guaranteed investment contracts, and 75,000 annuities, Executive Life Insurance's failure threatened the value of hundreds of thousands of life insurance policies and the retirement income of thousands of individuals. The outcome of the rescue attempt by California insurance regulators poses a clear test of the current state system of insurance regulation and will be a major factor in whether federal insurance and regulation are ultimately extended to the insurance industry.

The Insurance Industry

To understand the problems of the insurance industry, it is first necessary to understand how the industry works. Insurance is the exchange of a small certain payment, called a *premium*, for a relatively large but uncertain loss. The uncertainty might be a point in time, as with life insurance, or a dollar sum, as with property and casualty insurance. The companies make their money by spreading the losses of a few policyholders over the premiums of many. In fact, providing insurance coverage is simply playing a game of calculated risks.

The insurance industry began in the marine merchant business, when individuals, for a fee, would guarantee the delivery of goods regardless of storms or piracy on the high seas. From these practical beginnings, the industry grew to write over 14 million policies annually in the United States alone. The industry provides a million jobs to upper-level managers, data processors, actuaries, salespeople, and clerical staff. It is a major financial intermediary, investing its assets in senior corporate debt and in real estate mortgages in order to generate the earnings and safety necessary to meet its obligations.

In the modern insurance industry actuaries assess risk by looking at historical trends and running thousands of regression analyses: with enough data, they can predict the number and size of the losses for any given coverage—life, property, or liability—and thus estimate the price each policyholder should pay for the risks the insurance covers. To calculate the size and number of losses, actuaries look at environmental changes, such as an increase in the price of oil or in terrorism in Europe, as well as at differences in behavior trends of policyholders: changing driving records, mortality rates, and length and number of hospital stays. In short, actuaries are masters at quantitative analysis.

Insurance coverages can be categorized as life products and "all others"—specifically, property, casualty, and suretyship. With life insurance, the risk covered is early death; with property, the risk is damage to an insured's possessions, whether from fire, theft, or natural causes such as wind or flood; and with casualty, the damage covered is suffered by a third party due to the insured's negligence or accident. Policies can be written to cover specific lines—such as home, auto, fire, boat, or personal articles—or can be written as multiline coverages. Most home policies include fire coverage and often have provisions for limited personal article coverage. It is no coincidence that the number of products available is directly related to the number and types of customers—lower- and middle-income individuals (auto, home), wealthy individuals (personal articles, boat and yacht), small businesses (limited liability), and large corporations (worker's compensation, group health, commercial liability).

Life Insurance

Life insurance is designed to provide, on the death of the insured, cash benefits to third parties called *beneficiaries*, although beneficiaries are not necessarily parties to the contract. The basic contracts are term, whole life (cash value available), and endowment, all of which can be sold on an individual or group basis; the group contract forms the basis for a common employee benefit.

Life insurance companies, the largest group of insurance companies in terms of assets and revenue, have offered risk protection services in the United States for over 225 years. The Presbyterian Ministers Fund—incorporated in Philadelphia in 1759 as the Corporation for Relief of Poor and Distressed Presbyterians and of the Poor and Distressed Widows and Children of the Presbyterian Church—is the oldest life insurance company in the world and one of the oldest corporations of any type in the United States. It predated by more than two decades the first commercial bank in the United States, which was established in 1781.

The popularity of life insurance increased after the Civil War. One innovation that fueled this growth was the introduction of small policies peddled door to door with weekly payments collected in person by the agent. Another innovation was the incorporation of systematic saving through tontine plans. Subscribers formed a pool of money that, together with interest, went to the final surviving member.

By the end of 1989, over 2,300 life insurance companies in the United States held combined assets of about $1.3 trillion. These companies had approximately 400 million life insurance policies in force, which generated annual premiums of $244 billion. Life and health companies directly employed 810,000 people, and several hundred thousand more were employed by agencies selling life and health insurance. Life insurance companies were the third-largest financial intermediary, offering public products involving both insurance protection in the case of death and a means of saving for over 80 percent of all families in the United States.

Life insurance is a maturing business, however. Its rate of asset growth is one of the lowest and its profitability is the lowest of all major types of financial intermediaries. This slow growth is a direct result of changing demographics. Most people buy life insurance when they are young: as the number of young people in the population declines, fewer new customers buy life insurance. The decline in the number of young people is reinforced by other demographic trends, such as the two-paycheck family. When both spouses work, there is less pressure on each to carry large amounts of insurance to protect their families in the event of their death. Similarly, the growing number of single people reinforces this drop in demand, since single people generally feel no need to purchase life insurance. Finally, the increased use of group term life insurance as a fringe benefit reduced the individual's interest in traditional whole-life policies.

Casualty Insurance

Casualty insurance companies are in the unique position of not knowing the costs of their products until months, perhaps years, after the product's sale has been completed. Actuaries can only guess at ball-park figures, and with unforeseen catastrophes anticipated profits can become real and costly losses. To prepare for later losses, insurance casualty companies are required by law to keep a certain cash balance in reserve. The size of the reserves varies with the size of the claims anticipated during any given period.

Casualty companies make their money in two ways—through direct profit on their products and through investments made with cash generated through premium payments. Especially during times of high interest rates, casualty companies can actually lose money on their insurance business (recording an "underwriting loss") but offset that loss with profits from their investment portfolios. In recent years, the pressure for the underwriting business to be profitable in its own right has mounted as a result of low interest rates and increased competition.

THE SOCIALIZATION OF JUSTICE

A major cause of financial problems of the insurance industry at the end of the 1980s was the skyrocketing number of liability cases in the court system and the growing size of damage awards. The growing number of liability cases results directly from the dramatic growth of the legal profession in the 1980s and the attractiveness of contingency fees as a source of wealth to many attorneys. Accompanying the growth in number of cases has been an attitude shift on the part of the public that injured parties should be made whole regardless of the cause of their injury, an attitude that has been termed the *socialization of justice*. Increasingly, juries award damages in the millions of dollars to a wide variety of plaintiffs. The number of cases and size of awards have led a growing number of property and casualty companies to experience losses on many of their insurance lines, threatening the overall health of those companies. In many cases, the actuaries had no inkling of these developments at the time the policies were written and thus did not set the premiums high enough. This situation has benefitted those who bought the insurance at the expense of the owners of the insurance companies.

Servicing the Customer

Because even a simple change in an insurance policy often results in price changes, all records must be kept current. Casualty insurance products especially involve massive record keeping, information flow, and rate processing—through policy descriptions, reports of changes and accidents, endorsements, claim verification, and quantification of demographic and environmental changes that directly affect premium rates. In the 1980s, paperless computer systems absorbed many of the functions previously done by hand, and well-designed and well-operated computer systems became a crucial factor in determining a company's success.

Another crucial success factor for all insurance companies is adequate service. Servicing an account—whether for a major company, a nonprofit organization, or an individual—involves many functions, including the following:

1. Understanding the needs of the customer and recommending suitable products;
2. Assessing the value of the insured's property to ensure proper coverage;
3. Pricing the individual policies;
4. Handling the cash transaction;
5. Reporting the claim;
6. Investigating the claim;
7. Reimbursing the claim.

Because many companies' products are similar (having been based on similar actuarial studies), timeliness and accuracy distinguish good service from bad and good companies from poor ones.

Traditionally insurance companies have shared the burden of providing good service with middlemen—insurance agents and brokers. Agents represent the insurance company and usually are licensed to sell only one company's product for each line of business carried. The agents assume responsibility for their customers' payment of premiums. Brokers are agents for buyers, are licensed to do business with more than one company, and take no credit risk. A broker may secure quotes for a client from several sources. Brokers also sell other types of financial instruments, occasionally even mutual funds, whereas agents tend to concentrate on insurance products only. The brokers vary in size and sophistication and thus in the amount of service they provide. Large, national brokers, referred to in the industry as "the alphabet houses"—Alexander & Alexander ("A&A"), Marsh and McLennon ("M&M"), Johnson and Higgins ("J&H"), and others—usually have computer link-ups with the companies they serve. These brokers wield considerable power over the companies, since the companies depend on them for sales and claims management, especially for large and lucrative corporate accounts. Small agents are valuable to large insurance companies because they can build personal relationships with individual customers in the communities in which they live.

A few insurance companies have almost circumvented the

middleman by doing all sales and service themselves or through captive agents. For example, Sears's Allstate markets auto insurance directly through its retail customer base. Often considered budget insurance, these companies are known for their simple product lines, low prices (since selling costs are low) and, not surprisingly, sometimes a reputation for poor service.

Because of extremely high service costs, distributors who are customarily paid on a commission basis, costly fixed expenses of sophisticated data processing equipment, unpredictable losses and susceptibility to costly catastrophes, and fierce competition, the underwriting business runs on very tight margins. Underwriting losses in property and casualty insurance are not unusual. Analysts refer to underwriting profitability by using a combined ratio—the total losses and the total costs divided by the premiums received. A typical combined ratio is 1.1 or 1.2; an excellent ratio is 0.98 or 0.99.

Challenges of the 1980s Environment

The financial-services industry experienced dramatic change in the 1980s. Rocked by rapidly changing interest rates, inflation turning to deflation, new technology, and deregulation, the 1980s were a period of turmoil for a traditionally conservative industry. Overall, the insurance industry experienced squeezed profits and increasing numbers of insolvencies as its members diversified and moved into riskier, interest-sensitive products. The most notable casualties were Baldwin-United and Charter Company, which collapsed in the early 1980s after heavy losses on a single-premium deferred annuities scheme. The barriers between various segments of the industry, such as banking, securities, and insurance, blurred as major insurance firms bought securities firms, commercial banks moved into a wide range of investment-banking activities, and securities firms began to sell insurance products and bank products such as mortgages and depository services.

Because of the tight margins, the cyclical nature of the business, and the synergies between insurance products and other finance-related products (e.g., real estate mortgages and IRAs), many insurance companies diversified into other financial services. The companies that diversified hoped to become broad-based financial-services companies. The merger of different industry segments, however, was not without its casualties. In 1988 Sears and its insurance subsidiary, Allstate Insurance, closed its California thrift, which had been operated for many years, after using it to make a much publicized but apparently unsuccessful thrust into nationwide consumer banking in the early 1980s. Equitable, the third-largest life insurance company in the United States, experienced mass resignations of senior executives and the designation of a new chairman in 1988, the result of a disastrous fall in profits in 1987 caused by losses on guaranteed investment contracts (one of the hot insurance company products of the early 1980s). And the problems in south-western real estate created difficulties for some companies in their more traditional mortgage investments. The life insurance business was becoming more difficult: in 1989, forty-two insurance companies (mostly life companies) were declared insolvent, up from zero in 1981.

It became clear that some strategies for diversifying were more successful than others, and for some companies not aggressively diversifying has proven the best strategy. We look at the stories of three different companies—the Prudential Insurance Company, the Equitable Life Insurance Company, and the Massachusetts Mutual Insurance Company—whose experiences highlight the difficulties that insurance companies will face in the 1990s in a slow-growth industry facing increasing competition internally, rapidly changing markets and technology, and new competitors.

The Rock Diversifies: The Story of the Prudential Insurance Company

Although it has had problems, the Prudential Insurance Company is a model of successful diversification by a large insurance company. The "Pru" is the largest insurance company and one of the largest financial-services organizations in the United States in terms of total assets under management (directly held in its portfolio or managed for others). At the end of 1990, Prudential had $110 billion in consolidated assets and managed an additional $97 billion for others.

Its most important business is life insurance, but Prudential is also very active in other financial-services businesses, including mortgage origination, home and auto insurance, reinsurance, commercial lending, mutual fund distribution, securities underwriting, and investment management. Its subsidiaries include a major brokerage firm, Prudential Securities, and Prudential Investment Corporation, the entity that holds all of Prudential's internal investment-related activities. During the 1980s the story of Prudential Insurance was the history of its evolution from a mutual life insurance company into an innovative diversified financial-services giant.

In the early 1980s, Prudential entered the securities business with its acquisition of Bache and Company, a major securities firm. In June 1989, it expanded its reach in the securities business by acquiring Thomson McKinnon, the ninth-largest U.S. retail brokerage firm, with 4,700 employees and 154 branch offices. Although the acquisition made Prudential-Bache (precursor of Prudential Securities) one of the nation's five-largest retail brokerage firms, with over 8,000 retail brokers, Prudential did not ignore investment banking and related businesses. In addition to the investment-banking activities housed in its Prudential Bache unit, Prudential had significant investment-banking functions in other parts of the company. Also under its Investment Division, headed by a vice chairman, Prudential provides a range of merchant banking activities through subsidiaries in Europe and Asia and through Prudential Capital, which is also the largest medium-term lender in the United States.

Prudential Investment Corporation is responsible for a variety of investment activities ranging from real estate investments, directed by the Prudential Realty Group, to money-management activities, handled by Prudential Equity Management Associates. Prudential Investment Corporation is the largest purchaser of private placements in the United States as well as the premier private placement originator through Prudential Capital Corporation. A major term-lender to the middle market, at its peak in 1987 to 1988 Prudential Capital handled an annual deal flow of $5 billion in new term loans with a professional staff of 150 located around the United States. Both staff and volume declined, reflecting a lower volume in the market, to about $3 billion in 1990 and a staff of 105. Prudential Capital's loan portfolio includes traditional term loans to manufacturing companies of all sizes as well as alternative energy and leveraged buyout loans. This origination ability has contributed to Prudential's profitability, since it avoids the need to buy participation in loans originated by other institutions.

In 1987, Prudential entered the commercial banking business with the establishment of its "nonbank" bank, Prudential Bank and Trust Company. By the end of 1990, Prudential Bank and Trust Company had over a billion dollars in assets and had developed a broad product line, including certificates of deposit, money-market deposit accounts, home equity and second mortgage loans, small business loans, and a collective trust product for 401(k)-type retirement plans. The bank was growing at 15 to 20 percent a year.

By 1991, Prudential had completed its transformation from a life insurance company into a diversified financial services firm. It was competing head to head with Citicorp for the title of the United States's largest financial service organization. Prudential had a few bumps along the road, in particular with its Prudential-Bache securities unit, whose chairman resigned in 1991 as a result of the unit's profitability problems and his loss of credibility following an unsuccessful effort to build an effective investment banking unit. Nevertheless, Prudential's diversification had been a general success.

The Bigger They Fall: The Story of Equitable

Not all the large insurance companies have been as successful in the new financial-services environment as Prudential has been. A major life insurance company that has fallen on hard times in the new environment is the Equitable Life Insurance Company. It tried to diversify in the 1980s and improve its profitability, but unlike Prudential the results were disastrous. Equitable succumbed to many of the plagues of the late 1980s including the real estate debacle and the junk bond craze, but its biggest crisis arose from a purely insurance company product, the GIC or guaranteed interest contract. Serious management problems compounded its difficulties, but to some degree

Equitable's subsequent embarrassments arose from its efforts to compensate for the GIC situations.

GUARANTEED INVESTMENT CONTRACTS

A guaranteed investment contract (GIC) between an insurance company and an investor, such as a corporate profit-sharing or pension plan, guarantees the investor a specific rate of return on capital invested with the insurance company over the life of the contract. Although the insurance company takes all market, credit, and interest-rate risks on the investment portfolio, it can profit if its return on invested GIC funds exceeds the guaranteed amount. However, if its return on invested GIC funds is less than the guaranteed amount, the insurance companies will lose money. This reality caused many insurance companies in the 1980s to invest their GIC funds in high-yielding but risky assets like real estate and junk bonds. For pension and profit-sharing plans, guaranteed investment contracts are a conservative way of assuring beneficiaries that their money will achieve a certain rate of return. Because they are perceived as safe, carry an insurance company guarantee, and offer relatively high yields, GICs have been extremely popular with investors. In 1990, there were $180 billion in GICs outstanding; they were attracting large amounts of new funds, including large sums from the millions of 401(k) savings plans, where almost 65 percent of the funds were being invested in GICs.

In the mid-1970s, Equitable began an expansion binge that by the late 1980s threatened the survival of the company. Equitable started its expansion program by actively marketing its guaranteed investment contracts. By the mid-1980s, after an aggressive decade of marketing GICs, Equitable had $17 billion outstanding, 40 percent of its total liabilities. Then the risk inherent in GICs—that interest rates would drop and that Equitable therefore would pay out more than it was earning on the GIC funds—made itself felt. By the end of the decade, Equitable had lost more than $1 billion on its GIC portfolio.

GICs were the first wave of Equitable's problems, which began to multiply in 1982 when John B. Carter became its new president and CEO. A Harvard MBA with a background in sales and a penchant for corporate strategy, Carter launched Equitable on an aggressive drive to become a diversified financial-services firm. He gave the Equitable Life Assurance Society of the U.S. a new name—the Equitable Financial Companies—and started an active acquisition program focused on investment-management firms, acquiring almost two dozen subsidiaries in a period of three years. Donaldson, Lufkin and Jenrette, a major investment-banking firm with a strong base in money management and investment research, was acquired for $430 million in 1985.

In addition to expanding Equitable's investment-management business through aggressive acquisitions, Carter also sought to aggressively expand its basic insurance business. From the beginning of the decade to 1987, individual life insurance sales quadrupled, peaking at $43 billion in face value. Equitable also entered the health insurance business through a joint venture that subsequently encountered difficulties. Equitable was fortunate enough to sell its interest before the write-offs became serious.

As the company expanded through acquisition and aggressive sales, it adjusted its amenities and compensation to remake Equitable's corporate surroundings and compensation consistent with its new role as a diversified financial-services giant. In 1985, Equitable moved into a new corporate headquarters in New York with dozens of private bathrooms and expensive art. Executive salaries skyrocketed: one executive vice president's pay doubled in two years, while Carter's jumped 28 percent in his last year in office.

By 1987, the strain of Equitable's aggressive expansion began to show. Battered by losses on GICs and growing overhead costs, the company lost money for the first time since 1983, and capital ratios slipped from 4.2 percent of assets to 3.9 percent of assets. While its capital to assets ratio slipped, the quality of its assets declined. The company began to commit major amounts to leveraged-buyout transactions, entering this market late when the better deals were gone and the risks were much higher. Equitable invested so heavily in junk bonds and real estate that over 10 percent of its assets were junk bonds, loans for leveraged buyouts, and directly owned real estate. Equitable had 37 percent more of its portfolio in these high-risk assets than the averages for the insurance industry, although its capital-to-assets ratio was 20 percent below industry norms. In addition, it had aggressively but somewhat more carefully invested in mortgages. Nevertheless, Equitable held nearly 50 percent more of its portfolio in mortgages than the industry average.

As a result of Equitable's growing problems, Carter was retired by Equitable's board of directors in 1990 and replaced as CEO by Richard Jenrette, the investment banker who had been named chairman and chief investment officer in 1988. Jenrette, one of the founders of Donaldson, Lufkin, and Jenrette, changed direction at Equitable, emphasizing consolidation over expansion, in an effort to reverse the sagging fortunes of the giant insurance company. The new program included slashing overhead by 15 percent or $150 million a year through a salary freeze, reducing Equitable's direct payroll by 7 percent by eliminating over 500 jobs, eliminating executive perks like chauffered limousines and fresh flowers on the chairman's bookcase, and making major efforts to raise new capital including converting Equitable from a mutual company to a public company and issuing up to $1 billion in common stock. The jury is still out on whether Jenrette's turnaround will be successful, but Axa, a French insurance group, appeared interested in making a major investment and in securing control.

Conservatism Pays Off: The Story of MassMutual

One major insurance company that followed neither the path of aggressive expansion into other financial services from insurance nor aggressive investment policies was the Massachusetts Mutual Insurance Company. Founded in 1851, MassMutual is the nation's eleventh-largest life insurance company. At the end of 1989, MassMutual had over 1.5 million policyholders with over $100 billion of life insurance in force. Supporting its insurance-in-force were $25 billion in investments and various other assets. As a mutual insurance company, like Prudential and Equitable, MassMutual is owned by its policyholders. Industry sources suggest, however, that MassMutual is controlled to a much greater degree by its agents, who form an unusually strong network. The company's major product lines include life and disability insurance for individuals and businesses, life and health benefits management services, group pension plan management services, mutual fund management, and retail securities brokerage services.

At a conference sponsored by Coopers & Lybrand in April 1989, the president and CEO of MassMutual, Thomas B. Wheeler, explained how MassMutual deliberately avoided aggressive expansion of many of its product lines and diversification into new financial product lines in order to maintain its profitability and relatively strong capital base: "Our approach is that the best way to preserve capital is through adequate margins and lower risks. ... During the past decade, we maintained favorable margins and lower risk, in some cases at the expense of growth. ... Our role is first and foremost as a life insurance company—not a financial services company. We do not plan to open a bank, buy a restaurant, or underwrite Broadway shows." As a result of its cautious philosophy of concentrating on the life insurance business, MassMutual showed slow growth in the 1980s but also avoided the problems of companies like Equitable. If this was the result of the agents' influence, it was a happy outcome.

At the beginning of the 1990s, MassMutual was one of only five life insurance companies with a AAA bond rating from Standard & Poor's and Moody's, making it one of the safest companies to insure with because of the low risk of company failure. The key to MassMutual's financial soundness was avoiding high-risk products like GICs, maintaining conservative investment policies, and reducing operating costs. MassMutual's operating strategy used advanced computer technology to reduce the personnel required in its back office. MassMutual's investment policies emphasized high-quality, low-yielding securities. Its aggressive agents could be counted on to bring these advantages to the attention of prospective clients.

As many of the banks discussed in Chapter 3 have done, MassMutual has adopted a strategy of strengthening its position in its market niche in a consolidating industry rather than expanding aggressively into new areas. For MassMutual this strategy appears to be succeeding. As with Continental and First Wachovia, a conservative low-risk strategy can be the soundest when faced with stagnant, slow-growth markets and increasing competition.

Junk Bonds and the Insurance Industry

A major factor in the difficulties of the insurance industry has been high-yield or junk bonds. Many insurance companies used junk bond investments extensively as a way to avoid losses on guaranteed investment contracts that had been sold at high fixed rates of interest. In fact, in the 1980s the insurance industry was the largest buyer of junk bonds, holding 30 percent of all junk bonds outstanding. Junk bond problems and defaults have played a major role in the various troubled insurance companies like Equitable and Executive Life. At the time of Executive Life's failure in 1991, over 60 percent of its assets were in junk bonds ($6.4 billion out of total assets of $10.1 billion). As the problems of the junk bond binge of the 1980s play out, it is clear that more insurance companies will be adversely impacted.

There is a double irony for the insurance companies in their use of junk bonds to fund their GIC obligations. The first is that using junk bonds has made repayment of principal of those contracts much less certain. The second irony is that junk bonds to a significant extent replaced the direct insurance company loan, which was the traditional source of medium- and long-term debt financing for smaller or lower-quality companies.

By buying junk bonds instead of making the loan directly, insurance companies theoretically increased the liquidity of their asset portfolios—but at the cost of safeguards that historically had been in the portfolio. When the insurance companies made loans directly, they included loan covenants that gave them some protection against future problems in the companies they were lending to. Their dominant position in a company's credit structure, when they were direct lenders, usually gave them a great deal of leverage if the company floundered. As junk bond holders, insurance companies have far less direct leverage with troubled companies because junk bond loan covenants are generally less restrictive than the traditional direct insurance company loan agreements and because the insurance company may be only one of many bond holders (who must act as a group to have any impact). However, the greater liquidity of the junk bond has often proved a mirage; the market for a particular junk bond often dries up just when the issuing company is in trouble and the insurance company wants to dispose of the bond. Nevertheless, if the underlying value vanishes, the form of the loan may make little difference. In one recent real estate bankruptcy, the insurance lender settled its direct but subordinated claim for 7 cents on the dollar.

The Future of the Insurance Industry

The decade of the 1990s promises to be difficult for the insurance industry. The continued slow growth in many of its basic markets as a result of demographics, the continued socialization of justice in the casualty business, and the growing impact of technology on operations all promise to squeeze profits and point to growing failures. Continued consolidation of the insurance industry is likely, and the insurance business will become even more competitive as new players enter from the banking sector. Savings banks in the Northeast had already written $32 billion in policies, and Congress was debating allowing commercial banks to sell insurance. Of the over 2,000 companies in the industry at the beginning of the decade, many will be gone in ten years. However, unlike the savings and loan industry but like the commercial banking industry, the need for the insurance industry continues: it will be in business in the year 2000 as a more efficient industry with fewer players.

5

The Rise and Fall of the Investment Banker

The rise and fall of the house of Drexel Burnham Lambert was unusual primarily because of the firm's long period of spectacular prosperity. Its comet, Michael Milken, the brilliant analyst of low-quality bonds, began to capture the public's attention in 1979; by the mid-1980s, he was glowing incandescently. At the end of 1988, Drexel had equity capital of over $2 billion, was the fifth-largest securities firm in the United States (in terms of capital), and employed over 10,000 people: fourteen months later, it filed for bankruptcy.

The financial markets are notoriously volatile, and Drexel's experience dramatically illustrates that volatility. Pretax return on equity for the securities industry during the last decade ranged from a peak of 49 percent in 1980 to a low of 4.7 percent in 1987. The industry lost more than $200 million in 1990, opening the new decade with its first loss since 1973. Although spectacular losses at a few firms dragged the industry total into the red, even the profitable investment houses had their earnings dramatically trimmed.

The industry's historic market volatility is now compounded by a very short new-product cycle and by products that afford very little protection to their innovators. The individual or firm that creates a new product (or revives one that has been forgotten) usually wins applause from customers and clients for the imagination brought to a challenge. The innovator also makes a tidy initial profit, such as the 3-percent spread offered by the early swap products (arrangements whereby a borrower can sometimes tune its financial arrangements more efficiently by trading the obligations it has in one financial market with those a second borrower has in another).

Word of the innovation spreads quickly, however. The several parties to the transaction know the details and undoubtedly brag about what a great deal they received. Legal documents have to be filed and may be accessible to the public. Professionals change employers. The innovator advertises how clever the innovation is in order to attract additional business. In no time at all, the competition offers an improved product under a different acronym, firms in other countries introduce the product into other economies, and the product goes global.

Prices and fees eventually are cut, but not in time to stop additional competitors from offering the product. Because the value of proprietary skill and knowledge declines with the spread of information, however, margins are cut drastically. In the case of swaps, they dropped to levels of 0.5 percent or less, barely covering the variable costs of the time and effort involved in the transaction. The innovator usually hopes to escape with some benefits of the innovation rather than losing them all, as in the case of Drexel.

The rewards can be high, but the risks are high also. The investment banker can dine one year at the best restaurants and the next year work in a fast food outlet. Drexel was not alone in having problems adapting to changing financial markets. Four other major firms—Shearson Lehman Brothers, First Boston, Prudential-Bache Securities, and Kidder, Peabody—would probably have failed if their deep-pocketed parents had not injected over $3 billion in equity capital into them. In the annals of American business, no major industry had as spectacular a rise and as rapid a fall as the investment-banking industry during 1977 to 1987. Moreover, the existence of external deep pockets may have delayed the recovery by sustaining uneconomic capacity.

In this chapter we review the recent history of the industry and relate it to the turmoil in the financial industry. The general nature of the business is outlined, and then three specific cases are discussed. The Drexel Burnham Lambert situation shows how rapid product obsolescence creates problems for a firm. The Kidder, Peabody case raises questions about whether capital is needed to compete and, if so, whether it can be provided successfully by a large parent firm. Finally, the portion of First Boston's situation discussed in this chapter addresses the strategic question of whether the future lies with the full-service firm or with the boutique.

The Investment-Banking Industry in Perspective

What is surprising about the rise and fall of investment-banking in the 1980s is that the industry was not a new one. Sharp and dramatic changes tend to be experienced by new industries created because of a technological advance. The rise comes when the technology is first introduced, is followed by rapid growth as the products are accepted, and ends with a fall when the technology and the industry mature. The investment-banking industry, in contrast, had been around for over 200 years. But the industry's *products* are notoriously short-lived. The effect of a significant new product on an existing industry is the same as the effect that a new industry has on an old one. Color television had this effect, for example, when it was introduced.

Investment banking derives its name from its traditional function—locating and collecting funds for clients that need capital to finance new projects. The investment banker is to the seller and purchaser of securities as the honey bee is to the flower: the bee brings the two parties together to create new fruit of greater value than before while taking a little nectar off the top to make into honey in the hive. Profits, the honey, from underwriting depend on the number of new issues in the money and capital markets. Sources of income for investment banking firms tend to vary also as a function of cost containment, interest rates, and market conditions; the volume of trading activity; and merger-and-acquisition fees earned. Profits are volatile and can vary dramatically from year to year.

A LONG BUT VOLATILE HISTORY

The first investment-banking house in the United States was founded in 1764 by Thomas A. Biddle in Philadelphia. In the nineteenth century, other investment banks were established as a variety of merchants found it was more profitable to sell credit than to sell goods. Major investment-banking firms that survive to the present (at least in name) include Morgan Stanley; Lehman Brothers; Goldman, Sachs; Kidder, Peabody; Smith Barney; and First Boston in New York and Alex. Brown and Company in Baltimore. The list of firms that did not survive is a long one. As the *Wall Street Journal* pointed out on February 22, 1991, of the forty-seven investment banks that were listed in a mocked-up "tombstone" proporting to announce a 1969 new equity issue, only one still exists.

Investment banks are part of the broader securities industry that consists of three types of organizations—investment banks, which arrange public offerings of securities; brokers, which service the buying and selling of securities; and exchanges, which provide a place to conduct transactions and a vehicle for setting price.

Investment banks traditionally were classified into two categories—originating firms and distributing firms. Originating firms were historically the major players in developing securities offerings. Their partners provided advice to individuals and companies needing capital, arranged the type and terms of the securities to be issued, and organized distributing firms to assist in placing the securities. Advice also was provided on mergers and acquisitions, capital investment, dividend decisions, and other financial and strategic problems. These firms generally operated out of one office with a small professional staff to supplement the partners' efforts.

Because of the nature of the business, which tended to respond in an exaggerated manner to the business cycle, the originating firms swung quickly from boom to bust. Unless the firm kept its overhead low or was prepared to shed overhead quickly, which are both notoriously difficult for investment bankers to do, the bust part of the cycle could easily threaten a firm's existence.

Under the guidance of an originating firm, distributing firms joined syndicates to share the risks of guaranteeing to the selling company that the issue would be a success: the underwriting firms agreed to buy any part of the issue that could not otherwise be placed. In addition, the distributing firms undertook to sell the securities to their institutional and retail customers, using large sales staffs and often a number of offices in major population centers. As telecommunications developed, these multibranch firms became known as "wire houses" because they needed to communicate by telegraph rather than in person or by mail.

In addition, these firms usually engaged in the brokerage business, using their resources to bring together buyers and sellers on a continuing basis, facilitating trades of existing securities by maintaining a marketplace, and ensuring that the trade was complete in the event that one of the parties failed to perform. Brokerage was an important source of revenue for the distributing firms and enabled them to maintain their selling staffs even in periods when the new-issue market was thin. In addition, the brokerage capacity helped reassure customers for new issues that a market would exist when the customer wished to sell.

The distributing houses usually required more capital investment in plant and equipment and sometimes for the securities inventory than the originating houses required. The originating houses seldom had significant activity of the brokerage type, although the partners might maintain an investment operation to invest and speculate for the partners' account.

The distinctions between types of investment banks have become much less marked in the last generation as the industry has consolidated. In the first place, the elimination in 1975 of fixed, uniform commissions cut deeply into the average commission per share sold. (Commissions per 100 shares for 1972 to 1989 are charted in Figure 5.1.) Even in 1989, however, the deep-discount, no-frills brokers were still charging only a quarter of what a full-service firm was charging.

A reflection of this change was the drop in the price of a seat on the New York Stock Exchange from the range of $450,000 to

Figure 5.1
Profit. Commissions. and the Cost of a Seat on the NYSE

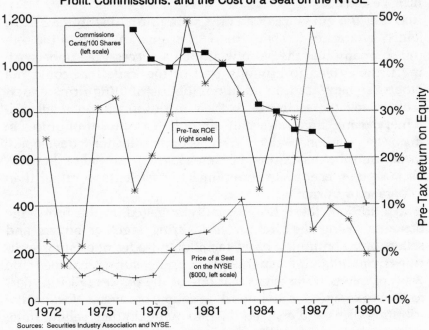

Sources: Securities Industry Association and NYSE.

$500,000 in the late 1960s to about $100,000 in the 1974 to 1978 period. The price of seats subsequently rose spectacularly, although in the mid 1980s apparently without relation to profitability, as Figure 5.1 illustrates.

Under the old rules brokerages had to charge the going rate for a security trade, but the customer could direct that part of the commission be paid to other members of the NYSE in compensation for a service such as research. When the commissions rates fell, there was little left to direct above the fees covering the costs of the executing firm. Thus, many small firms that had supported themselves as a result of market inefficiency or that provided research or other services in exchange for directed commissions were forced out of business as the fat in the commission structure disappeared. Mitchell Hutchins, Baker Weeks, and H. C. Wainwright were all prominent firms that lost their independence in this process.

Second, the Securities and Exchange Commission's Rule 415 brought about an organizational restructuring of the investment-banking industry, although probably not in the manner the SEC intended. Implemented in 1982, Rule 415 initially allowed over 1,300 large companies to file with the SEC most of the information necessary for an issue (or issues) of securities to be registered even though the details and date of the issues are not set. Once the SEC has accepted this information, the incomplete registration statement is left "on the shelf" at the SEC. A security issue (or issues) can be made at any time during the subsequent two years on submission to the SEC of the details of the actual security or securities to be issued. In addition, the financial data must be updated periodically. Formerly, each security issue was separately filed shortly before being offered to the market.

For the originating houses, the new arrangement eliminated much of the profitable business of preparing registration statements and negotiating them through the SEC process. In the first six months of operation, $14.7 billion of debt and $937 million of equity were sold under the provisions of Rule 415, and an additional $30 billion had been registered for delayed sale.

Rule 415 probably also cut the total cost of the issue to the company. Furthermore, provided that the registration statement was on the shelf at the SEC, a corporate chief financial officer could decide on very short notice that the market looked favorable for a security issue and call the company's investment banks to invite immediate proposals. There would not be time for the investment banker to leisurely prepare the registration statement on the one hand while organizing the syndicate on the other. Major originating investment banks were therefore forced to speak up themselves for large portions of the new issue and presume that they could syndicate it out. This practice reached its ultimate development when Credit Suisse First Boston introduced the "bought deal" in late 1979, whereby the firm agreed to be responsible for the entire issue.

As long as the originating banks were taking the entire risk, they decided to capture the sales profit by hiring their own sales staff to contact institutional buyers. Unless the issue was enormous, other investment banks might be invited to lend their names to the prospectus in exchange for an allocation of a few securities they could offer to their best customers. For a very large issue, a handful of major investment banks would form a syndicate to place most of the issue, again allowing in a few smaller firms as a courtesy. Rule 415 thus had the effect of further concentrating the investment-banking business with originating firms as they added distribution capacity. Smaller firms encountered problems from having too little volume of business to attract new customers and to cover the cost of their sales force and overhead.

The development of large, block trades, pioneered by Weeden & Co., and called the "third market," put capital pressures on both the originating and distributing firms. These blocks are positions of tens of thousands or even hundreds of thousands of shares (or bonds) that a fiduciary might want to sell from its inventory. In order to be responsive to sellers, the investment bank itself might have to buy and hold some of the shares temporarily until buyers for the entire amount could be found. This positioning took capital, which small banks could not raise as easily as large ones.

A new rule, Rule 144A, effective in 1990, allowed qualified large investors under certain conditions to bypass the investment banks completely by permitting them to trade unregistered securities directly among themselves or through a secondary market. This rule is too new to have demonstrated its effect on industry structure. On the one hand, it could improve investment-bank earnings because the enhanced privacy would encourage more European firms to use investment banks to help them raise more funds in the United States than they otherwise would. On the other hand, it could eliminate the middleman entirely in both placing and trading securities. In its first few months, the new rule appeared not to have a great effect on the industry, but the volume of issues was down substantially in any event.

Investment Banking in the 1980s

In the 1980s, the general public became aware of the investment banker for the first time since the 1920s and perhaps in a way they never had been before. Investment bankers were the subject of congressional debate for their role as architects of the takeover of major corporations by corporate raiders. Investment bankers, like Henry Kravis, were the lions of high society

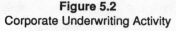

Figure 5.2
Corporate Underwriting Activity

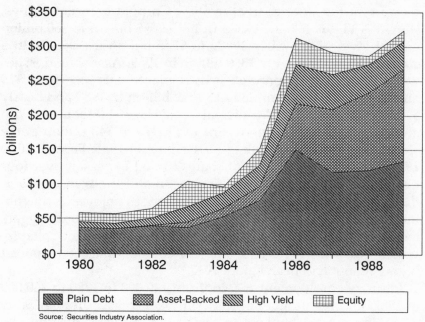

Source: Securities Industry Association.

because of their great wealth and apparent brilliance. And investment bankers like Felix Rohatyn of Lazard were the role models for thousands of business students. Others, such as Michael Milken and Ivan Boesky inspired awe, at least until the federal government successfully prosecuted them for a variety of crimes and sent them to jail.

The rise and fall of investment banking superstars Milken and Boesky reflected the broader rise and fall of the investment banking industry between 1978 and 1987. The recession of the early 1970s had hit the industry hard. It lost money in 1973 and broke even in 1974 (see Figure 5.1). The middle of the decade saw two years of prosperity in 1975 and 1976, and then in 1977 profits fell again. The pretax return on the industry's equity fell to 10.6 percent, only about 1.5 percent higher than the return on BBB bonds, which offered less risk.

Starting in 1978, as is shown in Figure 5.1, the investment-banking industry's fortune turned strongly for the better. Return on equity peaked at 49.2 percent in 1980 but maintained very high levels (with the exception of 1984, a year of uncertain interest rates and reduced corporate equity financing) until the collapse of the stock market in 1987. Corporate underwritings, shown in Figure 5.2, increased from the $55 billion to $60 billion annual level of the early 1980s to $285 billion in 1986, with a subsequent peak of over $300 billion in 1989. Asset-based issues were particularly important. Private placements rose from $15 billion to $20 billion annually to $119 billion in 1987 and nearly $200 billion in 1989. Municipal bonds also blossomed, with annual underwriting activity increasing from $40 billion at the start of the 1980s to a peak of $201 billion in 1985. From 1980 to 1987, the reported volume of shares traded increased over four times on the NYSE but over five-and-a-half times in the over-the-counter market. The regional exchanges enjoyed a fivefold increase. Only the American Stock Exchange volume lagged, increasing merely twice. Even after the stock market collapse, volume on the NYSE and over-the-counter market remained higher than it had been before 1987.

Industry employment soared, from 140,000 in 1980 to 260,000 in 1987, and the number of sales offices increased from 4,200 to 6,700. Investment bankers in their twenties were making six- and sometimes seven-figure incomes, and as many as a third of the graduating classes of leading business schools were going to work for investment banks.

Many of the new products introduced by the securities industry during the 1980s' upswing, such as placing clients' commercial paper with money funds and transforming pools of assets like mortgages, car loans, and credit card receivables into marketable securities (securitization to be discussed in Chapter 7), all came right out of the hide of the commercial banks. Commercial bank profitability was being eroded by the savings and loan industry, whose desperate attempt to survive had cut spreads in many markets; by foreign banks, which had access to much less expensive deposits and capital; and by the investment banks, which were creating new products to replace mainstays of commercial banking. The banks fought vigorously for the right to respond with investment-bank-like products of their own. Often only after extensive litigation, reflecting the failure of elective bodies to respond to changing economic forces, were commercial banks and insurance companies able to began com-

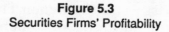

Figure 5.3
Securities Firms' Profitability

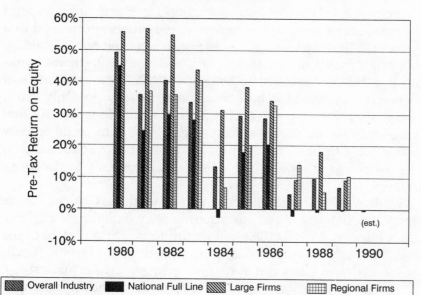

Source: Securities Industry Association.

peting even in limited segments of the business, such as the underwriting of revenue bonds, Eurodollar syndications, and commercial paper. Some banks, such as Morgan Guaranty, had been acting as merger-and-acquisition advisers since the early 1970s and had been assisting in raising money but not risking capital in the process. The total economic activity encompassing investment banking was thus much larger than figures for the securities industry itself show.

The prosperity was not uniformly shared throughout the industry, however, as Figure 5.3 illustrates. So-called national full-line firms, as classified by the Securities Industry Association, were the least profitable category, actually reporting losses in 1984 and in 1987 to 1989. The large investment banks were the most profitable, earning a minimum of 31.1 percent even in 1984. Regionals generally fared less well but did not lose money during the decade.

Furthermore, within the industry a consolidation of financial resources among a few large investment bankers took place. Historically, many investment-banking firms had specialized in one or more products, such as institutional brokerage, research, retail brokerage, or the financing of corporations, government agencies, and state and local governments. Some firms focused on a particular geographic region, while others specialized in a particular industry, such as energy, insurance, or banking. Although many securities firms offered both investment banking and broker services, by the early 1980s a dozen firms had emerged that provided broker services nationwide. Only about two dozen firms operated corporate finance departments that were capable of underwriting and distributing sizable new issues for corporations. Many smaller units consolidated into large regional groups, which competed vigorously for business in their areas.

Stock market trading, while still a vital part of brokerage firms' profitability, shrank as a source of income for the nation's top securities firms as the giant institutions that did most of the trading, such as bank trust departments and pension funds, pushed commissions down to an average of five cents a share. At the same time, deficit-laden governments and cash-hungry corporations began to raise huge sums of capital via bonds and other fixed-income securities. To increase profits, institutions traded these securities at more rapid rates, a function of interest-rate volatility (which was very high during the early 1980s) and new quantitative techniques in risk-return analysis. As a result, bond trading became one of the most important sources of revenue for the brokerage industry, doubling its share of revenue from 11.8 percent in 1980, the low of the decade, to a high of 20.4 percent in 1990. However, when interest rates were relatively stable, as in 1988 and 1989, there was less institutional bond trading, which adversely affected brokerage firm revenues.

In summary, the decade ending in 1987 was a rip-snorter for the investment-banking industry despite institutional and regulatory changes that threatened its most profitable areas and the arrival of new competitors. New products had been introduced to meet social needs (they are discussed in Chapters 7 to 9). American industry was undergoing a major restructuring in an effort to become more competitive, a process that contributed to the profits of all types of business professionals. Although the fortunes of retail-oriented brokerage firms had fluctuated with

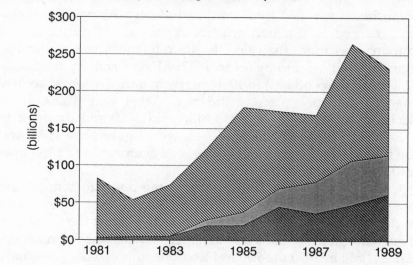

Figure 5.4
Completed Mergers and Acquisitions

LBOs   Foreign Acq'd   All Others

Sources: Securities Industry Association
and Sanford C. Bernstein & Co., Inc.

the movement of stock prices and the number of shares traded, investment banks in general averaged pretax returns on equity capital of close to 30 percent in the 1978 to 1987 period. At the same time, a number of select "wholesale" firms had been remarkably profitable, earning pretax returns of 80 percent or more. However, some analysts predicted that increasing competition would shave these enormous profits, as had happened to institutional brokerage commission rates and underwriting spreads.

The analysts' prediction proved correct. The securities industry in 1987 to 1988 did experience reduced revenues and profits, and many Wall Street firms announced large layoffs in an effort to eliminate unprofitable business lines, reduce high overhead, and curtail enormous trading losses that revealed meager management controls. The problems were caused in part by plunging bond and stock market prices and volumes. Competitive pressures also squeezed the profit margins of once-successful businesses, such as public finance and money-market instruments, as municipalities faced the realities of slower growth in revenues and less support from the federal government.

Although the restructuring of U.S. industry continued, the volume of securities activity was probably declining. Mergers and acquisitions handled by Securities Industry Association members reached $180 billion in 1985, as shown in Figure 5.4. This amount was more than double the rate two years earlier but then fell in 1986 and again in 1987. Merger activity reached a new peak ($265 billion) in 1988, partly in anticipation of tax-law changes that took place at the end of that year. The volume declined substantially to $233 billion in 1989 and dropped to $167 billion in 1990. This was the lowest figure since 1984, and the rate for the first quarter of 1991 fell even further, to the lowest level in eleven years.

Court decisions continued to open the doors to competition from commercial banks, holding in essence that banks could undertake to securitize their own assets and sell them without using investment bankers to intermediate the transaction. Finally, late in 1990 the Federal Reserve authorized a subsidiary of J. P. Morgan & Co., the commercial bank holding company, to underwrite a limited amount of securities, allowed Credit Suisse to become a majority owner of First Boston, and in early 1991 granted two Canadian banks permission to underwrite securities in the United States. Further approvals were expected. The divisions between the various types of banking had become less distinct than at any time since the Glass-Steagall Act had attempted to define them in 1933.

By the end of 1990, the pendulum had thus swung full arc and back again. The securities industry recorded a loss for the industry as a whole for the first time since 1973. Thousands of highly paid investment bankers were being laid off. From a peak employment of 260,000 jobs at the time of the 1987 stock market crash, securities firms' employment had declined about 25 percent. Approximately 60,000 jobs had been lost in the industry, and further reductions could total 40,000. In early 1991, even blue-chip securities firms, including Goldman, Sachs and Morgan Stanley, announced major staff reductions. Competition was increasing for a much smaller pie.

The following sections present stories of three investment banks illustrating three different problems the industry faced during 1978 to 1990. The first, Drexel Burnham Lambert, represents the most spectacular rise and fall of the decade as a result of its excessive reliance on one man and one product. The second, Kidder, Peabody, raises the issue of whether capital is needed in the business and what effect a parent organization can have on the traditionally free-wheeling investment banker. Finally, the initial part of the First Boston saga is discussed—the question of whether to attempt to be a full-line firm or concentrate in a narrow product line. The second part of the First Boston story, relating to its affiliation with Credit Suisse, is told in Chapter 12.

The Story of Drexel Burnham Lambert: Single-Product Hubris

Hubris is a Greek word designating arrogant self-confidence resulting from pride in one's abilities that angers the gods, who ultimately strike down the individual having the attitude. There is no English equivalent, but the Greek word describes succinctly the experiences of Drexel Burnham Lambert.

On August 12, 1970, Michael Milken's first research report, "Speculative Bonds: Attractive Yields to Maturity," was released by the firm of Drexel Harriman Ripley, Incorporated, which was taken over in 1973 by Burnham and Company. In 1974, after earning 100 percent on the small amount of Drexel Burnham capital he was managing, Milken was granted 35 percent of his group's trading profits as a bonus to be used as he saw fit. This arrangement continued for the rest of his association with the firm.

In 1979, Milken held Drexel's first high-yield bond (as junk bonds were known in polite society) conference, attended by sixty people. His point, one that he had been using to build a very successful record of investment and trading for Drexel and its clients, was that bonds with poor investment ratings can only improve, whereas those with high ratings can only fall. Therefore, he argued, seeking bonds whose time was coming was an excellent way to make more money at less risk than by investing in equities. Moreover, he was a brilliant analyst, pouring incredible amounts of energy into researching the prospects of outstanding high-yield securities in order to identify those that were undervalued.

As time passed, Milken discovered that his salesmanship was so effective that the demand for these higher-yielding securities was greater than the existing supply. The profits were attractive, and investments at higher yields were just what the thrift industry was looking for. The thrifts needed help earning themselves out of the problems caused by holding mortgages that paid less than the thrifts paid for deposits. Insurance companies, both life and casualty, were also seeking higher yields on their portfolios so that their insurance products could be priced more competitively to their customers. Pension fund managers were aspiring to better performance rankings. What was more natural in these circumstances than to create a greater supply of high-yield securities?

The demand for high-yield securities coincided with a restructuring that was taking place in the American economy. Many companies had been very profitable over the years but had not found opportunities in their own industries for expansion. Nevertheless, some continued to invest in projects that offered increasingly less attractive returns. A few companies effected major transformations, such as W. R. Grace, which changed over a twenty-year period from owning a bank, a shipping company, and businesses in Latin America into a major chemical, retail, and food company. Other managements gradually paid down whatever debt the company might have left from earlier, more aggressive days. Some looked to unfamiliar industries, developing portfolios of companies through friendly acquisitions that were then administered as financial investments. Major players in this game were companies such as LTV, Gulf & Western, Litton Industries, Textron, and IT&T. Their managements argued that these conglomerates were creating little mutual funds, but mutual funds in which the investor was also prepared to be an active manager and create core groups of companies that could work together to create value.

In some ways, these reactions illustrated the dangers identified by Berle and Means in the 1930s in their book, *The Modern Corporation and Private Property* and in 1959 in *Power without Property*. The authors argued that the public corporation had become completely insulated from the financial markets because it did not need equity capital or even much debt and that the stockholders were a sleepy bunch, unlikely to be active in defense of their interests against a management that was not maximizing value. Unhappy shareholders, especially institutions, would sell rather than fight.

The corporate raiders of the 1970s and 1980s, from the United States, the United Kingdom, and Australia, demonstrated that the Berle and Means line of thinking was no longer entirely valid. These individuals, such as T. Boone Pickens, T. Roland Berner, T. Mellon Evans, Alan Bond, Robert Holmes a Court, and Sir James Goldsmith, together with firms such as Kohlberg Kravis Roberts; Gibbons, Green, van Amerongen; Clayton & Dubilier; Wesray; and Forstmann, Little, sought undervalued companies, bid for control in a variety of ways that gave considerable value to the old owners and restructured the firm to create (or find) some value for new investors.

Even "white-shoe" investment bankers and major respectable insurance companies began to suggest to management groups that they might benefit from participating in a buyout of their division or of the public shareholders, run the company while it was being restructured, and then take parts of it public again. These friendly buyouts were pioneered by Jerome Kohlberg of Bear, Stearns, who initially brought a series of deals (such as Incom International, a gathering of divisions spun off by Rockwell International) to Prudential Insurance, an innovator in this business. In 1976 Kohlberg and two of his associates at Bear, Stearns set up their own partnership, Kohlberg Kravis Roberts & Co., and together with Prudential ultimately arranged to buy out such public companies as Congoleum Corp. and Houdaille Industries, which in 1979 was the first major public LBO. Another early leverage buyout that got publicity was arranged by William Simon, a former Secretary of the U.S. Treasury, whose investment group made $70 million in the year they held ownership of Gibson Greeting Cards. These large deals caught the public's attention and resulted in the acceptance of the leverage-buyout label for a type of transaction that had long been in existence without a special designation.

Buying out the old owners often required obtaining significantly more debt than the target company formerly carried on its books, at least while the restructuring was in process. Often the company was an established one with a good track record and sound, predictable cash flows. Even though the debt used to purchase control was risky compared to the debt that had been on the books, the risk was not judged by investors to be nearly as high as that of a new venture. Furthermore, the rates offered to the bond buyers were very high, and in the booming stock market the prospects were good for a rapid repayment. The more junior and risky debt would have "sweeteners" in the form of warrants that would allow the lender to share in the equity value, if any. The structuring of the financing began to dominate the analysis of value, leading some of the early participants like Prudential to curtail their involvement.

Milken realized that this need for funds could be matched with the demand for high-yield securities he had helped to create. He appears initially to have been assisted in this effort by at least four entrepreneurs: Carl Lindner, Victor Posner, Meschulam Rikles, and Saul Steinberg. Milken would issue securities for their companies, but they each would put aside a portion of the funds raised to invest in other issues that Milken sponsored. This helped create the strong demand necessary to support the market price and to attract new investors. As investors gained confidence in the high-yield securities, these securities were adapted to finance many other types of investments than LBOs. Overall, only between 20 percent and 35 percent of the high-yield securities were issued on behalf of LBOs. The wide range in the estimates of this figure may reflect the difficulty of accounting for debt that was taken on as a defensive measure by managements anxious to ward off a predator.

Little wonder that by 1985 the sixth high-yield conference had become a four-day production in Beverly Hills for 1,500 guests and the proverbial cast of thousands. Milken's admirers, including both buyers and sellers of high-yield securities whose personal wealth and prestige had been enormously increased by Milken's activities and innovations, extolled his talent and contributions to society.

In that year, on $2.5 billion of revenues, Drexel reported net income of about $300 million after taxes and after a $40 million bonus (roughly 8 percent of all bonuses the firm paid that year) to Milken. The next year, 1986, was the peak year for Drexel, with revenues totaling over $5 billion and profits of about $500 million after bonuses of $600 million.

THE BOOM YEARS

The ten years from 1976 to 1985, despite an economic slowdown in the early 1980s, had generally been kind not only to Drexel and Michael Milken but to investment banking worldwide. Competition for staff was intense. As one investment banker later commented, business was so strong it was being turned away because the firms didn't have the people to handle it. New hires, right out of business school, could sit down at a desk and a phone, and with modest competence they would immediately be generating revenues of far more than their cost even at the big salaries they were being paid. Salaries and bonuses for first-year investment bankers rose from $80,000 in 1984 to a high of about $130,000 in 1988. (For those few new employees, the figure was approximately $110,000 in 1990.)

The financial bubble burst for Drexel in October 1987 when the stock market melt-down heralded a much more cautious attitude toward aggressive financing, especially from those who foresaw a return of the 1929 economy. In addition, questions about whether various trading activities had been conducted lawfully attracted the attentions of ambitious district attorneys and politicians. Drexel's profits in 1987 fell to about $175 million, but the company was still ranked as having the fifth-largest capital ($2.2 billion) among investment banks. Profits disappeared in 1988, when a loss of nearly $200 million was recorded despite disallowing (under terms of a settlement with the Security and Exchange Commission) Milken's claims for bonuses due of some $200 million.

The twelfth high-yield conference, which had become known as the "Predator's Ball," was scheduled for April 1990 even though Milken was no longer with the firm. Drexel's filing for protection of the Bankruptcy Court on February 13, 1990, aborted the event. Drexel's equity of some $2.2 billion evaporated, 10,500 employees were released, and Drexel's twenty-two largest creditors (including thirteen foreign financial institutions) were left holding unsecured claims of over $400 million.

These will undoubtedly take years to settle. Milken ultimately pleaded guilty to several counts of violating the security laws and was sentenced to ten years, subject to adjustment for cooperating with the district attorney.

The Story of Kidder, Peabody, Inc.: Piper Payer Calls Tune

The changing fortunes of the investment-banking industry in the 1980s are amply illustrated by the experience of Kidder, Peabody, Inc. In the late 1970s, Kidder was one of the fifteen largest securities firms in the United States and one of the oldest on Wall Street, with a history dating back to the Civil War. A privately held partnership, Kidder was known for the competence of its investment bankers and its "carriage trade" retail brokerage business. During the first half of the 1980s, Kidder enjoyed the investment-banking boom with growing revenues and profits. Total profits for Kidder reached a record in 1986 of $81 million.

In June 1986, the partners cashed in on their prosperity by selling 80 percent of Kidder, Peabody, Inc. to General Electric Company for $600 million, 9.25 times earnings, which was approximately the price-earnings multiple that the common stocks were receiving of publicly traded firms such as A. G. Edwards, Merrill Lynch, and Paine Webber. This seemed modest compared to the price-earnings ratio of Standard & Poor's 425 industrial stocks, which was averaging about 17.5 times during 1986. On the other hand, the physical assets of an industrial company, which generate its earnings, cannot just walk out the door if they are dissatisfied, as the employees of an investment bank can.

GE'S SHIFT FROM COMMAND-AND-CONTROL

The General Electric Company has long been recognized as one of the best-run companies in the United States, with tremendous depth of management, and as a leader in management innovation. Of particular importance to GE's future in the 1990s was GE chairman Jack Welch's efforts to redefine the GE culture to make the company operate like "a

big company and a small company simultaneously." Underlying
Welch's efforts was his belief that GE had to shift from a command-
and-control organization, which had served so well for a generation, to
an information-based organization. In a command-control organization,
large corporate staffs and elaborate planning processes oversee decentralized enterprises. The new structure moves knowledge specialists to
dominant positions. Their task is to ensure that information is dissemi-
nated quickly and efficiently throughout the organization (and especially to front-line decisionmakers) and to the top of the organization.
As part of his refinement of GE's culture, Welch tried to reduce the
layers of management, increase the span of managerial control, and
make managers think more entrepreneurially. He put special emphasis
on increasing participatory management. Whether this change will be
sufficient to support the free-wheeling environment of an investment
bank remains to be seen, although General Electric was perhaps the
best industrial company to attempt the experiment.

General Electric Financial Services, Inc. (GEFS), a subsidiary
of General Electric Company, held the ownership of the organizations that, together with their affiliates and other investments,
constituted General Electric Company's principal financial-
services activities. GEFS owned all of the common stock of
General Electric Capital Corporation (GECC) and of Employers
Reinsurance Corporation (ERC). GE's 80 percent ownership of
Kidder, Peabody was assigned to GEFS.

GEFS thus was one of the most diversified participants in the
global financial-services market, having almost $75 billion in
assets and operating seventeen different financial and asset-
management businesses. GECC, which had $42 billion in earn-
ing assets, was a major supplier of capital and financial
expertise to U.S. businesses. ERC, with $4 billion as assets, was
the second-largest property and casualty reinsurer in the United
States and fourth-largest in the world.

Despite its strong growth and profitability, GEFS was apparently placed by security analysts in the same category as
money-center banks because of the nature of its customers and
the types of financing provided. Consequently, it was accorded
an earnings multiple similar to that of money-center banks
when analysts computed GE's overall earnings multiple. GE
management considered this valuation incorrect because it
believed GECC had superior management to that of the money-

center banks. GE expected GEFS to continue to show superior growth and profitability in the 1990s compared to other financial institutions because of its management strength and culture.

The investment-banking and securities activities of GEFS were conducted principally through Kidder, Peabody and perhaps would help raise the value placed on the financial-services segment of GE. At the time of its acquisition in 1986, Kidder's principal businesses included securities underwriting; sales and trading of equity and fixed-income securities; financial futures activities; advisory services for mergers, acquisitions, and other corporate finance matters; merchant banking; research services; and asset management.

With its acquisition by GE, Kidder was expected to become one of the top five securities firms in the United States, along with Merrill Lynch, Shearson Lehman Brothers, Salomon Brothers, Goldman Sachs, and Morgan Stanley, and one of the top two or three leading investment banks. Kidder believed it had the high-quality staff and client list to obtain opportunities to lead major merger and leveraged-buyout deals, provided it had the capital necessary to handle the bridge financing. This would enable it to issue letters to potential clients to the effect that it "was reasonably confident" the deal would be completed. The clients would then be comfortable about proceeding without concern that the deal would fall apart for lack of funding. In addition, capital was required to trade large blocks of securities.

GE's capital and financial strength would provide the necessary funds. In addition, GEFS could feed to Kidder ideas that came in through the other parts of its financial empire rather than having to turn them over to an unaffiliated investment house.

These expectations have not yet materialized. A first important complication arose in November 1986 when Martin Siegel, Kidder's former star merger strategist, was implicated in the Ivan Boesky insider-trading scandal. Although he had left Kidder for Drexel in February 1986, the questionable actions had occurred while Siegel had been employed at Kidder. To settle the implications of this and other matters, but without admitting guilt, GE in the spring of 1987 agreed to pay the

Securities and Exchange Commission $25.3 million in penalties. GE management wanted to take no chances GE would lose its investment in Kidder. The penalty of $25.3 million was modest compared to the $600 million invested that might be at risk.

Kidder chairman Ralph D. DeNunzio was soon replaced by GE director and Midwestern industrialist Silas S. Cathcart. To reduce the possibility of further securities violations, Cathcart installed new management controls. The staff was increased to provide the controls, along with additional people hired to expand Kidder's business, using GE's capital resources. Cathcart did not claim to have investment-banking experience; his purpose was to straighten out the control system to ensure that no further laws were violated.

The initial result of these changes was a rapid increase in Kidder's expenses. These expenses, coupled with a downturn in Kidder's business as a result of the October 1987 stock market crash and the one-time cost of the SEC settlement, resulted in a major swing in profits for Kidder in 1987. From a record high of $81 million in profits in 1986, Kidder reported a $28 million loss in 1987. The losses in 1987 stimulated GE's management to exert greater influence on Kidder's operations. By the end of 1987, Kidder had cut employment by 1,500 people, 20 percent of company staff.

Profits rebounded in 1988 to $46 million, but mutual dissatisfaction and disenchantment between Kidder's management and its GE parent were growing. This disillusionment came to a head in January 1989 when GE selected Michael Carpenter, a forty-one-year-old GE strategic planner, as Kidder's new CEO. Kidder's president and twenty-year Kidder veteran, Max Chapman (age forty-five), immediately resigned. Soon after, three other senior executives left, including the head of investment banking, amid predictions that many additional Kidder executives would resign in June 1989 when their three-year, noncompete contracts with GE expired. GEFS was also forced to purchase $550 million of securities from Kidder's high-yield portfolio in order to maintain the firm's liquidity and capital position.

In early April 1989, there were predictions of a significant downturn in business for Wall Street generally. In Kidder, Peabody's case, the GE ownership seemed to create special apprehension. Because of the apparent dissatisfaction with the existing Kidder management, experts anticipated that Kidder would be folded into GE Capital with the Kidder name retained only for specialized marketing purposes. The impact such an integration would have on Kidder's various lines of business was unclear, but there were serious questions whether GE's structured, controlled environment would fit with Kidder's traditional free-wheeling, entrepreneurial activities, essential to the creative investment banking game. The bearish sentiment on Kidder was not shared by Carpenter, however, who had stated that he believed Kidder could thrive in the 1990s by combining its traditional entrepreneurship with GE's discipline.

GEFS had shown continuous growth in revenues in the five-year period of 1983 to 1988 despite the problems at Kidder. This increase came both from internal growth of existing businesses and from acquisitions. Existing businesses showed strong internal growth, with full-service leasing at that time being one of GE Capital's fastest-growing areas. Leasing products included auto leasing; trailer and space leasing; the leasing of more than 47,000 railcars; Genstar Container Corporation, the world's largest lessor of shipping containers; Polaris Aircraft Leasing, the world's largest lessor of commercial jet aircraft; and a truck leasing business with more than $1.5 billion in assets and 55,000 vehicles. Through its various subsidiaries, GECC authorized more than 3 million consumer purchases each week. These were all businesses in which competition was strong, and it was clear that GEFS could compete effectively in them. These businesses are, however, relatively cookie-cutter deals subject to standardization in processing and risk assessment.

By 1991, the jury was still out on the experts' predictions for Kidder, Peabody. It had not been dismembered, and it appeared that General Electric was continuing efforts to create a new type of investment bank. GE clearly had the resources to ensure that in the future Kidder would be more disciplined and institutional than its predecessors and could work effectively within the confines of a larger organization. This implied that its product line would concentrate on those suitable for mass production and distribution using the latest in technology, such as programmed trading. The brokerage portion of the firm was to be upgraded and oriented toward the affluent investor, which might provide leads for the corporate finance department.

Kidder's announced strategy for its European office, at least as reported in early 1990, raises some questions about the consistency of strategies, however. The London branch was given a charter to develop capacity in originating, placing, and trading high-yield debt. This is an art form that does not appear to fit the high-volume, low-risk, automated business to which GE's traditional skills apply. GECC, for example, had stubbed its toe badly in London when three deals they had done during 1988 and 1989 all experienced serious financial problems. In fairness, however, GECC's LBO record in the United States had been quite good.

The problem is to find a way to utilize effectively the free-wheeling, individualistic investment banker, creating one-time deals. This challenge had so far escaped even John Reed, Chairman of Citicorp. He had been enormously successful in applying efficient industrial practices first to the operations department of a major financial institution and then to the consumer finance function, which is characterized by a large number of small transactions. The bank's record in commercial real estate and in its institutional and investment-banking groups raise questions about whether these activities had been making the proper risk-and-return assessments.

If GEFS and the management it has installed in Kidder are able to work out a new role for Kidder, it may be a prototype for some of the many investment banks that are subsidiaries of larger organizations. For instance, out of the top twenty-five investment banking firms at the start of 1988, two have failed, and analysts argue that another four or five would have failed except for support by their parents. Three firms remain in private hands; six are held by the public; and the remaining fourteen are owned by other institutions, including GE and Xerox from the industrial sector, financial conglomerates American Express and Primerica, four banks, and four insurance companies. The insurance companies, notably Prudential and its Prudential Securities investment banking subsidiary, have not yet shown the way to success despite the expenditure of a vast amount of money and managerial time. Thus, GE still has a chance to demonstrate the superior management skills for which it is famous and to find a big-firm/small-firm structure that will work in a volatile industry.

To Boutique or Not to Boutique? That Was First Boston's Question

The First Boston Corporation originally acquired a deep-pocket investor when Credit Suisse, the third-largest and oldest bank in Switzerland, arranged to buy 30 percent of the firm in 1978, but that part of the story is covered in the discussion of the reglobalization of finance in Chapter 12. The concern at this point is with the issue that raged among investment bankers, and particularly violently at First Boston, about whether it was feasible to be a full-service firm or whether specialization was required.

Originally incorporated in Massachusetts in 1932 as The First of Boston Corp., following the Glass-Steagall Act it was divested by its bank owners and became the first publicly owned securities firm in the United States. Over the years, it effected skillful mergers with other firms and built an enviable stable of top corporate clients. At the end of World War II, it was considered one of the four top investment banks in the country. The 1970s brought a dimming of its status, and management sought a connection with a premier European universal bank. In addition, access to new capital would permit First Boston to underwrite very large segments of an offering or even entire deals.

Also in 1978 Peter Buchanan, blunt-spoken and a long-time trader for First Boston, became president of the firm, which at the end of 1978 showed net income of only $1.8 million on $94.2 million in revenue, the lowest income level in its history since the Depression. Those results were not aberrations, as both revenues and profits had been slipping steadily during the 1970s. Teaming up with then-chairman and CEO, George Shinn, Buchanan engineered a recovery that established First Boston as one of the strongest of the big five investment banks. In 1983, First Boston had $515.4 million in total revenues and net income of $80.2 million.

The Shinn-Buchanan strategy was to position First Boston Corporation as a full-service, international investment banking firm serving both suppliers and users of capital around the world. First Boston's business was broadly divided into four areas—financial advisory services and underwriting, merchant banking, sales and trading, and research. The Investment Banking Department provided comprehensive financial advisory services, specialized merger, acquisition, and divestiture services, underwritings in conjunction with the Capital Markets Department, and other corporate finance activities. Through its merchant banking activities, First Boston facilitated major client transactions and invested in mergers and acquisitions, recapitalizations, leveraged buyouts, venture capital, and real estate transactions. First Boston's sales and trading area, including the Taxable Fixed Income, Equity, and Municipal Securities Departments, used the firm's own capital to trade and assist in underwriting securities of corporate and other private issuers, as well as government and agency securities. First Boston's Equity Research, Fixed Income Research, and Economic Research Departments performed a wide array of analyses covering such securities and domestic as well as international economic conditions. Through subsidiaries, First Boston was a member of major security exchanges in the United States, Europe, and Asia.

To guarantee a comprehensive range of financial advisory, capital raising, and sales and trading services to clients and customers throughout the United States, First Boston had regional investment-banking offices in ten major domestic markets and eight foreign offices on four continents. First Boston employed approximately 5,000 employees worldwide in the mid-1980s, 3,000 of whom constituted the professional staff including 127 managing directors, 93 directors, and about 750 vice presidents. Some 500 investment-banking professionals were responsible for developing and maintaining client relationships and executing transactions with domestic and foreign clients. Approximately 1,000 professionals were engaged in principal trading and customer sales activities, and about 175 were in securities research. In addition, First Boston had approximately 2,000 operational, administrative, and support personnel.

PROFIT DISPARITY AMONG FIRMS

The statistics of the Securities Industry Association showed that national, full-line firms were less profitable than either the large investment-bank category or those firms based in New York City. (Figure 5.3 shows industry profitability by category of firm.) In 1984, for example, the national firms showed a combined loss of 2.6 percent of equity capital, whereas the New York City classification showed a positive return of 19.9 percent and the large investment-bank category returned 31.1 percent. The full-line firms returned to profitability in 1985 and 1986, but they attained half to two-thirds the level of profitability the other classifications reported.

At First Boston, profit disparities among departments were emphasized when much of the credit for the firm's turnaround in profits was attributed to the Mergers and Acquisitions (M&A) Department, headed by Joseph Perella and Bruce Wasserstein. Perella had joined First Boston in 1972 and ran the one-man department in relative obscurity until George Shinn became CEO in 1975. Because Shinn's strategy emphasized M&A, Perella was allocated the resources necessary to hire talent and expand business. This included hiring Bruce Wasserstein in 1977. Perella and Wasserstein pioneered the use of M&A specialists instead of generalists. They wanted to be perceived as the most professional M&A department on Wall Street. First Boston's M&A bankers had to become the most knowledgeable as to the conceptualization, analysis, and implementation of transactions.

In 1977, the M&A department of nine professionals generated just over $3 million in fees. By 1985, the group had grown to 100 bankers and analysts generating close to $200 million in fees at more than the firm's average margin. This represented almost one-quarter of First Boston's total revenue that year of $888 million. In 1986, First Boston was ranked first in both the number and dollar value of those M&A transactions in which it served as adviser; it was expected to maintain that number-one position for 1987.

By mid-1987, tension was mounting. First Boston's M&A department generated more than $350 million in fees in 1987, but the firm reported only $108 million profit on $1.3 billion in total revenue. This profit included a one-time, $80 million pre-tax gain from selling the headquarters building. Wasserstein was reportedly very critical of the firm's direction. He blamed the problems on the trading side of the firm and wanted that business eliminated as a profit center; he thought it should function strictly as support for his department's activities. According to press reports, he and Perella had come close to leaving in early 1987, but then Buchanan asked them to initiate a detailed analysis of the firm's direction. In January 1988, Buchanan reviewed the analysis and, realizing Wasserstein's recommendations would result in huge layoffs, announced that there would be no change in the firm's full-line strategy.

Wasserstein and Perella were also reportedly rebuffed in their request for more influential positions in the strategic management of the firm. They told senior management it was time to retire, but that wasn't what senior management's watches showed.

Wasserstein and Perella made their objections to the First Boston strategy public when they announced their resignations on February 2, 1988, and formed their own investment bank. First Boston's stock dropped 13 percent the next day, compared to a 1 percent decline in the Dow Jones Industrial Average.

By the time Perella and Wasserstein resigned, Wall Street was full of rumors that other major firms were having similar internal conflicts. Salomon's investment bankers were publicly complaining that they did not have enough representation on the firm's board. Investment bankers throughout the industry resented subsidizing the traders. To throw more wood on the fire, the trading losses resulted in smaller year-end bonuses than in the past. With the investment banking side of the business so profitable, especially mergers and acquisitions, top management at the firms had some serious issues to contend with, issues that needed to be resolved quickly before other employees followed Perella and Wasserstein.

The industry seemed evenly divided between those who were sure Wasserstein and Perella were the backbone of First Boston and those who felt First Boston had competent, albeit not as creative, replacements.

The industry was also divided about whether there was strength or weakness in attempting to be a full-service firm. On the one hand, those supporting a full-service institution admitted that it would inevitably be less profitable than whatever product line was hot at the moment because other product lines would be in the doldrums. When the hot products cooled and the cold products warmed up, the full-service firm would still be profitable and maybe even at an advantage because it would be first in a line from which others had dropped out. Trading had been king before, but First Boston had lost $100 million in 1987 in fixed-income securities. M&A was hot now. Tomorrow, the shoe might again be on the other foot.

Proponents of this point of view admitted, however, that a firm should not attempt to compete in a business to which it brought no strategic strengths. They also pointed out that one-stop shopping had its conveniences for the customer and, if properly used, provided sales tools and opportunities for the corporate finance group.

The opponents of the full-service strategy argued that an investment bank should be small and flexible and should move with the market rather than maintain a large investment and hope that the market would come back to it. This position maintained that because investment banking was a people business, the high producers in the hot product lines could simply walk away to join another firm or found one of their own that would not require them to support the losing departments. The idea of a full-service firm was like a dinosaur—overweight and becoming obsolete.

The industry environment at the time seemed to favor those opposed to the full-service concept as expenses in most firms continued to outpace revenues in the third quarter of 1987. Many firms had revealed profit-action plans even prior to the October 19, 1987, stock market crash. Staff reductions and cost controls were being instituted by the industry. By Black Monday, Wall Street had already laid off 1,100 employees. More layoffs were expected, and the crash accelerated the pruning process the industry was undertaking. By the end of January 1988, more than 10,000 layoffs either had occurred or had been announced on an employment base that had been 244,000 at the end of 1986.

The departments most under scrutiny were the municipal, corporate, and government bond businesses, money-market and commodities operations, and mortgage and real estate brokerage units. The plunging bond market and huge trading losses revealed many unprofitable departments, poor management controls, and the huge overheads built up during the rapid expansion in the industry. The *Wall Street Journal* headlined an article even as late as July 20, 1989, "Along Wall Street, Once-Mighty Traders Are Reduced to Pawns."

In addition, the high number of deals in the pipeline in late 1987 led to heavy risk arbitrage losses. (Risk arbitrage is the name given to the process of investing in stocks of companies on both sides of an acquisition.) First Boston lost $60 million in these risky investments. Underwriting losses were also widespread. Many firms lost as much as $50 million, and four firms stood to lose $100 million each just from the $12.33 billion underwriting of British Petroleum Co. even after the British government had modified the terms to ameliorate the problems the underwriters faced.

The outcome of the strategy debate remained unclear in early 1991. Many full-service firms redefined the meaning of full service to exclude products for which they had no inherent advantage. Morgan Stanley, for example, curtailed investment advisory service to institutional clients who were not using enough other products to be profitable. Banks and investment banks withdrew from various product categories in which they had formerly made markets on the ground that their share of market was inherently too small to justify the capital exposure. Even those who had invested heavily in anticipation of opportunities expected from the deregulation of the London trading markets found themselves taking big losses as they exited overly competitive situations.

"TOUGH TIMES AS MERGERS DECLINE"

On February 9, 1990, The *Wall Street Journal* ran a story on "Wall Street Niches Pay Off as Megafirms Suffer." In November, a story appeared with the headline, "Wall Street's Boutiques May Face Tough Times as Mergers Decline." The highest-paid executive on Wall Street in 1990 was reputed to be a bond trader at Salomon, whose salary and bonus totaled $23 million. Another star was the head of petroleum trading at Salomon, who earned about $20 million. Meanwhile, the M&A

departments at major investment and commercial banks were being reduced, consolidated with other corporate finance functions, or eliminated altogether. "*Sic transit gloria mundi*," wrote Thomas à Kempis in the fifteenth century: "Thus passes the glory of the world."

It is not possible to evaluate the proper strategy by looking at the subsequent events at First Boston and Wasserstein and Perella. First Boston allied itself much more closely with Credit Suisse (see Chapter 12). Its later problems arose not so much from its efforts to be a full-service firm as from its being left standing up when the music stopped in the leveraged-buyout game of musical chairs, precisely the product line Wasserstein and Perella were promoting.

Wasserstein and Perella's firm fell from third place in merger deals completed in 1989 to eighth in 1990. Its merchant-banking fund, which had gotten a late start and hence paid relatively more for its investments, was not flourishing. Wasserstein and Perella, who in July 1988 had allowed Nomura Securities, the major Japanese investment bank, to invest $100 million for a 20 percent share of the company, reportedly planned to ride out the recession by continuing their strategy of working with complicated financial transactions. They admitted that in order to stay in business, the firm would probably be doing smaller deals than they were accustomed to doing in the past.

Conclusion

The morals of these three stories, each of which involves a major strategic issue for investment bankers during the period following the 1974 recession, are not easy to draw. It does appear that an innovator like Michael Milken can have significant influence if the environment is receptive. Ultimately, the discipline of economics applies to all, however. One consistency seems to be change. Drexel forgot, among other things, that trees don't grow to the sky; some trees are vulnerable to high winds when they get too large. Whether a full-service firm, such as First Boston aspired to be, or a boutique, such as Wasserstein and Perella founded, is most likely to flourish in the environment of the 1990s is not yet clear. General Electric and Kidder,

Peabody may be trying another alternative—developing portions of the investment-banking business that take careful management and the low cost provided by economies of scale but sacrificing the traditional entrepreneurial spirit and innovation that have often characterized the industry.

A second consistency in behavior among these three firms was a shift away from acting as the pollinating bee, which did not expose its own capital to much more than the overnight risk associated with a guaranteed underwriting, to investing its own funds for an intermediate term of one to five years while the client companies were restructured. This has been a successful strategy for some firms, but those were generally private enterprises specializing in only that line and not attempting to deal with the public. The one more broadly based firm successful so far in this effort is Morgan Stanley.

On closer examination, a number of critics have argued that Morgan Stanley actually did not invest its own cash capital. They claim that by the time Morgan Stanley took out its fees for a transaction, the net effect on its cash flow was positive even after deducting the investments it nominally made in the equity of the deal.

If this assertion is true, it suggests that Morgan Stanley was wise enough to maintain its role as a financial bee, contributing its human skills and knowledge capital to a project rather than its cash. It is a strategy certainly consistent with the approach of J. P. Morgan, whose influence was far more the result of his intellect than his money. It was said that the head of the table was wherever Morgan sat, but at his death, when his estate was probated, Andrew Carnegie remarked, "We always thought he was a rich man."

A major challenge for those attempting to marry technology and financial artistry, such as Welsh of General Electric and Reed of Citicorp, is whether they can identify and implement a better strategy than J. P. Morgan's. It may turn out that the two dimensions are not reconcilable: as products become more routine and capable of being processed more efficiently by computer than by individuals, these products are dropped by the artistic firms and picked up by the batch-processing ones. The challenge for the artists, then, is to find new products for which their knowledge can command a premium.

Furthermore, the investment-banking industry in the early 1990s entered one of its periodic times of concentration after over a decade of great expansion and profits, which provided room both for experimentation and for error. The tolerance of the industry for either will be limited until the economy recovers strongly. Until then, the market will be harsh in its treatment of the firms whose strategic choices are not perceptive and whose skills are not highly effective.

Considering the highly leveraged state of U.S. business and individuals, even a return to normal growth is unlikely to produce the profits the investment-banking industry enjoyed in the 1977 to 1987 period because opportunities for buyouts and new products will be fewer. Corporate America might pay the investment bankers to unleverage it and restore balance sheet ratios to their more traditional levels. Short of this prospect, the weather for the industry looks distinctly foggy and wet.

Ironically, the commercial banks have received permission to play in this field just as the game has gotten very muddy and threatens to break up completely. Some of the weaker investment companies may attempt to find a strong bank parent in order to gain efficiencies of operation or other synergies. Considering the weak state of U.S. commercial banks, this attempt may provide opportunities for international banks. Before entering the market, commercial banks should reflect carefully on the experiences of Credit Suisse and First Boston, as described in Chapter 12.

II
THE RISE OF THE NEW FINANCIAL SYSTEM

6

The Rise of New Age Financial Institutions

One little recognized cause of the crisis in banks, savings and loans, and insurance companies is the rise of new forms of financial institutions that effectively replace many functions of traditional institutions. The current problems of the financial system do not reflect the collapse of the basic underlying economy, which occurred in the 1930s. The financial system that developed with the New Deal reforms of the 1930s is being replaced with a new financial system: the current financial crises are really the birthpangs of a new and more efficient financial system.

Major Financial Institutions in New Forms

Historically, the principal role of financial institutions was to serve as an intermediary between the individual saver and the ultimate user of funds, which was usually government or a business entity. This is still the role of financial institutions. What has changed is that the individual saver utilizes new forms of financial institutions to mobilize funds and transmit them into the global capital market. This change in the financial institution of choice for the individual saver is at the heart of the problems of the nation's commercial banks, thrifts, and insurance companies.

The two major new forms of financial institutions that channel the individual saver's funds into the market are pension funds and mutual funds. Both corporate and nonprofit institution pension funds in the United States and abroad represent a huge aggregate of capital that has grown rapidly over the last forty years. Mutual funds also have shown dramatic growth in recent years as individual investors have reentered the stock market through the mutual fund vehicle instead of direct ownership of the underlying stocks. Figure 1.2 in Chapter 1 shows the historical growth of pension fund assets and mutual fund assets compared to the asset growth of more traditional institutions such as commercial banks and thrifts. Figure 1.3 in Chapter 1 shows the growth in the number of mutual funds compared to the growth in the number of banks and thrifts.

Technology is playing a role in the rise of both types of institutions. Computer technology dramatically lowers the cost of aggregating capital and creating another layer of management for it. The process of issuing statements and marketing the services of these institutions has been dramatically streamlined. But even more important, technology has allowed these new forms of financial institutions to take over many of the traditional roles of commercial banks and savings and loans without some of their disadvantages.

For example, pension funds and mutual funds require no capital to cushion against a loss of value in assets because they are essentially pass-through intermediaries that do not promise their liability holders a specified return the way a bank, savings and loan, or insurance company does. Without a requirement to earn a return on capital, pension funds and mutual funds are able to pay more for earning assets than competing banks and savings and loans and still return a higher yield to their liability holders. Money-market mutual funds pay more to their shareholders than competing bank certificates of deposits even though money-market funds invest in bank certificates of deposits themselves and other low-yielding investments like Treasury bills and commercial paper.

The Pension Fund System

The first pension plan in the United States was established in 1759 for widows and children of Presbyterian ministers. The first employee pension fund in the United States was started at the time of the U.S. Civil War for retired New York City policemen. With the industrialization of the United States, pension funds grew steadily as more and more large employers provided pensions for their employees. Most of these plans were annuity plans invested in standard life insurance investments such as government bonds, mortgages, and other fixed-rate instruments. A few plans were profit-sharing plans, such as the Sears Roebuck plan, which was founded in 1916 and did so well investing in Sears Roebuck stock that long-serving lower-level employees such as janitors were able to retire in their forties and fifties as wealthy individuals. By 1950, the 2,000 pension plans in place in the United States held almost $17 billion in assets, and approximately 25 percent of the workforce was covered by some type of pension plan.

In 1950, the pension fund industry changed dramatically when General Motors introduced a pension fund for General Motors employees. Funded and managed by General Motors, this plan was unique in its intention to invest in the "American economy" through the purchase of private-industry equity securities and its use of professional "asset managers" to manage the fund. Unlike existing pension plans that invested in debt securities (primarily of the federal government) or in the company's own stock in the case of profit-sharing plans like that of Sears Roebuck, the General Motors plan would invest in the equities of a broad section of American industry. Of course, General Motors had the ultimate responsibility for financially supporting the plan, but the more the plan earned on its own assets, the less General Motors would have to contribute.

The General Motors pension fund concept was a tremendous success, and other companies rushed to copy it. Within a year,

private employer pension plans in the United States quadrupled to 8,000 and started a phenomenal period of growth.
Between 1950 and 1974, pension fund assets doubled every five
years. By 1974, there were approximately 50,000 private
employer and state and municipal employee pension funds in
place controlling $200 billion of assets. As a result of the growth
of private employer pension funds, over half the American
workforce was covered by pension plans in 1974.

In 1974, a landmark event in the development of pension
plans occurred. Responding to alleged widespread abuses and
deficiencies in the pension system, the Congress passed the
Employees Retirement Income Security Act or ERISA, which
overhauled the laws covering employer pensions. Before passage of ERISA, pension plan sponsors were not required by
statute to set aside funds for the payment of benefits in advance
of the date on which the benefits become payable. Some plans
used the pay-as-you-go approach, and others used the terminal
funding approach, where benefits were funded only on an
employee's retirement. Pension plan participants could be
totally dependent on their employer's willingness and ability to
fund its pension obligation in the future.

In response to the problems created by companies' failure to
meet pension obligations, ERISA required minimum funding
requirements and established the Pension Benefit Guaranty
Corporation (PBGC) to insure vested pension benefits. In addition, ERISA accelerated the mandatory vesting schedules for
employees' pension rights and required that the actuarial
assumptions used by the pension plan be signed off by an actu-
ary and that the corporation's mandated pension fund contribution be consistent with actuarial assumptions. ERISA's minimum
funding requirements coupled with the new vesting schedules
created a massive funding need for the pension system.

The result was that total pension fund assets increased from
$200 billion in 1974 to $2.7 trillion in 1989, almost equaling the
total assets in the commercial banking system. Between 1950
and 1989, pension assets grew at six times the growth rate for
GNP and total financial assets in the economy. During the
1990s, pension funds are projected to grow at an annual rate of
$100 billion to $200 billion per year. Fueling this growth will be

pension funds' special tax status, which allows pension fund contributions to be tax deductible to the corporation or individual making them. The earnings on those contributions are tax exempt until they are withdrawn from the pension plan. Pension funds', high growth rate coupled with stagnant growth of the commercial banking system and the disappearance of the thrift industry guarantees that pension funds will be the largest form of financial institution by the year 2000.

The Significance of the Emergence of Pension Funds

As pension funds have grown, they have become the largest source of intermediate-term and long-term capital in the United States economy. Pension funds are the most important buyers of new stock issued in both initial public offerings and in offerings of new stock by existing public companies. In addition, pension funds are the biggest source of funds for privately placed equity, particularly for formal venture capital companies.

Along with their influential role in the U.S. equity market, pension funds are also increasingly dominating U.S. debt markets. As more and more new corporate debt is placed with pension funds, they are replacing life insurance companies as the principal source of medium-term and long-term debt. Even more significant than their role in buying long-term debt is the role of pension funds in funding mortgages. As an increasing percentage of new home mortgages are securitized (the subject of Chapter 7) and sold to pension funds, pension funds are replacing thrifts as the largest holders of long-term mortgages and speeding the demise of the thrift industry. The match between the long-term of the mortgage and the long-term nature of pension fund assets is far more rational than the match was with short-term deposits of a thrift institution.

Of equal importance to the role of pension funds as the largest source of capital in the economy is their new role as the most important owner of American industry. In 1950, at the beginning of the pension revolution, private pension plans accounted for 1 percent of corporate equities and 13 percent of corporate bonds. By the end of 1989, pension funds owned 40 percent of all corporate bonds and 25 percent of all corporate equities. Pension funds' ownership of large public companies was even higher than their total share of equities. At the end of 1989, institutions owned 54 percent of the equity of the 250 largest companies in the United States and 48 percent of the 1,000 largest companies. Examples of large U.S. companies with more than 50 percent institutional ownership include General Electric, Merck, ARCO, Johnson & Johnson, Eli Lilly, American Express, and McDonald's. A wide range of U.S. industry groups—including the aerospace, electrical manufacturing, office equipment, and transportation industries—have more than 50 percent institutional ownership.

The significance of pension funds to both the financing and ownership of U.S. industry was first highlighted by management expert Peter Drucker in 1976 in his book *The Unseen Revolution*. In this book, Drucker highlighted not only the overall growth of pension funds between 1950 and 1974 but also their growing importance in the ownership of American industry. As Drucker pointed out, the growing pension fund investment was bringing socialism to the United States. Because pension funds legally belong to the workers of America, pension fund ownership of America's largest companies has effectively transferred ownership of America's industry to its workers from the mythical capitalists of Marxism and real-life capitalists like Mellon, Rockefeller, Ford, and Carnegie of the late nineteenth and early twentieth centuries.

At the same time that legal ownership of America's largest corporations has been transferred from legendary entrepreneurs to America's workers, effective ownership (in the sense of directing the business enterprise) has been transferred to the middle level corporate bureaucrats and civil servants who are the day-to-day managers of the nation's pension funds. This is a development of immense importance. It has given rise to a major money management industry (discussed further in Chapter 10); the replacement of the visionary leadership of the original entrepreneurs who founded America's major corporations with that of paid managers out to maximize their own welfare rather than that of the shareholders; and the replacement of patient shareholders interested in maximization of the long-term value of the enterprise by short-term risk adverse shareholder surrogates who operates in a lemming-like fashion.

Growth Creates Problems: The Corporate Governance Movement and the Difficulties of the PBGC

This transfer of ownership has had several major effects on large corporations in America. One is that top management of these corporations has been increasingly severed from contact with company owners. Pension fund money managers typically hold stocks while they perform and sell them when they don't. This readiness to sell when stocks fail to perform rather than to replace corporate management by voting for new directors was a major contributor to the corporate takeovers and leveraged buyouts of the 1980s. If the shareholders wouldn't effect change, outsiders would! Money managers sold out to the highest bidder regardless of the long-term impact on the company or the economy. In fact, many good arguments have been made in recent years that this readiness to sell companies for short-term profits has had a detrimental effect on the long-term growth of the American economy.

More recently, these sales have given rise to a growing corporate governance movement as a result of a combination of greater awareness among pension fund managers of liability under ERISA for failure to act as a fiduciary and increasing difficulty in selling the large blocks of stock that major pension funds hold without a significant loss. This growing movement seeks to have pension funds play a more active role in governing the corporations in which they are major shareholders.

SEARS RESISTS CORPORATE GOVERNANCE

In the spring of 1991, the corporate governance movement entered a new phase when one of its leaders—a respected former business executive and senior administrator in the U.S. Labor Department under the Reagan adminstration, Robert Monks—campaigned to be elected a director of Sears Roebuck. His stated goal in seeking institutional shareholders' votes was to be an outside voice on Sears's board so that management would feel more pressure to be effective in improving Sears's performance. Monks believed that top management of Sears was insulated from any pressure to turn the company around because so much of its stock was controlled by institutional investors, who traditionally voted with management. Sears's management felt that Monks's effort represented such a threat to the cozy status quo that it spent $5.5

million in a proxy campaign and restructured the board from fifteen to ten directors to make it harder for Monks to be elected. Apparently Sears's management was not interested in what shareholders had to say or in being responsive to the institutional owners of the company.

Even as pension funds become the largest form of financial institution in the United States, they are beginning to succumb to some of the problems of traditional types of financial institutions. When ERISA was passed in 1974, it established the Pension Benefit Guaranty Corporation to ensure that worker's would not lose their savings as represented by pension rights. However, as 1991 began, the PBGC began to report problems like those experienced earlier by the FSLIC and the FDIC. In March 1991, the PBGC reported that underfunding of pensions by a number of major corporations that were in or near bankruptcy had created a situation in which the assets of the PBGC could be exceeded by its liabilities to the extent of $14 billion dollars, a difference that would have to be made up by the U.S. Treasury and the American taxpayer. Even as the financial system changes, some things stay the same.

The Mutual Fund Industry

The first mutual fund was organized in Boston in 1924. Then, as now, a mutual fund was a company that pooled the financial resources of individual and institutional shareholders with similar financial goals to make investments that met those goals. Investors gained access to money managers' expertise and to financial diversification that was previously available only to wealthy individuals and large institutions. Like other parts of the securities industry, the mutual fund industry experienced some abuses of trust during the 1920s. The industry was brought under the New Deal securities rules by the Investment Company Act of 1940, which required all mutual funds to register with the Securities and Exchange Commission and to meet certain operating standards, and by the Investment Advisors Act of 1940, which regulated the advisors to the funds.

The industry reached $1 billion in assets in 1945 and 1 million accounts in 1950. By 1970, there were 400 mutual funds totalling over $50 billion in assets. Money-market mutual funds that allowed individual investors to participate in high short-term interest rates were introduced in the early 1970s, and their introduction signaled a turning point in the mutual fund industry.

Because novice individual investors were more willing to give money-market funds a try, money-market funds became the first mutual fund investment of 30 percent of all mutual fund investors and the largest and fastest-growing segment of mutual funds by the end of the 1980s. Although banks were authorized to offer money-market deposit accounts in 1983, money-market mutual funds have paid consistently higher rates, up to a 300 basis point differential in 1989. Money-market mutual funds have remained the primary competition for bank deposit dollars and hold assets equal to about 15 percent of bank deposits.

Before money-market funds, the mutual find industry was concentrated in equity funds, but during the 1980s the types of mutual funds exploded. Funds specialized in the assets of an industry such as energy or states such as Ohio or countries such as Germany. By 1990, the Investment Company Institute, a research organization for the mutual fund industry, classified mutual funds into twenty-two major categories by investment objective. Over the decade of the 1980s, mutual funds were the fastest-growing major financial institution.

Mutual Fund Owners: The Mythical Everyman

In 1980, the mutual fund industry controlled $135 billion in assets in 564 funds for 12 million shareholder accounts; one in twenty people invested in mutual funds. By 1990, one in four people—30 million people with 58 million accounts—invested almost $1 trillion in over 2,900 mutual funds. Mutual funds have attracted investors for three reasons. First, an individual investor actually hires a professional money manager by investing in mutual funds, often with an initial investment of as little as $250 to $2,500. The money manager can base portfolio decisions on economic and financial research that may be difficult for individuals to gather and use. Second, a fund can provide the benefits of diversification among a variety of industries or types of securities that would not ordinarily be open to an investor without a substantial portfolio. The third benefit for investors is the exchange privilege within a family of funds. This allows shareholders to exchange shares from one fund to another within a group under common management. In changing economic conditions, investors can easily move their money between short- and long-term investments, between industries, and even between mixes of debt and equity.

As the total assets in mutual funds have grown over the past ten years, so has the number of households that have invested in them. In 1980, 6 percent of households owned mutual funds. By 1989, 25 percent of U.S. households invested in mutual funds, an increase of over 18 million households. Although investors in all age groups owned mutual funds, 45 percent of investors were in the twenty-five to forty-four age bracket. Over 20 percent of all U.S. households had a head of household sixty-five years or older, yet only 14 percent of mutual fund owning households were within this age group, implying an interest in mutual funds by younger investors. This trend is encouraging for the industry when combined with the anticipated 28 percent growth rate in the number of thirty-five- to fifty-four-year-olds over the next ten years.

Mutual funds are owned by households from a wide range of income levels. Almost a quarter of all mutual funds are owned by households with incomes of $25,000 or less, although this figure may be distorted by the number of retired householders in this income bracket. Sixteen percent of households owning mutual funds in 1989 had annual incomes over $75,000. Sixty-five percent of households with income greater than $75,000 owned mutual funds, compared with 25 percent of the total population.

In the changing regulatory environment, many different kinds of firms provided a wide range of financial products and services to investors. Considering the fragmentation of the industry, it is not surprising that diverse mutual fund distribution channels existed. In 1990, the Investment Company Institute divided investment activity into six distribution channels: full-service brokers, insurance agents, financial planners, captive sales forces of mutual fund underwriters, direct marketers, and deposit institutions or banks. In effect, every segment of the financial-services industry is involved with mutual funds.

The Rise of Money Market Funds

Because mutual funds require no equity capital to protect their shareholders against risk, they are much more efficient than commercial banks. This reality has fueled the growth of the most rapidly growing part of the mutual fund business, the money-market fund. First introduced in the early 1970s, money-market funds have increasingly replaced bank deposits as the place where consumers keep their cash and near cash assets. Figures 1.2 and 1.3 show how the number of money-market mutual funds and the assets of money-market mutual funds have grown since their introduction in 1974. Given their growth and the thrifts' shrinkage, money-market funds will replace thrifts as the largest alternative for consumer liquid savings in the early 1990s.

What is particularly interesting about money-market funds is that they look very much like commercial banks of the 1950s and 1960s except that they have no capital, are not insured by the federal government, and have no prudential supervision over the quality of their assets. From the consumer's standpoint they certainly operate like a bank; consumers can write checks on them or make other types of withdrawals as they would from a traditional savings account. Through cash-management accounts such as the one pioneered by Merrill Lynch and now offered by most brokerage firms, consumers can even access their money-market accounts through an automated teller machine using a credit card. And most important to the consumer, they offered regular interest payments, which often exceed competitive bank rates by 1 percent to 3 percent.

From a balance sheet standpoint, the money-market funds also look like banks (except for the lack of capital). Money-market funds invest in liquid assets like Treasury bills and notes, municipal bonds (the tax-exempt funds only), bankers' acceptances, and commercial paper (high-quality, short-term corporate loans)—essentially the same investments that banks held forty years ago. However, because the money-market funds have no shareholder capital (or *only* shareholder capital, if you consider money-market fund holders as equity holders rather than depositors), they do not have to earn a spread over the cost of their funds and do not have to guarantee a return of those funds. They are a true pass-through intermediary.

THE RELATIVE EFFICIENCY OF BANKS AND MUTUAL FUNDS

The relative efficiency of commercial banks and mutual funds can be seen by comparing the Chase Manhattan Corporation, the second-largest commercial banking company in the United States at the beginning of 1991, and the Fidelity mutual fund group, the largest mutual fund manager in the United States. Both institutions had approximately $100 billion in assets under management in early 1991, but the people and capital required to support the two operations are markedly different.

To create, fund, and manage its assets under management, the Chase Manhattan Corporation required 40,000 people, $5 billion in equity capital, and a 3 percent margin between the return on its assets (principally business and consumer loans) and what it paid its source on funds (principally interest to depositors) to cover the expenses of its operations such as personnel costs, to provide a reserve for losses on its loans, and to provide a return to its equity shareholders. To create, fund, and manage its assets under management, Fidelity required only 6,500 people, less than $500 million in equity capital, and a 1 percent margin between the return on its assets (principally debt and equity securities) and what it paid its source of funds (principally dividends to its mutual fund shareholders) to cover the expense of its operations such as personnel costs and provide a return to its equity shareholders.

A bank is distinquished from a money-market fund by its guarantees to its sources of funds (its depositors) that it will return the face value of their money with interest. The mutual fund promises its source of money (its mutual fund shareholders) only that it will manage that money to the best of its ability and hopefully return the face value of that money plus a handsome profit to its source of money. The difference between a guarantee and a best-efforts basis requires the bank to have much more equity capital in its business than the mutual fund and to make sufficient profits in order to provide an attractive return to its equity supplier. This guarantee of security of principal and interest to its sources of money makes the bank's job much more difficult than that of the mutual fund.

Commercial Banks and Mutual Funds

The old saying "If you can't lick them, join them" applies to commercial banks and mutual funds. The mutual fund industry is attractive to investors as well as to commercial banks. Banks are realizing that they cannot compete with mutual funds, so they are establishing and selling their own. The sales fees that the banks receive from the mutual fund companies provide noninterest income, a much needed revenue source in times of shrinking net interest margins. But banks forego a profit opportunity when they sell others' mutual funds; they receive a one-time sales fee but miss the continuing management fees.

Changes in the regulatory and legal environment have encouraged commercial banks to introduce and manage their own mutual funds. When in 1987 the Basle Committee on Banking Regulations and Supervisory Practices recommended increasing banks' capital requirements, banks began to search for assets that could be managed without additional capital, a criterion mutual funds fit. Norwest Bank successfully tested a limit of the Glass-Steagall Act by allowing one subsidiary to manage a fund that another subsidiary sold. Prior to the Norwest test, banks had been prohibited from underwriting their own mutual funds since the 1930s. They usually hired a distributor, regulated by the Securities Exchange Act of 1934, to file their fund with the Securities and Exchange Commission.

With the Norwest decision, commercial banks realized that the structure of the financial-services industry would continue to change. The barriers surrounding banks, erected after the Depression, would be eliminated, allowing banks to become stockbrokers, sell insurance, open branches nationwide, and underwrite bonds and mutual funds. Banks began to think of themselves as financial-services companies and rushed in large numbers to establish their own mutual funds. By 1990, seventy-nine of the 100 largest U.S. banks, forty-seven of the top fifty banks, and all the top ten banks offered their own mutual funds.

Investors at present, however, choose to purchase mutual funds through a bank only 18 percent of the time, although they use banks for 65 percent of their total investment activity. These findings seemed to contradict a 1989 *Wall Street Journal* study that found commercial banks are better positioned with investors as a source of investment advice than any other channel. Furthermore, studies by the Investment Company Institute in 1989 showed that 80 percent of investors used one channel for all their investment needs three-quarters of the time. This customer loyalty highlighted banks' potential advantage as the holder of an investor's most basic financial relationship—a transaction or checking account. Banks should benefit from cross-selling mutual funds to their transaction and savings account customers and from gaining deposits from new mutual fund customers.

Analysts have determined that investors do not buy mutual funds from banks because banks have only recently begun to offer the funds and usually do not offer a sufficiently wide variety of mutual fund investment alternatives. Investors are also uncertain about who in the bank they should contact for information about mutual funds. Banks have to eliminate these obstacles, and similar obstacles in other new products such as insurance, for investors if they hope to remain viable in the changing financial industry. As banks become diversified financial-services companies, their role in the mutual fund and other segments should grow. Increasingly, banks will minimize their requirement for capital and increase their net income by offering their customers money-market funds and other types of mutual funds and services instead of seeking to have their customers deposit their funds directly in the bank itself.

The Future of New Age Financial Institutions

In the future, pension funds and mutual funds can be expected to continue to grow and become increasingly dominant in terms of total assets under management compared to traditional types of financial institutions such as commerical banks and insurance companies. At the same time the role of many traditional financial institutions will change, as banks and insurance companies increasingly become originators of the assets they sell to others and managers of assets for others. In the process, the assumption of risk by the traditional intermediaries will be reduced. By the year 2000, pension funds and mutual funds should account for most of the nation's financial assets.

Several factors should contribute to this trend, including some already discussed in detail in this book. The first will be the savings boom that many economists expect in the decade of the 1990s as the baby boom enters its prime savings years. This savings boom should significantly increase the nation's financial assets, and the majority of these savings will be directed to small company and individual pension funds or mutual funds. The second factor will be the special tax status of pension funds, which will continue to encourage people to save through a pension fund whenever possible. The third factor contributing to the increase in relative share of assets in pension funds and mutual funds will be the demise of the thrift industry and the consolidation of the commercial banking system (discussed in earlier chapters). The fourth factor will be the relative efficiency of mutual funds and their low capital requirements compared to depository institutions, which will increasingly make them the financial institution of choice of the average consumer. The final factor will be the growing use of securitization by traditional financial institutions to increase fee income and move assets off their balance sheets to improve their capital base and their return on capital. The role of securitization in creating the new financial system and hastening the demise of the old system is the subject of the next chapter.

7

The Securitization of the Financial System

The evolution of financial-service institutions and instruments has resulted in the creation of some of the ugliest words to enter the English language in recent years. Polysyllabic for the most part, they have little of the brevity and charm of computer terms such as "debug," "bootup," and "floppy disk." One of the earliest terms to emerge was "disintermediation," which appeared in the mid-1960s to describe the removal by corporate financial officers of deposits from banks in order to invest them directly in Treasury bills or other instruments. Sidney Homer, long the portfolio timing strategist at Salomon Brothers, even ran a contest offering a significant cash prize for the best, attractive word that could be used as an alternate. He eventually called off the contest, admitting defeat. It should be no surprise, therefore, that the most important factor in the transformation of the financial system has been given one of the least attractive names: *asset* (or *loan*) *securitization*.

Banking expert Lowell Bryan of management consultants McKinsey & Company has described asset securitization as a "new technology" that is reshaping the financial landscape.

Asset securitization is speeding the demise of the savings and loan industry, accelerating the consolidation of the commercial banking system, and supporting the dramatic growth of pension funds and mutual funds. Asset or loan securitization has made obsolete the traditional role of savings and loans as a holder of home mortgages and is increasingly making obsolete the traditional role of commercial banks as a holder of consumer, business, and commercial loans. The new technology of asset or loan securitization will be the most important factor in the development of the new financial system.

Loan Securitization

Loan securitization is a hybrid form of financing that combines features of two well-developed systems—the traditional credit system and the securities system. Securitization can take place without being loan securitization. Commercial paper and junk bond issuance, for example, are forms of securitization that do not involve the literal conversion of loans into securities. The earliest securitized loan was the banker's acceptance. In addition, just as commercial paper has essentially replaced large bank loans with a security, junk bonds have replaced medium- and long-term insurance company loans with a security.

Assest securitization is quite simple in concept, but it rapidly becomes quite complex in practice. At its most elementary, a financial institution makes loans for a purpose such as purchase of a single-family house. When it gets enough of these loans, it puts them all in a bag and sells to investors the rights to receive the payments made on the loans in the bag. In order to ensure that it is not liable in any way for the payments and that it will have no rights to them, the financial institution puts the bag in the possession of a fiduciary or trust, which has the responsibility for making sure that payments are collected and disbursed according to the contracts.

Once the bag is in the hands of the trustee, the credit risk associated with the originating institution has been completely separated from the bag of assets. Therefore, the price of the bag reflects the quality of the assets in the bag rather than the quality of the originating institution. The institution with the worst credit risk would get the same price for the same bag that the best credit risk would get. The worst-credit-risk institution can therefore compete directly with the best to make these loans. It could not do this if it had to raise the money itself to pay for the assets in the bag and had to charge the borrower the premium it paid in the market because of its own risk.

In reality, loan/asset securitization is an incredibly complex and carefully structured five-part process. Figure 7.1 (see page 139) shows a diagram of it using an an illustration a Citibank transaction to be discussed in a later section. The five parts are: origination, structuring, credit enhancement, placement and trading, and servicing. The securitization process begins when a financial institution originates and puts together a pool of underlying primary assets, which it then sells to a special purpose vehicle (SPV) set up for the purpose of structuring the transaction. The assets sold can be either specific receivables with fixed maturities such as mortgages, or they can be earmarked accounts (e.g., credit card accounts) whose balances revolve over time. The nature of the SPV—which can be a trust, a special limited partnership, or a special purpose corporation—determines the tax and accounting treatment of the transaction and the structure of the relevant operational details, such as the way payments are to be made to the ultimate investors and any extra protection to be provided against bankruptcy risk.

Once the pool of assets has been sold to the SPV, the SPV itself then issues a security such as a note or a bond, which represents either debt of the SPV or an equity interest in the SPV (known as an asset-backed security, or ABS). ABS's isolate the assets in the pool from the credit of the financial intermediaries selling the loans and servicing the pool and protect investors against losses on the underlying collateral. Because the SPV is legally separate from the originating institution, the financial condition of the seller does not influence the credit quality of an ABS it organizes. Even if the seller were taken over by the regulators, the assets of the SPV would not be affected nor could they be claimed by the creditors of the orginating entity.

Credit rating agencies assign ratings to ABS issues just as they do to corporate bonds by assessing the ability of the underlying assets to generate the cash flows necessary for principal and interest payments to investors. Rating agencies assume a worst-case scenario for losses when determining the level of loss coverage necessary to attain a given rating. Ratings are based on repossession frequency and severity of losses under an assumed disaster economic scenario. The rating agencies evaluate the historical default experience of the portfolio, the specific characteristics of loans within the pool, and the selection criteria used to form the pool. Loss coverage required to earn a high rating is usually several times the actual historical losses on the portfolio.

To obtain the investment-grade credit rating for the ABS and make the transaction attractive to investors, some type of credit-enhancement arrangement is usually necessary. An irrevocable letter of credit (LOC) from a commercial bank is the most common form of ABS credit enhancement. LOCs generally cover losses up to either a fixed dollar amount of principal or a percentage of a declining principal balance. Alternatively, an SPV may obtain insurance to guarantee against a portion of potential losses on the assets, typically a *first loss guarantee* from the originator of the primary assets, and then obtain a *wrap guarantee* (similar to a reinsurance contract in the property/casualty business) from an insurance company for a multiple of expected losses.

One way to meet the net flow requirements imposed by the rating agencies is to overfund the pool of securities. The originating institution puts securities into the pool to give the pool a cash-flow present value in excess of the expected proceeds of the sale of the ABS. For example, if a rating of AAA requires the investor to be safe even if 40 percent of the pool defaults, a pool of $100 million can be sold for only $60 million. The originating institution would be the residual owner of the balance of the pool when the securitized obligations had been retired. In some instances, this residual amount will also be securitized, although at a much higher discount rate to reflect the risk of its inferior position.

The level of credit enhancement, as well as the quality of the enhancer, are evaluated by the rating agency. An issue can be rated no higher than the credit rating of the credit-enhancer. An issue, however, can receive a lower rating if the level of enhancement for that particular issue is judged insufficient in light of the ABS's structure.

With this credit protection, the ABS's typically are very highly rated and are usually bought by institutional investors, such as mutual funds or pension funds. The underlying assets and payments to the investors can then be serviced either by a third party or by the originator, which in any case retains the spread between the yield on the underlying assets and the interest paid to the investors, net of credit enhancement and other fees.

The Growth of Loan Securitization

Securitization of loans made by banks and other financial institutions began in 1970 when the recently created Government National Mortgage Association (GNMA) offered investors the opportunity to buy into pools of FHA and VA mortgages by purchasing a new type of security, a mortgage-backed security (MBS). During the fifteen years after the initial MBS was offered by GNMA, the market for MBS's grew rapidly. By 1985, MBS's represented the second-largest pool of securities outstanding after U.S. government securities. A total of $334 billion of MBS's were outstanding from the three leading issuers—the Government National Mortgage Association (Ginny Mae), the Federal Home Loan Mortage Corporation (Freddie Mac), and the Federal National Mortgage Association (Fanny Mae).

MBS's were originally issued only by government-related entities. By 1987, however, private issuers were becoming increasingly important. During 1987 new MBS issues (both public and private) represented about two-thirds of all mortgage originations in that year. There were over 360 privately sponsored new issues in 1987, or 1.5 every business day, for an annual volume of $70 billion.

Until 1985, securitization of loans was confined principally to securitization of residential mortgages. Then, the market for ABS's changed dramatically. The first public securitized transaction of nonmortgage assets occurred in March 1985, when participations in a group of computer leases were offered by Sperry Rand Corporation and its investment banker, First Boston. Following the securitization of computer leases, Marine Midland Bank, in conjunction with Salomon Brothers, securitized $60 million of automobile loan receivables in May 1985, and the feasibility of securitizing of nonmortgage assets was clearly established. Since then, securitization of nonmortgage assets has been dominated by securitization of automobile and credit card receivables.

A review of the history of securitization of automobile loan receivables shows an impressive record. Between the first public offering of automobile loans, in 1985, and 1988, there were sixty-two issues, with initial balances totaling approximately $21 billion. In addition, substantial private placements of ABS's of automobile receivables also were made. Issuers included General Motors Acceptance Corporation (GMAC), Ford Motor Credit, Chrysler Finance Company, and Nissan Motor Acceptance Corporation as well as major financial institutions such as Bank of America, Marine Midland Bank, and First National Bank of Boston. GMAC was responsible for over half of the total, issuing 58 percent and 85 percent of all automobile loan ABS's in 1985 and 1986, respectively. During 1987, GMAC sharply decreased ABS issuance; however, a broader group of participants entered the market, including commercial banks and the finance subsidiaries of other automobile manufacturers.

Credit card ABS's, first publicly offered in 1987, has rapidly become the second-largest sector of the nonmortgage ABS market. Issue volume was $2.5 billion in 1987 and $5.2 billion in the first nine months of 1988. Commercial banks and thrifts had been the primary originators of credit card ABS's backed by MasterCard or VISA receivables. Then Sears introduced in June 1988 the first public ABS supported by retail credit card receivables. Montgomery Ward and J. C. Penney followed with issues backed by their card receivables. By the end of 1987, securitization of nonmortgage assets had reached an annual level of $10 billion, and the volume was growing. By this time, ABS's were backed by a wide range of loans including loans on boats and recreational vehicles, airplane leases, unsecured personal loans, and life insurance policy holder loans.

By the middle of 1991, asset securitization was becoming the single most important activity of Wall Street. Total ABS's outstanding were in excess of $800 billion, an amount larger than the assets of the S&L industry. New issues of ABS's in the first six months of 1991 were estimated at $125 billion, making it likely that 1991 would surpass 1990's record of $180 billion in new issues of ASB's. At the rate of $250 billion, the new issues of ABS's would equal 10 percent of commercial bank assets. Though mortgage-backed securities still dominated the market, accounting for $710 billion, other types of ABS's were rapidly increasing in importance. In 1990, almost $50 billion of non-mortgage ABS's were issued, and the pace of new issues of non-mortgage ABS's in the first half of 1991 was outrunning that of the first half of 1990. The turnover of non-mortgage ABS's was higher than of mortgage ABS's. Almost 40 percent of the non-mortgage ABS's had been issued within the year, whereas the comparable figure for MBS's was less than 20 percent.

An Example of Loan Securitization: Citibank Mortgage Pass-through Certificates

The broadest use of loan securitization has been in the mortgage area. Between 1981 and 1986, the percentage of new mortgage originations securitized rose from less than 20 percent to approximately 70 percent. Since 1986, the percentage of new mortgages securitized on an annual basis has ranged between two-thirds and three-quarters of all new mortgages. The majority of mortgages securitized have utilized some form of federal credit guarantee. Often this guarantee comes at two stages, with federal credit guarantees being used at both the individual loan stage and at the securitization stage. For example, a lender may pool a group of FHA- or VA-insured loans (credit guarantee at the individual loan level) and then have Ginnie Mae (the Government National Mortgage Association) guarantee the ABS's. However, an increasing percentage of mortgages are being securitized without any form of government protection. Citibank's issuance of mortgage pass-through certificates for nonconforming mortgages in November 1986 is an example of such a transaction. In late November of 1986, Citibank sold $110 million in mortgage pass-through certificates with 9 percent coupon. The transaction occurred in the following manner and is diagrammed in Figure 7.1.

Over a period of several years, Citibank originated fifteen-year, fixed-rate mortgages in New York, New Jersey, and

Figure 7.1
The Loan Securitization Process

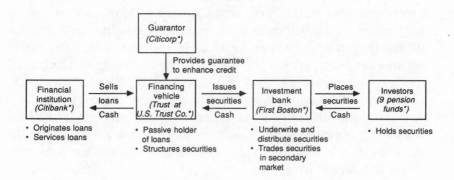

*Refers to participant in Citicorp mortgage securitization example.

Connecticut. These loans varied in size and type with some having outstanding principal balances of over $350,000 while the majority had balances of less than $150,000. Over two-thirds of the loans were for single family homes; the balance were for condominiums and row houses. A few exceeded 80 percent of collateral value but had private mortgage insurance so that the uninsured amount of the loan was no more than 75 percent of the collateral value. For a variety of reasons, these mortgages were not suitable for sale in government guaranteed securitization programs, but Citibank wished to securitize them anyway.

To accomplish that purpose Citibank contracted with the United States Trust Company of New York to establish and be trustee for a tax-exempt trust. Citibank then sold $110 million of its fifteen-year, fixed-rate mortgages to the trust and received back $110 million in Series 1986-Q Pass-Through Certificates each representing a fractional undivided interest in the pool of mortgages. The certificates were designed so that investors would receive monthly payments of interest and principal. Each month investors would receive their proportional share of principal payments made by borrowers in the preceding month and their proportional share of 9 percent annual interest on the outstanding principal accrued the previous month.

To enhance the attractiveness of the certificates to investors, Citibank agreed when it sold the mortgages to the trust to protect the trust against losses from default on the mortgages. This protection was in the form of a Citicorp guarantee to make up any losses on default over 4 percent of the original face amount of mortgages up to a maximum of 10 percent. When the establishment of the trust, the sale of the mortgages (including Citicorp's guarantee), and the issuance of the certificates to Citibank were complete, the certificates were rated by Standard & Poor's. Because of the high quality of the mortgages and the Citicorp guarantee against default, Standard & Poor's rated the certificates AA, making them suitable investments for conservative institutional investors.

After Standard & Poor's rated the certificates, Citibank joined forces with First Boston to sell the certificates to institutional investors. Each took responsibility for placing half the securities, $55 million. Ultimately, the issue was placed with nine nondepository institutional investors (primarily pension funds), illustrating how depository institutions are being replaced as the funding source for mortgates.

INVESTMENT BANKS LOVE SECURITIZATION

The growth of securitization has been a bonanza for investment banks. Investment banks such as Salomon Brothers that are oriented to the bond market have found that securitization has created a new, extremely profitable market for them. In the early 1980s, Salomon Brothers made hundreds of millions of dollars in profits as a result of its leading role in securitizing the residential mortgages of savings and loans. Salomon's real estate department under the leadership of Lewis Ranieri bought billions of dollars of mortgages from thrifts and resold them to pension funds and other investors as ABS's at spreads of up to 300 basis points or 3 percent of the face value of the mortgage. This equaled $3 million dollars in revenue (most of which was profit) for Salomon Brothers for every $100 million in mortgages the firm bought and securitized.

Citibank remained the servicer for the loans even though it had sold the loans to the trust. As servicer, Citibank receives all payments from the borrowers, to whom it appears that Citibank still holds their mortgages. All principal payments together with the portion of the payments necessary to pay interest at the pass-through rate are then deposited into a trust account. For its role as servicer, Citibank receives the difference between the 9 percent interest paid on the certificates and the actual interest paid on the mortgages in the trust. Since the average rate on the mortgages sold was about 10.4 percent, Citicorp receives about 1.4 percent annually on the balance of the mortgages in the trust ($110 million initially and then declining over time as the principal of the mortgages is paid off) in return for its serving expenses and the risk it assumed for partially guaranteeing the mortgages in the pool. By selling the mortgages to the trust while remaining the loan servicer, Citibank reduced its assets, its liabilities, its required capital level, and its exposure to loan losses while increasing its fee-based income, its return on assets, and its return on capital.

Other Types of Securitization

Even though mortgage loans have been the depository institution asset securitized to the greatest degree, other types of bank and thrift loans are increasingly being securitized. Since 1985, automobile loans, credit card loans, and other types of consumer and business loans have all been sold as ABS's. Some banks have securitized portfolios of LBOs and highly levered transaction (HLT) loans. Investment bankers have even arranged securitization for portfolios of accounts receivable of commercial companies, thus bypassing the depository institutions completely.

Many of the nonmortgage ABS's utilize structures developed by automobile loan ABS's because automobile loans are relatively short term (three to five years) compared to residential mortgage securities. Each type of asset being securitized has its own little quirks that must be properly allowed for in designing the securitized security. Automobile loans, for example, are seldom prepaid when interest rates fall. Unlike mortgages, which can be refinanced at a lower rate, the refinancing of an automobile loan has to be done at used-car rates. These are usually sufficiently higher than new-car rates that refinancing is not attractive. Credit card receivables present structural challenges because of the very short duration of the balance in any given credit card account compared with the typical investor's wish for a security with a known return over a period of three to five years. Credit card securitization thus requires an elaborate arrangement for replacing balances in accounts if they are run down, allocating the incoming cash flows to the investor as interest or principal, and closing out the pool at the end of its life.

Virtually all these types of issues, public and private, have featured some sort of credit enhancement, which protects against credit losses on the collateral. Credit protection can be provided by an issuer guarantee, insurance, or letter of credit. (Third-party credit enhancement can enable an issue to have a higher rating than the issuer.) The form of credit enhancement depends on the issuer. Banks, which are governed by regulatory accounting, rely on third-party credit enhancement because recourse financings by banks are treated as debt and are subject to capital requirements. Finance companies or nonbank issuers can provide their own guarantee, but entities rated lower than AA can generally obtain a better issue price by using third-party credit enhancement. Debt covenants prohibiting recourse transactions can also be a factor in deciding whether to seek third-party credit enhancement.

Credit protection usually takes a form analogous to a "pool policy" on pools of mortgages: it covers losses up to a fixed percentage, typically 5 to 10 percent, of the pool balance. An alternative to third-party credit enhancement is a senior-junior (and subordinated) securities issue in which two classes of securities are created for an SPV, with the senior class of securities being sold in the market and the junior class being held by the loan originator. This alternative is actively used by companies selling credit card receivables.

Apart from the credit enhancement devices, investors are protected from losses in several ways. Most issues require that delinquent payments be advanced by the servicer or guarantor. Theft or the destruction of a vehicle is covered by insurance policies on the individual loans. Death of the borrower can be covered by credit life insurance. Some losses on indirect loans can be covered through dealer recourse. The pool policy covers the remainder of the losses up through specified limits of the policy. Although prepayments can create some uncertainty, the short maturity of many of these issues means that scheduled amortization is a much larger component of cash flow than for mortgage securities. As a result, wide swings in prepayment rates have only a minor effect on the investment properties (yield, weighted-average life, and duration) of these short-term ABS's.

Loan Sales Distiquished from Loan Securitization

Where lack of uniformity in loan terms, structures, and prepayment patterns make it difficult to securitize assets, whole loan sales are utilized. There are four principal types of secondary market sales of separate whole loans:

- Participation. In this type of transaction, a participant purchases either a full or partial participation interest in a loan or pool of loans from the original lender. There is no direct contractual relationship, however, between the participant and the borrower; the only parties to the loan agreement are the borrower and the original lenders. A specified share of the loan payments is passed to the participant through an original lender, who retains ownership of the note and continues to be responsible for all administrative matters relating to the loan.

- Syndication. In this type of arrangement, a primary lender brings other lenders to a transaction to take a share of a loan at the point the loan is closed. Each of the lenders is thus a direct party to the loan agreement and a named payee on the note. The negotiations concerning the loan may include only the primary lenders or all the lenders involved.

- Assignment. An assignment is an outright sale of a piece of a loan, with a pro-rata share of the owner's rights and interests, to a third party. As in a syndication and unlike a participation, the third party has a direct contractual relationship with the borrower.

- Sale. In this type of transaction, a loan is sold in its entirety to a third party. The sale ends the contractual relationship between the original lender and the borrower. A new note is issued to the buyer of the loan.

Loan sales once were made by banks exclusively to other banks. However, in recent years specialized mutual funds have been set up to purchase loans directly from banks. These mutual funds allow banks to sell a greater portion of their loans and are speeding the transfer of assets from the depository system to nondepository financial institutions. In addition, some trade associations and banks have been working to standardize the routine commercial loan so that sales of whole loans to a securitizing institution would be easy. Some loans have even been given ratings by credit agencies.

The Impact of Securitization on the Financial System

Historically, investors were willing to pay for the greater liquidity and credit transparency of securities over loans by accepting lower returns than the equivalent loan would provide. This, in turn, led borrowers who raised money through securities to have lower financing costs, provided the costs of issuing the securities did not exceed the differential between the interest rate on the security and its loan equivalent. Loan securitization took advantage of the cost differential between loans and securities. This cost differential could both pay for the cost of securitization and provide a profit to the securitizing institution. In addition to the reduction in required reserves and the profit potential, financial institutions received another benefit from securitization. Loans that were securitized reduced the overall balance sheet of the institution, thereby reducing total capital required and improving return on equity for a given level of profits.

During the 1980s, borrowing that traditionally flowed through the credit system increasingly migrated to the securities markets. Securities directly replaced loans (as in the case of junk bonds and commercial paper) and loans were securitized because securities are inherently a more efficient, more cost-effective method of borrowing. Their cost-effectiveness came from the three advantages that securities offer to the end investors. First, securities are liquid and tradable, while loans are illiquid; there is only a very limited secondary market for most loans. Second, debt securities are rated by credit agencies, while loans are not. Large classes of investors, including individuals and pension funds, have little ability or desire to assess or cope with credit risk. By investing in rated securities, these groups avoid the trouble and expense of dealing with credit risk, assessing creditworthiness, and working out problem loans to avoid large losses. Third, government regulators increasingly required financial intermediaries, such as commercial banks and savings and loans, to reduce their assets, and securitizing loans was an easy way to accomplish this without abandoning a market.

There are many advantages to be realized from asset securitization for financial institutions—the gains to be achieved from the reduced capital requirements resulting from a reduced asset base, access to cheaper funding, and greater manageability of risk. Asset securitization provides financial institutions with increased flexibility in terms of loan portfolio management and risk management because financial institutions now have the option of either keeping loans in inventory or selling them. Securitizing assets gives the manager of a financial institution control of when and how much risk the institution absorbs because a manager has the ability to eliminate interest rate risk and credit risk by selling loans. Similarly, by selling assets, institutions are able to reduce the cost of required reserves and FDIC insurance.

Probably the greatest advantage of asset securitization is the opportunity it presents financial institutions to improve ROA (return on assets) and ROE (return on equity) by reducing the required asset size and equity size for a given level of profits. Financial institutions can generate fees for originating loans without having the requirement to keep the loans in their own portfolio. By securitizing loans, financial institutions can keep their asset size and capital requirements below what historically has been required for a given volume of loan origination.

PRUDENTIAL AND THE SECURITIZATION OF COMMERCIAL LOANS

A study by a Prudential task force in the spring of 1988 had found a strong potential for secondary market sales of private placements either through securitized pools of assets or through sales of individual whole loans. A special company, PASS, Inc., was therefore established in August 1988 to provide the Prudential organization with an ongoing professional capability to sell assets from Prudential's investment portfolio and to sell those portions of assets that Prudential's investment organizations had originated but that Prudential Insurance did not wish to take into its own investment portfolio. The sales were planned to help keep the proper maturity and diversification in the portfolio. The intended market for PASS, Inc.'s product was commercial banks, insurance companies, thrift institutions, pension funds, mutual funds, and foreign financial institutions, particularly foreign commercial banks.

PASS's first new product attempt was a pool of seasoned short-term loans to be securitized and sold out of the portfolio of Prudential Insurance Company, PASS, Inc.'s parent. Security interests in the Prudential pool of "privately placed" loans would be sold in the form of a public Eurobond issue to investors, primarily to Japanese insurance companies. This initiative, was expected to raise about $400 million. The assets to be sold by PASS, Inc. were a pool of approximately 100 seasoned fixed-rate private placement loans with a remaining life of 1 to 4 years and an average life of 1.4 years. The quality rating was equivalent to Moody's Baa and Standard & Poor's BB-. While this particular offering was never made, it shows that almost every type of financial institution loan is subject to securitization. Other institutions have had surprising success, for example, securitizing a portion of the highly levered transactions in their books.

Although asset securitization provides many benefits to lenders, it has some disadvantages. These include reduced use of financial institutions as intermediaries, loan portfolios weakened by the selling of the best loans, and increased competition because institutions can originate far more loans than they are required to hold and thus do not curtail their origination efforts as their portfolios fill up.

The Future of Loan Securitization

The future of loan securitization is continued growth throughout the 1990s. By the end of the decade, commercial banks probably will be securitizing the majority of their loans and selling them to pass-through intermediaries like pension funds and mutual funds. In the process, commercial banks will reduce their need for deposits to fund the loans they are holding and reduce their need for capital to support their portfolio of loans because these portfolios will be smaller. At the same time that commercial banks reduce their need for deposits, they will also reduce their need for deposit insurance. Since banks that securitize a large portion of their loans will be more efficient, the spread of securitization will reduce the total number of banks needed to service the economy, adding to the overcapacity problem and intensifying the looming shakeout in the banking system.

8

The New Casino of Futures and Options

The new casino, filled with glitzy financial products, has run away with the volume of the financial marketplace. Its share of transactions exceeds those on the public stock exchanges, and analytical techniques have brought about fundamental changes that support the trend toward market efficiency. In order to discuss, even at an elementary level, the games found in the new casino, a brief historical perspective and an introduction to hedging are required. The implications of these techniques can then be identified. Readers familiar with these products may want to scan the introduction, skip the hedging basics, and turn directly to the latter portions of the chapter.

Historical Perspective

Although significant volume of trading in futures and options on financial instruments, such as common stocks, dates from only the early 1970s, these transactions are a modern extension of techniques that have been used for centuries in other arenas. The most common use of hedging, the category of transaction

148

into which both futures and options fit, has been with agricultural commodities. The farmer with crops in the field wants to lock in sale prices even before the crops are harvested, to ensure a profit (assuming, of course, that the price the farmer can get is greater than the cost of raising the crop). The farmer who sells a quantity of grain in advance for future delivery at a fixed price is thus protected from a subsequent price decline (as perhaps might result from an unexpected bumper crop). The baker, who has a contract with a grocery chain to supply baked goods at a fixed price over the course of the year, wants to lock in a fixed price for flour to protect the bakery's profits from an unexpected rise in price (as perhaps might result from crop damage late in the growing season). The farmer and the baker therefore each agree on a price the baker will pay and the farmer will receive on mandatory delivery of a specified amount of grain at a specific time in the future, such as the expected harvest time. (The details of this process are described in the following section.)

The obvious inefficiency of farmers and bakers searching for each other to make a match led to the development of commodity exchanges—institutions that allow parties with goods and those with the need for goods to work through agents to effect transactions. Because there was often an imperfect match between buyers and sellers at any given moment, third parties (perhaps those who also acted as agents) were allowed to take positions so that transactions could take place. The third parties, whose label as *speculators* is excessively pejorative, were betting that their knowledge of the market (fundamental analysis) or of trading patterns (technical analysis) would allow them, on average, to make a better return than investing capital in other ventures of comparable risk.

The translation of these techniques from commodities to the market for financial instruments, stocks and bonds, was slow for several reasons. First, there was a lack of information about the prices for the hedging alternatives. Whereas the commodity exchanges were public institutions, in which trading was conducted in the open and prices were recorded and reported, the market for hedges in common stocks was conducted among a network of brokers. Small advertisements would appear in the

Wall Street Journal, bordering the pages containing the quoted transactions on the New York and American Stock Exchanges, that offered options on a few common stocks. By the time an investor called, the price might have changed. Furthermore, the spreads between the buying and selling prices for these hedges were extremely large because the brokers offering them could not be sure what might happen in the considerable time before a position could be closed out. Finally, even speculators shunned the market because of suspicions that their transactions might not be executed properly; the opportunities for incompetence or dishonesty appeared to be too great to chance participation.

The lack of information, in turn, led to a lack of liquidity in the market, which made it difficult to buy or sell in any large amount without significantly altering the market price. As a result, the hedging market for financial instruments was small, left to a few brokerage houses and investors who were modestly active.

Two developments occurred in 1973 that dramatically altered the attractiveness of hedging transactions in financial instruments. First, after several years of study and negotiations with the regulatory authorities, the Chicago Board of Trade, a commodity exchange, opened the Chicago Board Options Exchange to trade options on selected common stocks listed on the New York Stock Exchange. This arrangement moved the trading of financial hedges off the periphery of the newspaper and into the open. The success of this initial venture led to other exchanges opening trading in contracts on a myriad of financial instruments. Mere opening of a contract in a financial instrument, however, does not necessarily ensure it will be traded any more than it would with physical commodities; some contracts were quietly buried after an initial trial period.

The second development was the publication by Professors Fisher Black and Myron Scholes of an article ("The Pricing of Options and Corporate Liabilities," *Journal of Political Economy,* May–June 1973) identifying the four parameters that were critical to the valuation of an option contract: the difference between the price at which the option could be exercised and the price of the underlying entity, the volatility of the value of the underlying entity, the time left before the option expired, and the interest rate for government short-term debt. (As the first element decreases or any of the others increases, the value of the option increases.) Although subsequent research has raised questions about the applicability of the formulation in many instances, the Black-Scholes model gave sufficient structure to what had been guesswork that many market participants felt comfortable enough to try using and trading options.

Hedging Illustrated

The following brief example shows how hedging and options can be used to reduce risk. Although this example is greatly simplified, the reader new to this topic may wish to refer to the glossary of terms at the end of this chapter. (Then the relevance of the blossoming of the hedging markets is related to the theme of financial markets in transition.)

It is also important to underscore an important difference between a futures contract and an option contract. A futures contract is a *commitment* to deliver (or receive) physical goods. For that reason, when an individual sells a futures contract (agrees to deliver in the future), the broker requires a deposit to help ensure that the seller can make good on the commitment to deliver the commodity. In the event the seller of the futures contract defaults, the broker can use the deposit to buy the necessary contracts to close out the position. If the value of the commodity declines, the broker periodically refunds enough to the futures seller to keep the margin at 10 percent (percentage subject to change) based on current prices. If the value of the commodity rises, however, the seller is required to deposit additional sums with the broker. (These payments are termed *margin calls*.)

In contrast, an options contract *does not commit* the buyer to accept physical delivery of merchandise. The buyer exercises the option only if it is profitable to receive the goods and resell them at a profit or if it is cheaper to exercise the option than to buy currently in the open market. Thus, if a farmer buys a call option on grain at $3.00 per bushel, nothing happens as long as the price of grain remains below $3.00; the owner of the option to buy lets it expire because to exercise the option would result

Figure 8.1
Profit at Production Cost of $2.25

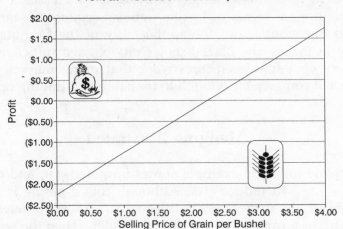

in a loss. The farmer would exercise the option only if the price of grain rises above $3.00. In this case, the farmer would ask for delivery but would immediately sell an equivalent physical quantity of grain on the spot market. The margin requirements for the seller of an option are thus virtually nonexistent as long as the spot price is "out of the money" with respect to the option price. The margin requirements for the buyer of an option are nonexistent because the buyer demands performance only in circumstances where the buyer will have the necessary cash by virtue of being able to sell the item immediately on the spot market at more than the exercise price of the option.

An Agrarian Example

Returning to our agricultural illustration, recall the farmer who sells a grain futures contract and the baker who buys a contract for the future delivery of grain. By selling and buying at a fixed price for future delivery, both sides set the price for the exchange regardless of subsequent price movements.

Suppose that part way through the growing season, the farmer decides with a high degree of certainty that the cost of the grain crop will be $2.25 a bushel. At this point, of course, the farmer does not know the price for which the grain will actually be sold at harvest time. Figure 8.1 shows the profits per bushel that will result from selling at prices between $0.00 and $4.00 a bushel. Presumably, the lower end of the scale is hypothetical, but the price could possibly drop below the $2.25 cost, which would result in a loss to the farmer.

By calling a commodity broker, the farmer learns that the price today of selling grain for delivery three months hence, about the time the crop will be harvested, is currently $2.50. The farmer can thus contract now to deliver a bushel of grain in three months and at that time receive $2.50 a bushel. If the farmer enters into this contract, the profit is "locked in" at $0.25 for each bushel sold. If the price of the crop falls to $0.00 at the time of harvest and when delivery is promised, which is represented at the extreme left of the figure, the farmer sells the crop on the "cash" or "spot" market at $0.00, buys a contract to take immediate delivery of grain, and presents this contract to the broker in lieu of grain itself. (The baker engages in a mirror transaction. This arrangement enables the owners of futures contracts to avoid the inefficiencies of having to make a physical delivery to one another.) The contract costs nothing because the value of the grain is $0.00. The farmer then collects $2.50 per bushel owed him on the original bushel contract. In sum, the farmer collects $2.50, the crop cost $2.25 to raise, and the farmer nets $0.25 a bushel.

Suppose that rather than falling, the price of grain rises to $4.00 a bushel at harvest time. In this case, the farmer will be able to sell the crop for $4.00 cash in the spot market, which would normally mean a handsome profit over the $0.25 a bushel the farmer initially anticipated earning. However, the farmer still has the obligation, under the outstanding contract he sold earlier in the year, to deliver grain at $2.50. The farmer must therefore use the money received from the sale of the crop in the cash market to buy a contract to receive grain. (The price of the spot market and the futures market should be close to one another at this time because we have assumed the cash transaction would occur at harvest, which was the same time the farmer selected as the delivery date in the futures contract.)

The farmer will present the contract (to receive grain) to the broker in lieu of physically delivering the grain owed under the original contract to deliver grain. The broker will pay the farmer the $2.50 a bushel due under the terms of the initial contract to deliver.

Figure 8.2
Profit from a "Futures Roundtrip"

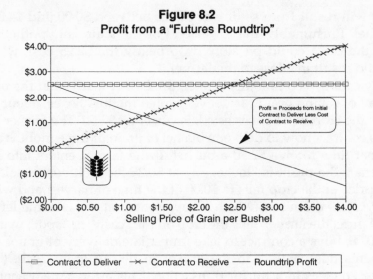

Selling Price of Grain per Bushel

—□— Contract to Deliver   —✕— Contract to Receive   —— Roundtrip Profit

The net position on the cash sale of the grain for $4.00 and the farmer's simultaneous purchase for $4.00 a bushel of the contract to receive grain is zero. The farmer collects $2.50 on delivery (in the form of the contract to receive which the farmer bought), netting a profit of $0.25 a bushel, just as in the case of the price falling below $2.50.

Thus, once the farmer sells a contract for future delivery against a crop in production, the farmer's profit no longer depends on the price of grain at the time the crop is delivered. This conclusion is illustrated by Figures 8.2 and 8.3 in combination. Figure 8.2 shows the farmer's profit or loss on the "roundtrip" in the futures market. The farmer contracted to sell in the future at $2.50 a bushel regardless of the price of grain at the time of delivery. (This agreement is represented by the horizontal line in the upper part of the figure.) At the time of delivery, the farmer has to buy a contract in lieu of physical delivery. The cost of this contract would be the same as the selling price of grain in the spot market at the time delivery is due, represented by the upward-sloping line. The difference between the contract price to deliver and the cost of the price to receive (to cover) is the profit, represented by the downward-sloping line. If the delivery price is less than the contract price, the farmer loses money.

But don't forget that the farmer also gets the cash proceeds

Figure 8.3
Total Effect of a Futures Transaction

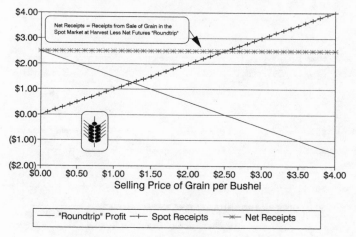

Net Receipts = Receipts from Sale of Grain in the
Spot Market at Harvest Less Net Futures "Roundtrip"

Selling Price of Grain per Bushel

——— "Roundtrip" Profit —+— Spot Receipts —✳— Net Receipts

from selling the grain itself in the spot market. Figure 8.3 shows this amount as the upward-sloping line. The downward-sloping line is the profit on the futures "roundtrip," just as shown in Figure 8.2. The farmer's ultimate position is the net, the horizontal line at the top of the figure at $2.50 a bushel. The net profit is the net receipts ($2.50) less the costs (given at $2.25), a constant $0.25 regardless of what the market price of grain becomes.

In summary, if the price of grain drops, the farmer loses money on the crop but makes it back by being able to "cover" the outstanding futures obligation at the lower price. If the price rises, the farmer makes money on the crop but loses the same amount buying the "cover" at the higher price.

To gain this certainty, however, the farmer has given up the possibility of making a larger profit if the price of grain rises. A farmer who wants to maintain some possibility of enhanced profits if grain prices rise significantly can buy an option to buy grain at a fixed price in the future. The higher the exercise price of the option above the spot price, the lower the cost of the option, as indicated by the Black-Scholes option model. Buying an option at a high price (above current market) will enable the farmer, at a modest transaction cost, to cash in on a price rise if it is substantial enough.

Figure 8.4 shows how the farmer would profit by purchasing

Figure 8.4
Payoff from an Option at $3.00

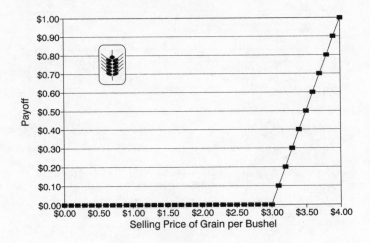

Figure 8.5
Profit from $3.00 Option Costing $.05

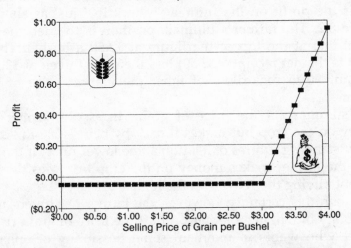

an option to buy a bushel of grain during a specified period at $3.00. As long as the price of grain is less than $3.00, the farmer would not exercise the option because grain can be purchased at less than the $3.00 option price. The option is thus worthless at expiration. Once the price rises above $3.00, however, the option has a payoff. At a price of $4.00 for grain in the spot market at the maturity date of the option, the farmer would make $1.00 per bushel by exercising the option.

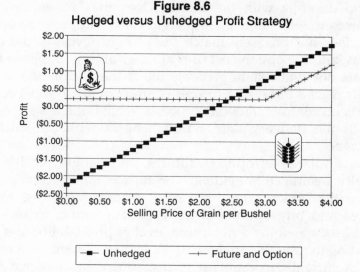

Figure 8.6
Hedged versus Unhedged Profit Strategy

Options have a cost, however. In the circumstances described, it would not be unreasonable for the farmer to have to pay $0.05 per bushel to purchase the option to buy grain at $3.00. Figure 8.5 shows the profit the farmer would make by purchasing such an option: the farmer would lose $0.05 until the price had risen to $3.00 a bushel and would break even at $3.05. Thereafter, the farmer's profits would increase as the price of a bushel of grain increased.

Figure 8.6 is a chart of the profits (and losses) the farmer would make from remaining unhedged, on the one hand, or from combining a *futures* contract to sell grain at $2.50 with an *option* to buy at $3.00 a bushel. If the spot price at harvest was $2.50 or less, the farmer's profits with the hedge would be greater, $0.20 ($0.25 profit on the futures contract less $0.05 for cost of the option) versus an increasing loss per bushel with an unhedged position. Above $2.50 per bushel, the farmer's position would be less attractive hedged than unhedged. By purchase of the option, however, the farmer does share some of the benefit if the price rises significantly above current levels.

There are risks in both futures and options transactions, however. Suppose the farmer's crop fails, leaving the farmer with no crop to sell to raise the funds to buy a contract to offset the outstanding futures contract. Suppose the price of grain rises dramatically, which would require the farmer to make further margin deposits with the broker. Does the farmer have the resources to withstand these margin calls? Suppose the option term does not precisely match the physical cycle of the commodity, and the option cost rises at renewal time. Suppose markets are not available in precisely the farmer's crop: the farmer raises broccoli but sells a futures contract in artichokes because there is no contract traded in broccoli. What if there is a broccoli glut at the delivery date simultaneously with an artichoke shortage?

The similarity of options, futures, and hedging to life and casualty insurance is evident. The farmer makes certain payments (the broker's fees and other transaction costs) to sell futures and buy options, thereby cutting profits in order to avoid loss, obtaining a minimum level of profitability, and participating in growth. Purchase of life insurance requires a reduction in current consumption or investment in exchange for a cash payment at death; purchase of casualty insurance requires a reduction in consumption or investment in exchange for compensation under specified conditions.

A Financial Example

Now that we have looked briefly at how futures and options can serve to control risk for a producer of goods, let us look at how these hedging instruments reduce risk in the financial markets. On March 12, 1991, the common stock of CBS, Inc., was trading at $169.25. In order to buy a share, an investor would have to pay $169.25 (or 70 percent of that amount if the purchase were made on margin with the rest borrowed from the broker) plus fees. If the stock price goes up, the investor will make $1.00 in profit for each $1.00 increase in the share value above $169.25. Likewise, if the share price drops, the investor will lose $1.00 for each $1.00 the price declines below $169.25. Figure 8.7 shows the investor's profit or loss from the purchase of a share of CBS at $169.25.

As an alternative to buying the CBS common stock outright, the investor could purchase a *call* on the stock, which would give the investor the option to buy the stock at a fixed price (known as the *exercise* or *strike price*) for a fixed time period. If the stock rises above the strike price, the investor will exercise

Figure 8.7
Common Stock Profit Chart

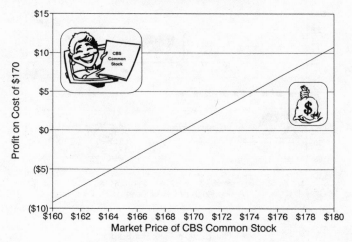

Market Price of CBS Common Stock

the option; if the stock falls below the strike price, the investor will allow the option to expire.

On March 12, 1991, a call expiring in May 1991 on a share of CBS common stock at a strike price of $170 could be purchased for $8.75. If an investor purchased this option, the investor would own the right to pay $170 and receive a share of CBS common stock at any time before the expiration date. Of course, if the shares trade below the strike price, the option will be allowed to expire without being exercised.

Figure 8.8 shows the "payoff table" for the $8.75 call on CBS stock. This is *not* the profit on the transaction; it merely charts what the rational investor will receive (the payoff) depending on the price of the stock at the expiration date of the option. (The profit will be the payoff less the cost of the option.) As Figure 8.8 illustrates, the investor will receive nothing if the CBS stock price is less than the strike price of $170. The investor will receive $1.00 for each $1.00 the market price is higher than the strike price, represented by the line taking off at a 45 degree angle to the northeast.

The risk, of course, is that the investor will lose the entire $8.75 if the price of CBS stock does not rise above the strike price. To reduce the potential magnitude of the loss, the investor might sell a *put*, which would give someone else the right to force the investor to buy a share of CBS stock at a fixed

Figure 8.8
Call and Put Payoff Table

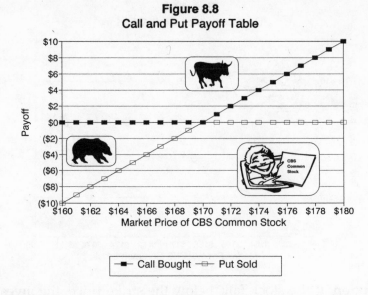

Call Bought — Put Sold

price for a given period. On March 12, 1991, the right to put a share of CBS stock at $170 to another investor at any time until the May expiration date was quoted at $7.75. This is the amount the seller of the put would receive (before transaction costs). This receipt would reduce the investor's outlay to $1.00 (plus transaction costs), the difference between the cost of the call and the proceeds of selling a put.

Figure 8.8 also charts the potential exposure to the investor from having sold a put. If the price of CBS common stock rises above $170, the put will be allowed to expire by its owner. If the price falls below $170, however, the investor will be required to buy a share of CBS at $170 from the owner of the put. In order to get cash back, the investor will then have to sell this share at the going price, now below $170, taking a loss to close out the position. The investor is thus exposed to potential costs equal to the strike price, costs that could by far exceed the proceeds from initially selling the put. (This exposure makes selling puts a very dangerous transaction for a novice.)

But look at the effective position of an investor who has bought a call and sold a put on a share of CBS common stock. The results (charted in Figure 8.9) are exactly the same as if the investor had purchased a share of the common stock, except that the investor has had to put up only $1 net rather than $170. Figure 8.9 demonstrates this equivalency by charting the *profits*

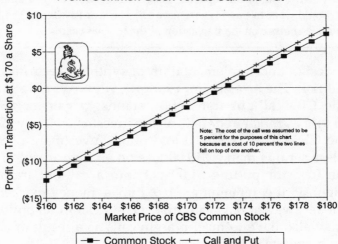

Figure 8.9
Profit: Common Stock versus Call-and-Put

from both transactions, attempting to allow for the costs of each. The difference between the call-put combination and the common stock alternative is caused solely by the transaction costs. A cost of 10 percent for the call-put transaction equates to a 1 percent transaction cost on the "round trip" of buying and selling the stock. (The cost in Figure 8.9 was set at 5 percent so that the lines did not fall exactly on each other.)

The call-put combination is an example of what is known as a *synthetic security* because it artificially creates the same effect on the investor's position as if the investor actually owned the security itself. This particular transaction is one of the least complex; many others of far greater complexity have been created by the "rocket scientists" employed by financial institutions.

SYNTHETICS PRODUCTS DEPARTMENT CONFUSION

Before a recent visit to Japan, members of an Australian bank's Synthetic Products Department had their business cards translated into Japanese. On the group's first call on a prospective client, their cards were studied by the Japanese executives with appropriate seriousness and then with apparent increasing confusion. The Australians became aware that something was causing a problem. To ease the situation, the Australians produced the gifts they had brought—small stuffed koala

bears. This action seemed to heighten the confusion rather than allevi-
ate it. Finally, one of the Japanese hosts asked, "Why do you think our
bank would want to buy toys from you?" The word *synthetic* had been
rendered as *plastic* on the translation of the business cards.

The design and implementation of synthetic securities is not
without risk. The investor, for example, who pays only $1.00 net
into the CBS call-put transaction stands to gain or (what is
worse) lose as much in dollars as the investor who pays $170 to
buy the CBS share. A $10.00 loss on an investment of $170 is
much less serious than a $10.00 loss on an investment of $1.00.
But the investor putting $1.00 net into a call-put transaction
may deposit the remaining $169 into a money-market bank
account as a way of balancing risk. (The seller of an option contract may also have to meet margin calls as a result of adverse
price movements in the underlying stock.)

The risks to the designer and issuer of synthetic securities
come in two forms. The security may be designed and priced
improperly. In that case, investors will buy all of the under-
priced part of the security and leave the issuer holding the over-
priced portion. This happened to Merrill Lynch in the
mid-1980s, hitting the firm with a loss of over $100 million. The
second risk is that the traders themselves may get out of control
and incur hundreds of millions of dollars in further losses while
they are trying to speculate out of a loss position by doubling
the bets. This apparently happened to Volkswagen, also in the
mid-1980s, again with losses of over $100 million.

Effect on Financial Intermediation

The development of the market for synthetic securities (including the instruments and strategies dealing with futures, options,
hedges, short-sales, swaps in a variety of instruments such as
foreign exchange, common stocks, and interest rates) has been
another in the series of new "institutions" undermining the traditional system of financial intermediation. This new casino of
instruments enables the parties to a transaction to work directly
together with only the intermediation of an exchange or a broker rather than to work through an intermediary that actually

puts up capital and takes the risks. For example, a company whose lowest-cost financing is short-term, floating-rate debt but that wants long-term, fixed-rate debt can now arrange an interest-rate swap with another company (maybe even in another country) whose situation is the reverse. Formerly, the borrower would have gone to a bank to arrange a fixed-rate loan, and the bank (perhaps through a foreign branch) would have located a source of funds appropriate to the risk the bank thought it profitable and prudent to take. The counterparty to what is today a swap, looking for short-term money, would have formerly used the same institutional arrangements. Now, each can borrow directly in its own markets in the most advantageous form and then work out the most appropriate overall deal by use of properly structured synthetics.

Ironically, it was precisely the aversion of many financial intermediaries to taking more than the credit risk, as interest rates became more volatile in the 1970s and 1980s, that created an environment encouraging the development and elaboration of these new instruments. Borrowers did not like exposure to these interest-rate risks either. The rocket scientists in investment banks and corporate-finance departments of commercial banks could thus charge significant fees for finding ways to reduce the risks (and costs) to the principals in the transactions.

The development of a system of (comparatively) direct dealings between principals substantially reduced the amount of financial-intermediary capital required because the intermediary risk exposure was reduced. Credit could still be extended to the borrowers, but the intermediary was taking only credit risk rather than credit, rate, term, and perhaps international risks. In turn, new players could enter the market without having to provide full-service risk protection. For instance, investors willing to buy commercial paper could provide funds efficiently to a borrower (combined with the borrower's making suitable adjustments through the synthetics market) from whom a commercial paper investor would never purchase long-term Eurobonds.

The existing intermediaries, primarily large commercial banks, thus had their franchises undermined in two ways: first, less capital was needed for the same volume of transactions, with easier entry increasing the potential competition; and second, the number of competitors increased because of the new methods being used. Furthermore, as a result of competition, the compensation for structuring the deals was high if no capital was being committed, but it was not sufficient to support the amount of capital required for traditional intermediation.

Although this aspect of the synthetics markets enhanced the competitiveness of investment banks versus commercial banks, other aspects caused problems for the investment banks. As shown in the illustration of the call-put option, an investor could have the same effect on a portfolio by buying a combination of Treasury bills and a call-put alternative as by buying common stock directly. In the direct-purchase case, however, the volume of business done with the investment bank would be $340 (a purchase and a sale, at $170 if the price of CBS stock did not change over two months) versus $16.50, the sum of the purchase of a call and the sale of a put on the CBS stock. Clearly, the commissions on the call-put alternative are much less than the commissions on a corresponding trade in the common stock. This development compounded the loss in revenue to the investment bank resulting from the shift in customer profile away from small investors, who paid higher commission rates, to large institutions, which negotiated lower rates.

The investment banks have nevertheless benefited on balance from the synthetics because synthetic security techniques have been essential to the development of the complex securitized products the investment banks have designed and marketed, as illustrated in Chapter 7. The problem of converting an uncertain stream of receipts from a portfolio of mortgage loans (such as interest, scheduled principal, repayment on refinanced mortgages, and defaults) into a contractual, level, quarterly payment would be impossible without the ability to arrange futures and option contracts of a variety of sorts. It would also be impossible without fast computers to keep track of the bookkeeping. Computers are also essential to analyze a portfolio of assets being prepared for sale to the public ("securitized"), to determine its characteristics, and to ensure that the proper credit enhancement and synthetics are in place. Without this demonstration, the credit agencies would not be willing to provide the top credit ratings necessary to attract conservative purchasers of the securitization at a sufficient spread to pay the investment bank for the process.

The increased competition, the better information, and the

faster communication of both information and decisions permitted by computer technology also should mean that the markets will respond faster to new developments. Market volatility should increase, as indeed it appears to have done in the last five years. This does not necessarily mean that the positions ultimately reached would be different, but they should be reached faster. The physical analogy of the greater dangers of overshooting when an object is moving rapidly, other things being equal, does come to mind.

In contrast to commercial banks and possibly to the investment houses, the insurance industry does not seem to be as vulnerable to adverse effects from the new synthetic-product casino. Its position in the intermediation market has tended to be at the long-term end, where competition is much less intense than in the short-term end. It is much harder to structure efficiently priced hedges in the absence of a liquid and quoted market.

Instead, because of their position in these longer-term markets, insurance companies may be in a position to take advantage of imperfections that might develop between the short and the long terms. By properly analyzing the opportunities, insurance companies can use their more stable flow of funds and long-term investments to write contracts at a profitable spread for those who want long-term certainty. Some insurance companies, such as the Prudential Capital Corporation subsidiary of The Prudential Insurance Company of America, have entered this market aggressively. (The alternatives cited in the accompanying box also illustrate the proliferation of the games available in the casino.) Other companies, such as Equitable and Baldwin-United, were badly damaged by apparent misassessments that exposed them to costs that were unanticipated or to risk protection that was improperly structured.

EXCERPTS FROM THE OCTOBER 18, 1990, NEWSLETTER OF
PRUDENTIAL CAPITAL CORPORATION

- What can you do about all the gloomy, uncertain news in the financial marketplace? Today's steep yield curve offers opportunities and swaps can help you take advantage of them. Here are a few ideas which may address your needs.

Do you have ...

Low-coupon fixed-rate debt? Receive fixed in a swap. You may be able to achieve a sub-LIBOR rate. Of course, rates may increase, but this risk can be mitigated with a cap.

- *Fixed-rate debt and think that rates will fall?* Buy floors. This is a good strategy if you think that short-term rates will fall. If you own a collar, buy back the floor to participate in a rally.

- *A view that rates will decline in the future but want protection now?* Enter into a swap to pay a fixed rate. At the same time, sell the right to cancel the swap later. If rates fall, the option will not be exercised. The fixed rate is lower because of the option you sold. Or, better yet, buy an option to cancel the swap.

- *A need for long-term financing but expect rates to decrease?* Sell a cap in the future. The premium lowers your all-in cost of financing. As long as rates stay below the cap level, you pay nothing! This strategy is for companies who can tolerate some interest-rate risk. You could also sell a put swaption.

- *High-coupon fixed-rate debt and expect rates to drop further?* Enter into a combination of swaps. Receive a fixed rate in a long-term swap. Pay fixed in a shorter one to lock in savings during the short-term. Revert to a floating rate after short-swap expires.

Don't let a steep yield curve and volatility stop you from making important financial decisions today. Instead, take advantage of swaps to achieve your financial objectives.

Cautions

Despite all of the apparent protection provided by the hedges and the synthetic securities, it is important to realize that there is no such thing as the perfectly safe hedge; very small apparent exposures may create big losses. The counterparty may be unable to perform. The counterparty may refuse to perform, as in the case of the sovereign members of the Tin Council, whose action caused enormous problems for the London Metals Exchange and its members. Fraud may exist, or traders may violate the prudential rules within which they are supposed to work. The structure of the deal may be flawed or so complex that critical steps are not implemented properly. Historic relationships may cease to exist. These have all been causes for major losses by, in most cases, very sophisticated investors. Less sophisticated investors, searching for high returns, have often not understood or assessed the exposure they have, as some who sold puts during early 1987 learned at their expense in October 1987 when the stock market fell sharply.

In addition to these problems, there are two other serious handicaps in attempting to control risk by use of hedges and similar techniques. In the case of futures transactions, the need to meet margin calls can present a serious cash-flow problem. Recalling the farmer who sold corn for future delivery, if the price of corn rises, the commodities broker will demand that the farmer put up the appropriate additional margin on a daily basis. The value of the farmer's crop should be rising, of course, but that will not be turned into cash until the end of the growing season. The farmer must therefore be able to provide the additional margin out of spare resources or be able to obtain a loan against the value of the crop. Given the uncertainties of crop yields, the local banker should be cautious in advancing funds. Even if the funds are available, the farmer must pay interest on them (or lose interest on spare resources). This will increase the cost of the transaction and could indeed eat up the entire profit the farmer expected to lock in.

The use of options has similar potential problems. Because an option contract may not be available for the term of the underlying transaction, the investor may have to plan on buying over time a series of options to maintain the desired position. If there is a significant change in the market, the cost of maintaining the option cover may go up so much that it is less expensive to close out the position at a loss than to continue until the end. This apparently happened to a major regional bank in the Midwest, which had bought a very long-maturity portfolio of bonds and planned to protect itself from increases in the interest rate through the use of options. The bank was forced to unwind its position at enormous cost, with serious damage to its equity capital and to its competitive ability. An Australian firm was supposedly caught in a similar problem while hedging its international portfolio of debt and investments. Although its investments were profitable, the firm did not have enough cash for the parent to maintain its foreign-exchange hedges when adverse currency movements took place. The parent ran out of cash, and the company was forced into liquidation with serious results for some of its subsidiary investments.

Finally, many of these new casinos are subject to little or no regulation. Where they are, the regulation may be structured without proper regard for the true risks of the markets. In the United States, for example, the Commodity Futures Trading Commission regulates financial instruments traded on the Chicago Board Options Exchange because the CBOE grew out of a commodity exchange, the Chicago Board of Trade. The fact that the commodities traded are financial instruments that are listed on exchanges supervised by the Securities and Exchange Commission, rather than in corn and pork bellies, is less relevant than the parentage. This regulatory bifurcation has led to turf battles that have hardly been conducive either to orderly regulation or to orderly product development. The energies spent on turf battles could have been far more productively spent in designing proper protection for the players in what are highly interrelated markets. As is usually the case in the United States, however, the rapid change in economic realities and technical capacity have left the regulatory agencies far behind.

Implications for the Financial System

As with many other developments that have had a serious impact on the financial systems in the United States, the casino of options and hedges has flourished because it substitutes technology and human intelligence for the use of capital. The synthetic securities have increased the ability of participants in the financial markets to get together directly, paying a fee for intelligence and technology to do the job, rather than use an intermediary whose capital has traditionally helped buffer the risks of the principal parties. Not every new type of option, hedge, index, or basket of securities will meet the test of the market. But it seems likely that the usefulness of the securities casino will remain, even if the rate of growth slows dramatically.

Although efforts to do so have been made after major market dislocations, it will be hard to turn back this particular clock. These financial devices now perform important market functions that financial intermediaries used to provide but cannot any longer: the margins became too thin as a result of competition from new, more efficient techniques.

The synthetic casino is also part of the general unbundling of the financial markets, which allows participants on both the providing-of-using-of-funds sides to select precisely the instrument needed to accomplish a specific objective and to price that instrument as it stands alone rather than carrying the burden of shared costs. Needless to say, this is not popular with those who view the financial markets as monopolies that can be saddled with social costs.

It is also highly likely that as long as the regulation of the casino is divided among a number of agencies, the regulation will be costly but not very effective. It is as though one regulator determined who would be allowed into the casino, another determined what games would be played, and a third managed the cashier's cage and the extension of credit. If the three parties do their jobs poorly enough that the market is choked off, the game will shift outside to the plaza in front of the casino. If they fail to exercise appropriate and coordinated regulation, the games might get so hot that the building catches fire. Despite the American tradition of dividing power, the increasing importance of synthetic securities to the financial system dictates that its regulation should be moved squarely into the domain of those who regulate the financial arena.

GLOSSARY OF TERMS

Call option A contract in which the buyer of the call option purchases the right from the seller to force the seller of the option to deliver a good to the buyer at a time and price established by the contract. The buyer exercises the option only if the price of the good at the time the option expires is above the contract (exercise) price. At other times, it is usually more profitable to sell the option to a third party than to exercise it.

Commodity exchange An organized market in which transactions take place in agreed commodities using standard, specified amounts, qualities, and delivery dates.

Future contract An agreement between one party to deliver and another party to accept and pay for a specified amount of a good at a specified price at a specified time in the future. By custom, *selling* a future means contracting to deliver a good, and *buying* a future means contracting to accept delivery and pay for the good.

Hedge   An investment position structured so that a profit is protected (or a loss constrained) regardless of the price movements in the various components of the position. Usually, as prices change, the increase in value of some components of the position are closely offset by declines in the value of other components.

In the/out of the money   An option is *in the money* if the price of the good under option is greater than the exercise price of the call option or less than the exercise price of a put option on the good. The option is *out of the money* if the reverse is true.

Long   To be long in a good or to have a long position is to own the good.

Option   An agreement between two parties wherein the first gives the second the ability to force the first to take action at the discretion of the second. The second party, however, is not required to force the action; the second party has the option or right to force the first to act. The second party, if rational, will exercise the right only when it is economically advantageous to do so.

Option value   Because an option gives its owner the right, under certain conditions, to force someone else to take action, the option has value even if the option's exercise price is out of the money with respect to the current market price of the action. The value of an option is a marketable security that has been determined to vary with the distance between the exercise price and the market price of the optioned item, the variability of the market price, the time remaining before the option expires, and the interest rate.

Put option   A contract in which the buyer of the put option purchases the right from the seller of the option to force the seller to buy a good at a time and price established in the contract. This type of option will be exercised when the price of the optioned good is less than the exercise price.

Short   To be short in a good is to have borrowed the good in order to sell it. The good must subsequently be repurchased and returned to its source together with compensation for the loan according to the terms of the agreement under which the good was borrowed. This latter action is known as *covering a short position.*

Spot market   A transaction requiring immediate delivery (subject to the necessary time to handle the paperwork and shipping) of a good sold in exchange for immediate cash payment. Also called the *cash market.*

Write an option By custom, *writing an option* refers to selling the right for someone else to force the writer to buy (writing a put) or to sell (writing a call) a specified amount of a good at a specified price for a specified time.

9

The Money Business Goes Global (Again)

Richard Fisher, now chairman of the investment banking firm of Morgan Stanley & Co., has been quoted as saying that the best thing the firm did to improve its international competitiveness was to abolish its international division. In order to understand this apparent contradiction, it is necessary to review briefly how the international money markets have changed over the past 150 years.

Overview

Archaeology has clearly shown that trade between cultures and civilizations rose rapidly and covered extraordinarily long distances, considering the limitations of transportation available before the application of the steam engine. The French *coureurs de bois*, in order to collect furs from the Pacific Northwest for transport to Europe during the late 1700s, paddled their canoes up the St. Lawrence River from Quebec City and into the Great Lakes to Lake Erie, down the Maumee River; portaged a few miles to the Wabash in order to enter the Mississippi River system, and then worked their way upstream into the Missouri and to the Northwest. When they had purchased the necessary load of furs, they reversed their route, completing the journey back to Quebec in eighteen months.

The capital requirements for trading missions of this type were relatively modest—providing equipment for the voyage, maintaining the crew, and purchasing the items being imported or exported. The capital was provided by citizens of the country originating the transaction, and efficiency was increased by the financial services that soon developed. For example, boats and cargo could be insured against loss once the number of voyages became large enough to spread the risk among the ship owners and operators. Traders needed to establish credit at both ends of the transaction to minimize the risk of carrying precious metals. Financial institutions therefore developed relations with one another, each holding balances for the other that could be provided to merchants trading between the two locations.

More complex capital transactions were required for financing the other major international activity of the day—war. The absence of efficient tax collections made it difficult to raise funds to support military operations. Local assets, especially those belonging to the opposition, could, of course, be seized for the government's use, but funds were also provided by foreign bankers either in the form of precious metals or credit. Collecting, particularly from a losing side, was another problem. Even collecting from a winning side could be difficult. The extremely high interest rates and demands for collateral reflected these problems.

The difficulty of collecting illustrates the most important element necessary for the development of a multinational financial system—a low risk of default. The lender in international transactions is exposed both to *credit risk*, the risk shared with domestic lenders that the borrower cannot repay, and to *transfer risk*, the risk peculiar to international transactions that the borrower has local funds but cannot obtain the form of payment specified in the loan agreement. In other words, a perfectly sound Brazilian business may have access to all the cruzados it needs but cannot buy dollars to repay its foreign loans.

The lower the level of risk, the greater the willingness of

financial sources to finance cross-border ventures and hence the greater the volume of international transactions. The credit of the individual borrower must be assessed in all cases. Transfer risk, as events in Latin America showed starting in 1982, can be extremely dangerous yet hard to evaluate, adding considerably to the problems of maintaining trade in an uncertain world.

Risk may be reduced by technology, by a mutually understood structure of rights and obligations, by the ability to enforce these rules with some certainty about the outcome, and by a peaceful sociopolitical environment. Risk is not always reduced by relatively more democratic forms of government, however.

Historical Perspective

The Colonial Period

The development of trade between Europe and Asia and between Europe and the Americas was extraordinarily important in the development of the legal structure necessary for the Industrial Revolution to occur. To the merchants of the early seventeenth century, the financial requirements and risks of international trade were greater than most single individuals or even partnerships could afford.

In addition, whereas individual proprietors and partners were normally in direct charge of their firms, usually the investors in large enterprises had to leave the policy direction to a subcommittee of the owners (a board of directors) and the routine management in the hands of a management group. The individual owners thus could hardly feel they should be held personally responsible for the actions of their board and management. Consequently, limited-liability entities (such as corporations) were developed to permit individuals to contribute capital without exposing themselves to the unlimited liability associated with a sole proprietorship or a partnership. Companies of this sort were involved in settlements and trading all over the globe. The influence and responsibilities of the English East India Company, founded in 1600, grew to such an extent that it was practically a sovereign nation, with its own civil and military services, until taken over by the British government following the Indian Mutiny of 1857.

The need for more efficient transportation, the opportunities created by new markets and new materials, and the drive for efficiency in turn nurtured new methods of production, new technology, and new machinery to harness vast amounts of energy. In particular, the Americas, rich in raw materials and inexpensive land, needed massive investments in transportation (canals and then railroads) in order to enjoy the benefits of its resources. In fact, the United States' constitutional convention grew out of a meeting in Annapolis in 1786 to plan a route for a canal to the west.

FOREIGN INVESTMENT IN THE UNITED STATES

Net foreign investment in the United States was $60 million in 1789, $96 million by 1798, and languished between $56 million to $118 million until 1834. By 1839, however, it had risen to $292 million, where it remained until 1853. Thereafter, the net foreign investment rose rapidly, exceeding $1 billion in 1869, despite the Civil War.

Governmental entities in the United States relied on European sources to supply their needs for debt. In 1837, foreign investors held about one-seventh of the outstanding securities issued by private and public entities in the United States. By the middle of the nineteenth century, foreign investors held half of the federal and state debts and a quarter of the municipal debt. Subsequent defaults made the United States one of the first LDC debt problems. As the century continued, however, foreigners invested more heavily in basic industries such as steel and railroads. Not until World War I did the United States become a creditor nation, a status it relinquished during the late 1980s.

Development in the Nineteenth Century

Before the Erie Canal was opened, transportation for most agricultural products cost more than the merchandise was worth. It cost $100 to ship a ton of grain from the Great Lakes to New York City. After the canal was opened, the cost dropped to $10. The $7 million construction cost of the canal was financed by

New York State and was repaid through fees within a decade.

One reason for foreign investment was that U.S. companies purchased their equipment in Europe. The early railroads, for instance, bought their steel rails, locomotives, and rolling stock from English companies. With insufficient cash for their capital equipment and often little or no operating record, the new railroads paid for their purchases with bonds. The manufacturer then sold these bonds, perhaps at a substantial discount from their face value, to recoup its costs and profits. These transactions were arranged by investment bankers, who quickly established networks of relationships on both sides of the Atlantic.

An early prominent investment banker was George Peabody, born in 1795. After working in retailing with several relatives and relocating to the District of Columbia, Peabody ultimately went into partnership with Elisha Riggs, another great financial name, to open a dry-goods store. This concern flourished and became one of the largest of its type at the time. Peabody set up an operation in London in the late 1830s, combining importing of merchandise and financing. By the early 1840s, he had moved to England and was engaged primarily in international finance, raising funds for railroads and governmental entities. George Peabody & Co. was the major international financial house with American roots; the other two most active in the United States in the period before the Civil War were Baring Brothers and the Rothschilds, both English in origin.

In 1854, in advancing years and with no heir, Peabody offered a partnership in London to Junius Spencer Morgan, a young, aggressive New England merchant with connections in Connecticut and Massachusetts, whose mercantile rise in many ways paralleled Peabody's own. One son, John Pierpont Morgan, was sent back to the United States from London in 1857 to join a New York investment banking firm and ultimately in 1895 created J. P. Morgan & Co.

IT'S ALL IN THE FAMILY

Morgan's English banking house evolved into Morgan Grenfell & Co., which was bought for $1.6 billion by Deutsche Bank in 1990 to rescue it from a variety of problems. In 1934 and 1935, following the passage of the Glass-Steagall Act, which prohibited one institution from conducting both lines of business, J. P. Morgan & Co. was split into J. P. Morgan & Co., the commercial bank which continued to operate as a partnership until 1940, and Morgan, Stanley & Co., the investment bank. After a merger with the Guaranty Trust Company in 1959, the commercial bank became known as Morgan Guaranty Trust Company. When its holding company was subsequently established, it was given the name of J. P. Morgan & Co., Incorporated, like the phoenix rising from the ashes. Even though the name of the commercial bank has not been changed, the JPMorgan logo is used throughout the organization.

The Morgans had always been closely affiliated with the financial groups in Philadelphia. In 1871, J. Pierpont Morgan joined his firm with Drexel & Co., which had been founded in 1837. The new firm, named Drexel, Morgan & Co., was headquartered in New York City. After twenty-four years, it was restructured again into two partnerships with overlapping members, and each firm resumed its former name. Drexel, which had faded over the years, was in effect taken over by Burnham & Co. in 1973, although Drexel was able to insist that its name should come first on the masthead. Ultimately, the firm was known as Drexel Burnham Lambert, Inc.

The Paris branch of Morgan, which was part of the Drexel dowry, had been established in 1868. When Morgan and Drexel split in 1895, Morgan got Drexel Harjes & Co. and changed the name first to Morgan Harjes & Co. and later to Morgan & Cie. This component remained with the commercial bank, J. P. Morgan & Co., finally was converted to a corporation in 1945, and ultimately made a branch of Morgan Guaranty Trust.

Similar interrelationships can be found among many of the premier U.S. financial institutions. The First National City Bank of New York component of Citicorp, for example, was founded by the same family who founded the Chase Bank component of Chase Manhattan Bank. George F. Baker, who developed The First National City Bank of New York, received financial support at critical times from the Jay Cooke group of Philadelphia, which ultimately became Charles D. Barney & Co. (Barney was Cooke's son-in-law), the major component of Smith, Barney & Co., now a subsidiary of Primerica. (Barney was the stronger firm than Smith, and alphabetical considerations also should have dictated that the name be Barney, Smith & Co; perhaps that did not sound "tony" enough).

The Rothschild firm never established a similar presence in the U.S. markets, although various companies were set up by the London and Paris branches of this famous family even into the 1980s. Baring Brothers failed in 1890 as a result of having guaranteed English loans to the Argentine Republic.

By the turn of the century, the leading investment banking firms in the United States were thus no longer subsidiaries of European firms, although many were controlled by families recently arrived from Germany that used their European connections to sell the securities of U.S. institutions. New Englanders had migrated south to New York to establish investment banks. Like the Morgan bank, many of these investment houses grew out of merchant firms that had found the financial aspects of importing more profitable than importing the goods. And New York had eclipsed its Boston, Philadelphia, and New Orleans rivals (in part through luck rather than inherent advantage) as the mercantile and financial center of the country, second only to London in international importance. Even as early as 1852, a guidebook to New York City modestly informed visitors that Wall Street was known as the focus of "great monetary operations, that are watched with great interest not only over the United States, but in Europe."

The period from the end of the Napoleonic Wars until the beginning of World War I satisfied the conditions needed for the healthy development of international trade and finance. As new technology developed in all major industries, commercial law established what was expected in performance on contracts. In the United States, the adoption of more uniform legislation encouraged interstate enterprises, creating opportunities for economies of scale in production and distribution. The Pax Britannica allowed transactions to be enforced and collected in the large portion of the world where the English writ could be enforced. Finally, relatively speaking, it was a peaceful period. Altercations existed, associated with the unification of Germany and of Italy, the Civil War in the United States, the decline and collapse of the Spanish Empire, the conflicts between the Boers and the British in South Africa and the Russians in the Crimea, the Boxer Rebellion in China, and the Russo-Japanese War. These tended to be confined to relatively few parties; the devastations were not total and, indeed, provided opportunities for foreigners to benefit from the subsequent reconstruction. There was no pervasive breakdown of commerce and trade such as was experienced after the fall of the Roman Empire.

The Early Twentieth Century

The period of 1915 to 1945, with two multinational conflicts and an intervening major depression, interrupted international relationships. First, the great European powers dissipated not only their young men but their capital in two enormous conflicts. Because its geographic location protected its industrial capacity, the United States supplied a considerable amount of the military materials. In part, these were a contribution by the U.S. citizens in addition to the U.S. soldiers sent to the battlefield. In part, however, they were obtained by a transfer of capital—claims on assets in the United States held by foreign citizens and assumed by their governments and used to purchase war materials. Although firms such as J. P. Morgan & Co., which acted as the purchasing agent in the United States for the British government in World War I, and Kuhn Loeb, which underwrote issues for the Japanese during their 1904 to 1905 conflict with the Russians, were involved in these efforts, direct contact between governments tended to settle a much larger proportion of transactions than were settled in peacetime. The World War I debt of European governments for support by the United States government is still carried on the U.S. Treasury's books.

Second, the Great Depression reduced the total volume of international trade and finance because not as much was being bought and sold. The value of U.S. exports fell from $5.2 billion in 1929 to $1.6 billion in 1932 and 1933. In addition, the period immediately prior to the depression was characterized by an increase in mercantilism—buy-local-product sentiment. This beggar-thy-neighbor approach contributed both to a decline in the volume of trade and also to a drop in the level of total economic activity.

By the end of World War II, the international financial scene was in shambles. But although the economies of large parts of the world were in ruins, capital had flowed into the United States to such an extent that analysts could not see an end to the world's dollar shortage. In fact, business was sufficiently good in the United States that U.S. financial institutions had no reason to consider taking the risks associated with going abroad.

The Postwar Period

How quickly things change! In the forty-five years since the end of World War II, Europe and Asia have both been rebuilt despite the lack of natural resources in Germany, Japan, Korea, and Taiwan. By 1990, the economies of the three great trading areas of Europe, the Americas, and Asia were approaching the same size, with the Americas a bit ahead and the Asians a bit behind. By 2000, it has been predicted that the Asian economy will exceed that of Europe and be almost equal to that of the Americas.

Two other significant developments occurred during this period. First, growth in the industrialized economies combined with a decline in the rate of discovery of new petroleum (and an increase in the marginal cost of this new oil) allowed the countries exporting oil to boost the price to levels well above the cost of the newly located oil. Because of the long time required to adjust to the alteration in the price of this commodity, the price increase resulted in the largest, fastest transfer of capital in the history of the world.

The second development, the financial failure of many important less developed countries (LDCs), was in part related to the oil-price crisis. Because of the new oil prices, many LDCs had to borrow large sums in order to pay their oil bills. The funds were not borrowed directly from the sellers of oil, however, but from the financial institutions with which the sellers left some of their funds for safekeeping. In addition, the slowing of the world economy that resulted from this transfer of wealth curtailed the sales of LDC products and cut the generation of foreign exchange. This foreign exchange was needed not only to buy fuel but also for major projects to create a modern infrastructure in the LDCs and pay interest on debts already contracted. The governments in many countries elected to continue these projects even though this decision entailed yet further increases in the amount of borrowing done on the international markets. Finally, the citizens in some countries became suspicious about the ability of their government to manage their nation's economy and moved their funds out of the domestic economy into safe havens, such as Switzerland or the United States. This process added further to the amount of foreign-denominated debt committed by the LDCs.

THE ANGLO-AMERICAN DOMINATION CONTINUES

Despite the dilution of the economic power of the United States, which was unavoidable if both the United States and the rest of the world were to prosper, the Anglo-American domination of international finance appears likely to continue. It will be a great surprise to many who have viewed the United Kingdom's rapprochement with the Common Market as an abdication of financial power to German institutions and the Bundesbank.

Anglo-American Domination of Financial Markets

The Anglo-American domination of international finance in part stems from the English success in establishing a colonial empire that shared a common language in virtually all parts of the globe. With its powerful navy, the British authorities could use force reasonably rapidly to maintain the civic order essential to a flourishing entrepreneurial environment. Other European powers tried to develop empires, but Germany, Italy, and the low countries were preoccupied with their own internal difficulties during the great periods of exploration, and France likewise tended to look toward continental Europe. The Great Russians were developing their contiguous, ocean-to-ocean empire.

The contemporary English historian of science, James Burke, has argued that the role of the adherents to the nonconforming religions in England was also critical to its industrial development. Because people who were not members of the established Church of England were restricted in participating in the professions, the nonconformists turned to commerce. These individuals did not have the agricultural outlook of the landed gentry but were oriented toward manufacturing and trading. They were heavily involved in industries as diverse as confectionary and chinaware, in canals and railroads, and in trade. Unable to attend the universities, nonconformists established their own educational system, which emphasized technical and engineering subjects—skills that enabled English firms to design and build efficient machinery. Seeking larger volume and economies of scale, British industries turned toward foreign markets. And unlike the celebrants of minority religions in many places, English dissenters were not periodically massacred but were gradually integrated into established society.

The English legal system also was suited to commercial transactions, private ownership, collective ventures, and contractual arrangements that could be enforced. The result has been that English law has become the law of choice in international activities.

Furthermore, English as a language is relatively easy to communicate with because it is very fault tolerant. Genders are few, word order is flexible, and tenses can be ignored by the use of other devices that express timing. "I see you" and "You I see" amount to the same thing. "I go yesterday" makes the point the speaker intended. Merchants may thus have had been helped in establishing a market by their use of English.

Finally, the English government has long encouraged the use of London as a center of financial and commercial transactions. It was a convenient meeting place for any trade entering northern Europe by sea, and one of the closest points of land to the Americas. Transatlantic cables were anchored in the United Kingdom. In the modern world, a good communication system is essential for a mercantile and financial center. Athens and Cairo did not develop into the international financial service business centers that were expected after the fall of the Shah of Iran in part because of inadequate telephone and electric systems.

The United Kingdom retains most of its historical advantages—law, location, language, and a market position that is difficult to dislodge, provided the government does not implement regulations and take actions that would undermine the country's commercial tradition. The United States shares the same advantages plus the benefit of an enormous market, plentiful natural resources, and, with the dissolution of the Russian empire, a relatively unchallenged Pax Americana. The prospects thus appear good for the continued Anglo-American dominance of the international commercial scene. Japan is clearly very important, as is Asia, but despite the volume of trading on the Tokyo Stock Exchange, the number of people who learn Japanese is small compared with the number who study English.

The Public Sector in the Postwar Period

Decisions made as World War II was concluding helped lay the foundation for the world's successful economic recovery. Unlike the untenable settlements imposed at the end of World War I, rehabilitation and reconstruction of friend and former foe were emphasized, with the United States taking the lead because of its huge accumulation of capital.

Three financial institutions were established in the mid-1940s by multinational agreement. The International Monetary Fund was designed to create stability in the foreign-exchange markets so that international trade would not be hindered with uncertainty about currency values. The World Bank (officially The International Bank for Reconstruction and Development) was set up in 1944 to make funds, in the form of loans, temporarily available to economies that needed them to supplement governmental grants. As the economies recovered, the loans would be repaid and could be recycled to other deserving cases. Finally, the General Agreement on Tariffs and Trade (GATT) was established in 1947 as a mechanism to promote the orderly reduction in tariffs and other barriers to international trade. It was the belief of the founders that an outbreak of mercantilism, which encouraged local buying, had contributed to the depression of the 1930s. If a similar problem could be avoided in the aftermath of World War II, a third world war would be less likely, and the standards of living would be higher worldwide.

These three institutions worked well for many years. Once the economies in Europe and Asia had been restored, a few statistics indicate the speed with which international finance developed. In 1965, $3.2 billion (in U.S. dollars) of international bonds were sold; five years later, the total had nearly doubled, to $6.0 billion. By 1975, that total more than tripled, to $20 billion, and almost doubled again by 1980. The 1985 figure was

$166.5 billion and $225.4 billion in 1986. One equity trade in seven, worldwide, had a foreign investor on the other side, up from one in sixteen ten years earlier. Cross-border equity flows reached $1.6 trillion in 1989. *Net* funds raised on international markets reached a record level of $448 billion.

Stresses and strains have appeared more recently. For example, despite the conviction for many years that the dollar surplus existing in 1945 would never be cured, by 1970 the continual deficit in the United States' balance of payments had transferred ownership of much of these dollars to citizens of other countries. This put serious downward pressure on the U.S. dollar. Those who held dollars increasingly began to exchange them for gold or for other currencies. This pressure forced the U.S. Treasury in 1973 to suspend the convertibility of the dollar into gold at a fixed rate and to allow the dollar to float in value versus the other major currencies of the world. The volatility of this float has proven greater than initially anticipated and has contributed to the difficulty of engaging in international transactions. It has also contributed to the relative decline of the International Monetary Fund as an arbiter of value of the currencies of the major trading countries.

These changes, in turn, have provided opportunities for many private institutions to develop ways to match parties on opposite sides of a currency so that both parties are hedged against unexpected changes that would adversely affect their transactions. For example, a travel company selling a package tour to a German group wishes to be paid in advance and wants to be sure it will receive the amount of dollars it expects. The German group wants to be sure it pays only the amount of deutsche marks it expects to pay. By locating parties with reverse concerns (paying dollars and receiving deutsche marks) or willing to commit capital to a speculation about the future market rates, a financial intermediary can provide a way for both buyers and sellers to be free of foreign-exchange risk by matching off those with opposite positions.

The World Bank has also been less certain about its mission and hard pressed to continue its excellent record of collecting as loans have gone to more marginal nations. The nature and quality of the projects, and hence the ability of the project to generate the funds to repay the loan, have become less attractive because the best projects have already been implemented. The marginal-returns schedule is not static, fixed forever in 1945, so newly profitable projects should continuously appear as the economy changes. After forty-five years in business, however, it seems likely that there has been some diminution in the menu available.

Requests by the Bank for additional capital from its members have been harder to get approved and then funded as the major economies worry about competition that might develop as a result of the funds provided. The major economies have also been looking inward rather than outward because of problems resulting from the oil-price shock and cyclical economic dislocations.

Finally, the GATT has been a roaring success, reducing tariffs to an average in many instances of 12 percent of what they were forty-five years ago. There has been a corresponding increase in world trade and an associated increase in all the ancillary-service institutions that support world trade. The easier tariffs were addressed first and eliminated, leaving the more difficult problems on the agenda.

Two major sticking points arose that frustrated the latest round of negotiations, the so-called Uruguay Round, leaving the negotiations in recess in early 1991 after five slow years of work. First, the low-cost agricultural producers insisted that high-cost agricultural areas (such as Japan and the European Community) reduce the subsidies provided to their farmers and open their markets to foreign producers. The feint toward elimination of subsidies by the European Community administration produced such vigorous demonstrations that EC negotiators refused to make what were considered significant concessions. The European farmers are small in number but are politically very influential, just as their counterparts are in Japan and North America.

The second problem arose over inclusion of service industries, including financial services, in the tariff reduction efforts. The issues arose particularly about access to markets for financial services, such as banks, credit cards, mutual funds, investment banks, and insurance companies. These tend to be very sensitive issues for governments, which want control over the banking system and the quality of the insurance being sold to residents. Furthermore, the myriad of federal and state regulations restricting U.S. domestic financial institutions did not tempt international financial institutions to grant U.S. institutions access to the European Community in exchange for what they could expect in the United States.

In addition, the service-industry issue also included the protection of intellectual property, such as copyrights (on traditional printed matter but also on computer software) and patents (particularly on medicines and high-technology machinery). The creators of intellectual properties in the United States believed that their ideas and products were being imitated abroad without proper payment for the use of these products. This was an issue of particular importance to the U.S. government because its citizens have been maintaining leadership in these areas.

The intellectual property issue has not been completely resolved. Enough progress at the GATT talks had been made, however, that it appeared the question was not going to break the deal. The banking and financial issues were serious, but changes in the structure of the U.S. financial system appear to be reducing the number of points open to debate. It was primarily the agricultural question that derailed progress at the time the Uruguay Round drifted to an uncertain halt. How long the small number of farmers involved—100,000 or 200,000, at most—can sustain their position is not yet clear. History suggests that they will not ultimately prevail because the public will tire of supporting the subsidies, as happened in the case of European miners.

In the meantime, regional trading blocks appear to be developing. The most visible is the European Community, with its 1992 target for complete free trade within its bounds. The United States and Canada have also developed a free-trade treaty, and President Bush has announced his intention of negotiating the inclusion of Mexico as well in a North American common market. This is an extremely important set of developments, whose significence is only now beginning to emerge.

The Private Sector

The private sector responded to the reglobalization of finance without the benefit of the coordinated structure afforded the public institutions. In the first place, the financial institutions of the United States emerged from World War II with a high degree of liquidity, in part because they had not had any significant demands placed on them since the 1920s. The banks had made no loans to the private sector because there had been little demand for loans, the private-household and corporate sectors had accumulated a large amount of liquidity themselves, insurance products were traditional in nature, and the investment business was largely one of stock brokering for individuals and helping foreign governments raise funds to finance their reconstruction.

As the U.S. economy grew, it used up the spare liquidity in the system. The measures of liquidity for banks became tighter as the loan-to-deposit ratios rose from the 1945 low ratio of 17.3 percent. The effort of several presidents to finance the war in Vietnam without raising taxes drained resources by increasing the federal debt. By the late 1960s, the recovery elsewhere was making it comparatively less costly to raise funds abroad and transfer them to the United States.

Several innovations helped speed this process. First, because they knew of the propensity of the U.S. government to seize funds belonging to those with which it disagrees, Russian banks and institutions were reluctant to hold deposits of U.S. dollars in U.S. banks in their own names. They therefore asked whether European banks would accept deposits in dollars rather than in their own currencies. The deposits would thus appear on the books of U.S. banks as belonging to European institutions rather than Russian ones.

The European banks agreed to this proposition, which gave them a source of dollars that they could relend. The natural consumers of these Eurodollars were U.S. companies, which found the cost of these funds was less than the cost of borrowing the deposits from a domestic bank. In part, this happened because European banks had to maintain fewer reserves than the Federal Reserve required domestic banks to maintain, and the European banks did not have to pay deposit-insurance fees. The mutual benefit to borrower and lender was sufficient for the Eurodollar market to grow very rapidly, fueled by the dollars being accumulated abroad as a result of the U.S. balance-of-payments deficit.

U.S. banks were quick to establish branches in London to

accept Eurodollar deposits and relend them to their customers in the United States and elsewhere. In fact, because of political pressure to hold interest rates down, U.S. banks were at times in the position of charging less for loans than their domestic sources of funds cost them. It does not take much insight to recognize this as a losing proposition. Such loans became a bit like the *menu touristique* in an expensive French restaurant—politically required on the *carte*, but with the last portion always just sold. U.S. banks advised customers that if they wanted loans without waiting, they could appear at a bank's foreign branch, which could pay the going rates to raise funds from the marketplace.

U.S. banks were also active in recycling the petrodollars earned by the oil suppliers after the oil-price increases. The increase in oil prices disrupted the domestic economy, reducing the demand for loans and increasing the competition for them, to the detriment of profits. Many banks were faced with problems resulting from extending credit to the real estate investment trusts, some of which had seriously overbuilt in the boom period of the early 1970s. In comparison, lending abroad to oil-based economies such as Mexico appeared to be less risky and more profitable. Other favored countries, because of their excellent economic performance, good resources, and attractive prospects, included Argentina, Brazil, and several countries in Asia. U.S. bank exposure to non-OPEC developing countries rose by 73.5 percent from 1976 to 1982, although the U.S. banks' share of these loans declined from 52 percent to 37 percent. The profitability of international loans extended by many large banks was reported to be more than twice the level the banks were earning on domestic credits.

Smaller regional banks participated in international loans syndicated by the money-center banks, loans that appeared to require little administration and initially offered large spreads. Some smaller banks even opened representative offices abroad so that they could make direct loans to governmental agencies and private companies rather than participate only in sovereign or private-borrower syndicated loans on which the spreads had become very small as the demand for participations increased. More frequently, however, the smaller banks took what their managements thought were relatively short-term exposures, taking early maturities offering lower rates and leaving the longer-term and higher spreads to large institutions.

Bankers were not unaware of the history of defaults by Latin American and other LDC borrowers. They reasoned—inaccurately—that individual investors and insurance companies in the past had not gone after defaulters with any meaningful threat of retribution and that even a sovereign borrower would not stiff the banks and risk losing trade credit. Furthermore, a safety-in-numbers mentality existed despite the fact that the entry of new lenders, attracted by the profitability of the LDC credits, eroded profits. If the banks of enough countries were involved, the governments of those countries would present a united front if the borrower attempted to renege—or so the thinking went.

In the first several problem instances, the process worked according to expectations. When Turkey and Zaire encountered economic problems, the banking community drew together to use morals suasion on the borrower to get its house in order. Even Castro is supposed to have advised the Sandinista government of Nicaragua not to isolate itself from the international financial system and become dependent on the Soviet Union for economic support.

Unfortunately, when a sovereign borrower cannot repay, it cannot repay. If funds are needed to keep the borrower operating and in a position that enhances the possibility of future repayment, the funds probably will be provided. Once one or two borrowers worked out accommodations with their lenders, even those borrowers who could repay were tempted to ask for adjustments to their debt agreements. As one retired banker was fond of warning, "you can't land the marines in Brazil."

This particular aspect of reglobalization left a sour taste in the mouths of senior bank managers, particularly if they had thought they were buying shorter maturities. Confronted with apparently interminable negotiations and little prospect for repayment, executive management responded by shutting down banks' international departments. Even trade-finance departments, whose credit records were usually good, were terminated in the anxiety to distance the bank from any suggestion of an international orientation. One result has been that foreign-owned banks have been increasing their share of the market for financing U.S. exports. International banks hold some 20 percent of commercial and industrial loans in the United States, but they finance about 30 percent of the exports supported with guarantees of the Export-Import Bank of the United States.

For U.S. banks, reglobalization has thus proven to be a sword with two very sharp edges. As demands for more prudent action conflict with demands to support U.S. exports, the banks have gone the more prudent lending route. They are being redomesticated. Until either the nature of political pressure on the banks changes or the LDCs' crises are a generation in the past, it seems unlikely that U.S. banks will aggressively seek global activities. In a recent instance demonstrating this trend, in early 1991 Security Pacific announced it would record a $200 million pretax loss to terminate its international investment-banking and corporate-finance initiative. The bank's assets would shrink by $7 billion, or about 10 percent, as a result of this decision.

Property and casualty insurance has been a global business for generations, with the highest risks insured through the syndicates at Lloyds of London (now apparently beset with problems on the international risks it accepted). As the purchasers of insurance have themselves expanded their markets, their willingness to insure with multinational firms certainly has not diminished. If anything, the tendency of the U.S. political and legal system to socialize risk by forcing insurance companies to accept and pay for it will accelerate the movement offshore to escape these problems. The use of self-insurance through wholly owned, offshore subsidiaries that may reinsure part of their highest risks with regular insurance companies also contributes to the expanding international insurance markets. The estimate of alternative-market (as the offshore business is known) share of risk-financing facilities in 1991 was 31.6 percent, representing premiums of some $30 billion.

Life insurance, in contrast, has tended to remain more national in character. This is perhaps the result of a regulatory propensity to feel less comfortable about promises from companies not under a domestic jurisdiction. However, in order to diversify the risk exposure of their investment portfolios, U.S. life insurance companies have put an increasing amount of their resources to work in funding European and Asian companies and other borrowers. In this sense, the companies may be cautiously returning to the portfolios that characterized the early portion of this century, which were dominated by foreign, higher-yielding bonds. Given their experiences of the 1930s and the banks' experiences in the 1980s, caution would be in order.

A reverse-investment pattern also exists. European and Asian financial institutions, especially insurance companies, have been investing heavily in the United States. Japanese firms have been attracted by particularly well-known real estate landmarks such as Rockefeller Center in New York City.

Investment banking has probably seen the most dramatic shifts in business. Total international transactions in stocks and bonds were $66.3 billion (U.S. dollars) in 1975; by 1980, the figure had risen to $251.2 billion. By 1986, the figures were $379.6 billion in stock transactions and $2,613.5 billion in bonds. Between 1984 and 1987, the number of companies whose securities were actively traded in at least two liquid markets rose from 236 to 487. Although the United States had the most companies fitting the definition, the U.S. total only increased modestly during this period. As shown in Figure 9.1, Japan, Australia, and the United Kingdom all enjoyed far greater

Figure 9.1
Companies with Common Stock Actively Traded in More Than One Market

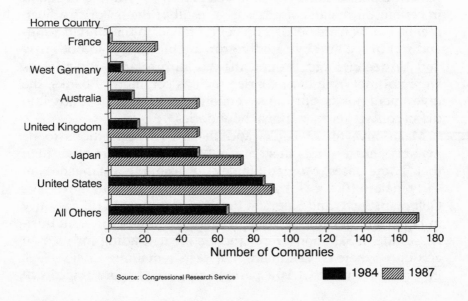

Source: Congressional Research Service   ■ 1984 ▨ 1987

increases, both absolutely and in percentage terms. West Germany and France were the league winners in the percentage increase in this type of multinational company.

Of the top fifteen underwriting firms (ranked by amount of capital) in the first quarter of 1989, which accounted for 74.2 percent of all underwriting, U.S. firms had the largest share, 40.5 percent; Japanese firms took 19.6 percent; and European firms underwrote only 14.1 percent. The prominence of Japanese firms reflects the fact that in 1988, for the first time, the volume of transactions on the Tokyo Stock Exchange exceeded the volume on the New York Stock Exchange. The market capitalization of the Tokyo Stock Exchange firms also exceeded that of the companies listed in New York. Out of a total worldwide market-capital value of US$8 trillion, $3.8 trillion was listed on the Tokyo Exchange, $2.4 trillion in New York, and $1.8 on European and other exchanges. The figures in 1978 had been only $327 billion, $870 billion, and $400 billion, which suggests that the growth in the Japanese markets had been particularly impressive compared with European growth.

Investment bankers have been key players in the redevelopment of these markets after decades in which global markets were not important to them. Pools of savings developed in Japan, where the population saved more than Europeans or Americans. Pools of savings developed in the Middle East and in certain European countries as a result of the oil-price adjustments. Funds were needed by governments in the United States and in Europe and by rapidly growing businesses in both new and old technologies around the world. Insofar as these needs were not met by intermediaries such as commercial banks, the investment banks put the savers and consumers of funds into direct contact across national boundaries.

Major investment banks and those with aspirations to be majors opened offices in significant financial centers other than their home bases. Morgan Stanley, for example, established an early major office in Tokyo and smaller offices throughout Asia. Goldman, Sachs and Salomon Brothers also opened offices early in Japan and developed very profitable but quite different businesses there. Salomon's reputation is for its trading for its own account, whereas Goldman, the last remaining major U.S. investment bank that is a partnership, offers more traditional relationship investment banking connected with its understanding of the U.S. financial markets. Goldman's relationship with its Japanese partner, Sumitomo Bank, which paid $500 million for 12.5 percent of the equity but received no voting rights or management control, reportedly has not yet resulted in the major flow of business that was expected.

Both Citicorp and Security Pacific Bank found expansion into international investment banking a costly experience. Citicorp paid $29.9 million in 1983 for 29.9 percent of the English firm Vickers da Costa, which had a strong presence in Asia, including a membership in the Tokyo Stock Exchange. Citicorp subsequently purchased an interest in another U.K. firm, Scrimgeour Kemp-Gee, which also had an Asian orientation. Ultimately, the two firms were merged, and Citicorp acquired complete ownership. The venture was apparently not successful: in 1991 the surviving combination of these firms was closed at an undisclosed cost estimated to have been $400 million. Security Pacific Bank in 1982 spent $13.7 million to buy 29.9 percent of Hoare, Govett, an English investment bank whose lineage can be traced to the 1600s. Ultimately, Security Pacific paid $95.6 million for 100 percent ownership of the firm. Industry sources indicate that the bank spent $1 billion in the ten years it attempted to develop its international corporate finance business before writing off some $200 million to terminate the effort. Clearly, success in international investment banking is not easy to achieve.

Knowledgeable sources, looking at volumes and costs, say that there is room for about ten to fifteen world-class financial intermediaries that combine commercial and investment banking and perhaps toss in a little insurance to round off the business. A few of the firms will specialize in commodity products in the sense that they will rely on high volume to create low-cost production and low price to win the volume.

A second group will take the risky strategy of investing their own capital in at least some of the transactions that flow through their doors. This strategy requires having the capital in the first place, a substance currently in scarce supply. It also requires careful monitoring because the commercial and investment banks make only the spread over the cost of funds, whereas the insurance company or similar "front-line" investor makes the entire gross interest rate.

Finally, members of a third group will intermediate without taking positions that expose their own capital to loss. These will perform the more traditional investment-banking function, using their presence in markets around the world to find and match needs for and supplies of funds.

This appears to be the strategy that Morgan Stanley has adopted and that, in part, accounts for the comment of Richard Fisher, the present chairman, quoted at the beginning of this chapter. Morgan Stanley believes that a winning strategy requires a firm to combine a local orientation in each market with skills and information bases that cross geographic barriers. The local orientation ensures that officers in that location know the needs of their customers and the opportunities the market affords. The cross-national orientation ensures that special technical knowledge is brought to bear in solving a problem. Hence, products are managed worldwide by the designated product managers. Officers with geographic responsibility handle housekeeping and regulatory matters but are not supposed to interpose themselves between the local product representative and the senior officers responsible for managing that product. The regional office head thus does not give orders to the firm's money traders located in that region.

It has been argued that effectively prosecuting this approach requires a large domestic market because, initially at least, markets must be known personally and thoroughly by the intermediary itself. This appears to exclude Swiss banks from aspiring to the ultimate status of world-class bankers—among the dozen global financial institutions. Credit Suisse, at least, appears to be putting this reasoning to the test. The creative efforts of its management are an example of the type of approach that may ultimately be successful for an aspiring global bank.

Credit Suisse First Boston

The story begins with an initiative undertaken by the venerable U.S. investment bank, First Boston, which is also featured in the to-boutique-or-not-to-boutique controversy discussed in Chapter 5. In 1978, when additional capital was believed to be necessary to support trading positions and leveraged-buyout bridge financing, First Boston sold a 30 percent interest to a London investment bank controlled by Credit Suisse, one of three major Swiss banks. The resulting corporate structure was convoluted: *The Economist* headlined a story about the firm as "More Names Than a Russian Novel." Corporate entities in New York (First Boston) and London (Credit Suisse First Boston) each owned a 40 percent share of the other. The New York and London offices were relatively independent, with the New York office to concentrate on business in the United States and the London office to handle the Euromoney markets and investment banking on the continent.

For some ten years the association was very successful. Credit Suisse First Boston, for example, grew to a dominating position in the Eurobond market and was active in standard investment banking. The group had a unique and broad geographic and currency mix in its international underwriting business. It relied neither on an individual currency nor on issuers from any single country for its capital market business. Credit Suisse First Boston also provided investment advisory and portfolio management services to institutional and high-net-worth individual investors worldwide. A subsidiary, Clariden Bank, was a fully licensed Swiss bank with offices in Zurich and Geneva and representative offices in Singapore and Hong Kong. To support its activities, Credit Suisse First Boston had approximately 1,000 employees worldwide, including 120 directors and officers.

First Boston enlarged its share of mainline investment banking and trading businesses in the United States. By 1987 it had the sixth-largest capital among investment banks in the United States, offering complete investment-banking services. A relaxed management style allowed aggressive and talented individuals to build a variety of strong departments. Although the relative profitability of various product lines was extremely volatile, the senior executives believed that it was important to have total-market capability rather than to build and shrink according to the vagaries of the economy. This strategy led two of the most productive investment bankers to depart and set up their own firm, Wasserstein and Perella, when First Boston's chairman refused to eliminate portions of the (then) money-losing trading functions.

The lack of coordination occasionally led both offices to make pitches for the same business, which created ill feelings. As financial markets became increasingly global, the managerial difficulties of the two firms increased to the point that readjustment was required.

In late 1988, Credit Suisse announced plans to develop a global investment-banking capability. First Boston and Credit Suisse First Boston would merge, with Credit Suisse obtaining the major portion (44.5 percent, the Glass-Steagall limit) of ownership in the new entity, CS First Boston, by virtue of buying out the public owners of First Boston. The managers of First Boston, who were significant owners of that company, would remain as minority owners holding 25 percent of the new firm. Metropolitan Life Insurance Company would also hold about a 10 percent minority interest. In addition to positions held by investors from the Middle East, a Japanese bank was to own 5 percent, and 7 percent would be divided among six Japanese insurance companies. The total Japanese interest, therefore, was 12 percent.

Credit Suisse planned to assign operating responsibility to three subsidiaries of CS First Boston: First Boston in the Americas, Credit Suisse First Boston (CSFB) in Europe and the Middle East, and CS First Boston Pacific in Japan and Asia. Although at this time there was an apparent trend on Wall Street toward small, specialized investment-banking firms, as integrated financial supermarkets stumbled, the Credit Suisse announcement indicated that some executives thought large financial institutions might have a significant advantage in the international arena.

THE CREDIT SUISSE NETWORK

Credit Suisse was Switzerland's third-largest bank in 1988 and the world's fifty-fifth–largest bank on the basis of assets and twenty-eighth in terms of capital. As a universal bank, Credit Suisse effected a far wider range of domestic and international banking transactions than permissible by U.S. financial law and regulation. Credit Suisse also engaged in a wide range of stock market, underwriting, and corporate-finance activities as well as investment counseling, management of mutual funds, and the safekeeping of securities. In addition, Credit Suisse was an active trader of foreign exchange, securities, bank notes, and precious metals.

In response to Swiss industry's emphasis on exporting, Credit Suisse had long been actively engaged in international-financing transactions. Credit Suisse's first branch outside of Switzerland was established in New York in 1940, primarily to provide safekeeping for the securities it and its customers owned in the United States. Since 1965, Credit Suisse had greatly expanded its representation abroad. By 1988 Credit Suisse had fourteen branches and agencies, fifteen major banking and financial subsidiaries, and twenty-four representative offices abroad, providing excellent representation in major financial centers. The bank had a total of 15,020 staff members worldwide.

Credit Suisse's investment-banking strategy was to position itself as the only financial institution with true global commercial- and investment-banking capabilities, with operations in the three major capital markets of the world—New York, London, and Tokyo—compensating for the fact that the Swiss market as such was very small. By taking in partners, Credit Suisse would ensure an eager market for the deals its investment bankers developed. And behind the investment-banking activity would be Credit Suisse, with a AAA rating and international network and a far greater ability to support its investment bank than the fondest hopes of U.S. banks that might look for possible changes in the U.S. banking system. If the two activities could operate cooperatively, they could feed each other customers and business.

The New York market was important, particularly as a result of deficit spending by the U.S. government, as an absorber of funds. In addition, its scale and sophistication made it a venue that attracted international transactions.

In the integration of the European Common Market after 1992, private and public enterprises are anticipated to be users rather than generators of cash to support the growth afforded by the potential of new economies of scale. This consolidation could become the world's most important capital market, given Europe's combined population of 320 million compared to 250 million people in the United States and Japan's 120 million. The proposed regulation that a single bank license in any of the European Community countries would open doors to offering all financial services in all countries of the Community would give Credit Suisse the power to compete in anything anywhere in Europe and to become a global bank.

The Asian marketplace, in contrast, is expected to be a major source of funds. Although still in a start-up stage, CS First Boston Pacific had a dozen Japanese institutions as equity participants, which was expected to strengthen substantially the subsidiary's position in Asian markets. These insurance companies and banks were looking for outlets in which to invest the funds accumulated by Japanese savers. The CS First Boston connection gave them instant access and an inside track to New York and London markets and gave CS First Boston similar access to the Japanese and Asian markets, which were generally considered to be labyrinthine traps to the outsider. Hence, the structure was a potential coup, enabling Credit Suisse to accomplish with a pen stroke what it had taken Morgan Stanley, Goldman, Sachs, and Salomon years to achieve.

The validity of the strategy may be sound, but its implementation appears to have been more difficult than expected. First Boston was a major player in the leveraged-buyout transactions of the late 1980s. It was one of the first to invest the firm's own money in a highly leveraged transaction (so-called merchant banking in the United States), and it had been very successful in some major early deals, such as Amerace. First Boston multiplied its equity investment in that company some six times in a couple of years and collected the associated fees. Other firms, such as Morgan Stanley, took title to and nominal responsibility for enormous collections of firms, including Burlington Industries, the textile company, and Fort Howard Paper. (The irony of the investment banks' exhorting conglomerate companies to slim and concentrate while they themselves were turning into conglomerate holding companies seems to have escaped most observers.) Needless to say, these extraordinary profits tempted the investment bankers into larger commitments of the firm's funds, as described in Chapter 5.

Unfortunately, when the LBO music stopped, First Boston found itself still standing with a number of large deals incomplete, including some $1 billion financed temporarily by funds that had been intermediated through First Boston itself. Thus, rather than acting as the ring master for the resolution of the problems created because buyout companies were unable to restructure their short-term debt, First Boston was trotting around with the companies like a trained pony while the lenders snarled and snapped like testy lions.

In addition, First Boston had also spent some $60 million in getting started on its own integrated securities-trading system. By late 1990, it was reported in *The Economist* that First Boston still had $40 million to go but could have bought something off the shelf for one-third of the outlay it was making.

The problems the potential losses created for Credit Suisse were serious. First, they eroded First Boston's capital base, which presented potential regulatory problems. They also made financial institutions increasingly reluctant to provide the firm with the operating capital it needed to conduct its day-to-day business. Finally, the adverse effect on First Boston's profitability meant that bonuses were threatened. This motivated managers of profitable activities to move to other firms that would recognize their contributions.

Controlling the operation was not an easy task and did not appear to have been completed as of early 1991. New executives were brought in from other institutions, and senior managers were moved back and forth across the Atlantic, clearly at the direction of the head of Credit Suisse, Rainer E. Gut. The most troublesome loans, totaling about $950 million, were either purchased outright or moved off the First Boston balance sheet into a separate limited partnership backed by CS Holdings, the parent company for the Credit Suisse bank and other investments. In addition, CS Holdings added $300 million in new equity (raising its ownership to 60 percent) to maintain First Boston's capital requirements. The outcome was clearly embarrassing to all concerned and required the Federal Reserve System to give its approval for the first time to majority ownership of a major U.S. investment bank by a commercial bank (and a foreign bank at that).

First Boston executives, many of whom reportedly had personally borrowed $1 million to invest in CS First Boston when it was set up in 1988, had little choice but to go along with the changes. Even so, the threat of personal bankruptcy was real.

Yet this was not a problem that could be easily solved by trying to duplicate the stability of the Credit Suisse home office. Well-experienced though they are, Swiss commercial bankers operate within the scope of well-defined policies and procedures. Even more than in the United States, if the manual had a rule, that was the answer; if it did not have a rule, guidance was requested from above. Uncertainty and entrepreneurialism was not encouraged. This is clearly not how successful investment banking was characterized in the past.

Despite the restructuring of CS First Boston, the problems faced by Credit Suisse became more complex in mid-1991, when it was announced that the parent holding company for the group, CS Holding S.A., would cut its dividend by about 30 percent. In addition, 20 percent of the bank would be sold to the public, and CS Holding would make a rights issue in order to raise about $1.6 billion in capital. These decidedly un-Swiss developments caused great concern in the financial markets, which Credit Suisse management tried to allay by pointing to the company's many strong operations.

Morals of the Story, If Any

The jury is still out on how to become one of the dozen global financial institutions. Perhaps, a universal global financial institution will not work in an unprotected global market, if different managerial requirements prove too much to house under a single roof. A headline for an April 1990 article in *Euromoney*, "The Giants Crawl Back into Their Niches," reflects this perspective.

Perhaps the Morgan Stanley strategy will prove to be the winning one for investment firms. It opened its own offices in the major markets and staffed them as quickly as possible with local citizens. It selected segments of the local market to which it could bring added value because of its international connections. It organized across markets and products rather than geographically. It established minor outposts in many markets (eight of twelve offices in 1991 had fewer than fifty employees) to support specific products rather than attempting full-service provision in all locations. It did not seek support of a commercial bank. It had access to the capital markets through its publicly owned stock, but its management also believed that a majority of the equity should be controlled by employees of the company. It financed even its short-term, speculative, leveraged-buyout investments by using special funds, to which its contributions were strictly limited and have subsequently been alleged in some cases to have been less than the fees it received from the transactions.

In the Japanese fiscal year ending March 31, 1990, Morgan Stanley was the second-largest U.S. securities firm in Japan, reporting revenues of $239.3 million and earnings of $1.7 million. Although the figures may not be comparable because Morgan Stanley is not organized on a geographic basis, Salomon Brothers earned $25.5 million in Japan, Goldman, Sachs earned $2.6 million, Shearson Lehman booked $10.6 million (on revenues of only $84 million!), and First Boston lost $5 million. Both Morgan Stanley and Kidder Peabody, which reported $4.4 million earned in Japan in fiscal 1990, have been leaders in using computer-based trading techniques in the Tokyo Stock Exchange. These techniques have been no more popular with the major Japanese brokerages than they were in the United States; despite their size and overwhelming market shares, the Japanese firms did not have the technical capacity to use computer-based techniques. In addition, because of the size of the Japanese firms, they were almost precluded from using them to avoid completely destroying the market.

Goldman, Sachs has adopted a follower strategy. Recently, that has translated into a 30 percent return for the partners' equity and thus questioned traditional wisdom that access to outside capital is essential for survival as an investment bank. A cautious approach seemed to have kept the firm's capital out of the bridge-loan business. A new computer system designed to track the firm's investment position arrived in 1987, just as the markets turned very volatile, again illustrating the importance of new technology in the financial business. Goldman was a relative laggard in opening international offices but has had considerable success recently marketing its ability to be marginally innovative to established practices.

Despite its profitability, it is unclear whether Goldman, Sachs can develop the local staff necessary to cultivate the special relationships with indigenous managers and owners that will allow it to develop its presence in the European and Asian mergers market. In addition, the partnership form creates special impediments with respect to the ability to envelop local executives into the home-office establishment. These problems may be overcome; but new management will have to accomplish it because John Weinberg, chairman for fourteen years, retired at the end of 1990.

Financial markets have been reinternationalized in the last quarter-century, but no one has yet built and managed a single entity that participates effectively in all aspects of the market. The objective may therefore be as chimerical as efforts to build a successful integrated textile company extending from the animal and fiber to the ultimate consumer. Watch this space: top billing on the marquee is still available.

10

The Golden Age of Investment Management

The rise of the new financial system has dramatically increased the importance of investment-management skills. Pension funds and mutual funds both require investment-management skills that are usually provided by outside investment managers. At the same time, the rise of the integrated global capital market, the advent of rapidly changing interest rates, and the development of the options and futures markets have increased the complexity of investment management. No longer can investment managers put the money in their care in long-term government bonds and forget about it as trust department officers did in the 1960s. Today investment managers must follow developments in financial markets around the world on a minute-to-minute basis and translate those developments into continual investment decisions using the latest computer technology and mathematical techniques.

The Investment-Management Industry

A sophisticated investment-management industry has evolved over the last twenty years and has become one of the most

Figure 10.1
Growth of Independent Investment Counsel Firms

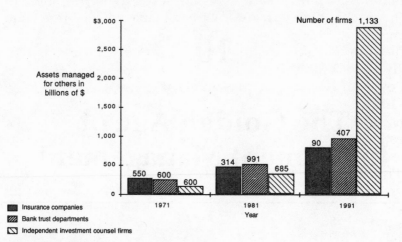

Source: Money Market Directory (Charlottesville, VA 1971, 1981, 1991)
Note: Money Market Directory is an annual directory of the leading money management organizations in the United States. The chart above is for the organizations included in the respective editions of Money Market Directory.

dynamic segments of the financial-services industry. The growth of large institutional investors, particularly pension funds, has spurred rapid growth of the investment-management field. Many small, independent investment-management firms have been established since 1970 to serve clients who have sought better performance than that provided by traditional dominant forces in the industry—bank trust departments and life insurance companies. Between 1981 and 1989, registered investment advisors more than tripled from fewer than 5,000 in 1981 to 15,700 in 1989. In 1988, the Securities and Exchange Commission estimated that 300 new money-management firms were being started every month. Figure 10.1 summarizes the tremendous growth of the money-management business between 1970 and 1990.

The money that Americans invested in mutual funds and pension funds grew from approximately $792 billion in 1979, or 17 percent of household financial assets, to $3.7 trillion in 1989, or 28 percent of financial assets. During that period, pension fund assets grew by about 15 percent per year, and mutual fund accounts by 27 percent per year. This high rate of growth allowed money managers to earn tremendous amounts for their services, with annual fees of 1 percent to 2 percent of assets managed not uncommon. Partners in small money-management firms routinely earn six- and seven-figure incomes. In 1989, the total fees earned by money-management firms were estimated at $10 billion.

The 15,000 active money-management firms vary significantly, with some firms managing billions of dollars in assets and others managing less than $100 million. At the end of 1989, the 100 largest money managers had combined assets under management of $1.9 trillion, half of the total amount. The investment orientation of investment-management firms was focused heavily on equities. A survey at the beginning of 1986 by *Pension and Investment Age* reported the following breakdown of money managers' portfolios: equities, 55 percent; bonds, 24 percent; cash, 10 percent; real estate, 5 percent; mortgages, 2 percent; mortgage-backed securities, 1 percent; other assets, 3 percent. The apparent difficulty of selecting equities that appreciate more than the market allows the money managers that succeed at stock picking to charge high fees.

Mutual Funds Create a Financial Giant

Probably the most successful money-management firm of the last twenty years is Fidelity. One of the oldest mutual fund organizations in the United States, Fidelity was in deep distress in 1946 when it was taken over by Edward C. Johnson II. With barely $3 million in assets, the company's survival was doubtful. To turn the company around, Johnson adopted a radically new investing strategy—investing in stocks with strong potential for growth rather than in blue chips. The new strategy paid off. Within twenty years, the firm was managing $4 billion in assets and had become one of the leaders of the mutual fund industry. By 1990, Fidelity managed over $100 billion in assets.

Fidelity manages more than 100 portfolio funds, compared to the dozen or fewer managed by other large mutual fund companies. These funds run the gamut of specialized types, including funds concentrating on high-growth opportunities, out-of-favor issues, turnaround companies, specific economic sectors like energy, and over-the-counter stocks. Handling

Fidelity's funds is an army of fund managers and security analysts that visits more than 10,000 U.S. and overseas companies annually. This intensive research effort has resulted in an excellent overall success record for Fidelity.

INVESTMENT MANAGEMENT AND THE NOBEL PRIZE IN ECONOMICS

The growth of investment management as a professional discipline has gone hand-in-hand with the development of investment-management theory in the overall discipline of finance. The growing importance of the financial theory supporting the investment-management discipline was recognized in 1990 when the Nobel Prize in economics was awarded to three leaders in the development of the theory of investment management and corporate finance. The 1990 prize was shared by Harry Markowitz (professor at City University of New York), William Sharpe (professor at Stanford University), and Merton Miller (professor at the University of Chicago). Of the three winners, Markowitz and Sharpe have had the greatest direct impact on investment management. (Miller's contributions, originally in collaboration with another Nobel economics laureate, Franco Modigliani, were in the area of corporate finance.)

Markowitz is the father of modern portfolio theory. His insight that the risk of an individual asset hardly matters to an investor and that what counts is the contribution it makes to the investor's total risk is the basis for most modern portfolio theory. These new concepts were implicitly recognized in ERISA when it abandoned the traditional "prudent man" rule that had governed pension investing, requiring each individual asset to be low risk; the new approach that allowed pension funds to balance low-risk assets with high-risk assets. Sharpe built on Markowitz's work to develop the capital-asset pricing model (CAPM), a staple of every business school curriculum today. The CAPM divides the risk of an investment portfolio into two categories: "systematic" or "market" risk and "unsystematic" risk. Systematic risk is the variation in a stock's price that is due to changes in stock prices overall; unsystematic risk is due to factors peculiar to that stock. Sharpe's work is the basis for much computerized management of investment portfolios including *passive indexing* (replicating to the extent possible the components and proportions of a market index), which is being applied to an increasing percentage of pension portfolios.

A key element of Fidelity's success has been the quality of its customer service. Although its investment results have been excellent, Fidelity's customer service distinquishes it from its competition. Fidelity invests heavily and wisely in technology, advertising, and support staff. Its telephones answer one call per second twenty-four hours a day. Its street-level Investor Centers, located all over the United States, are within an hour's drive of almost 90 percent of all Americans making more than $50,000 a year.

The recent star of Fidelity's family of mutual funds has been the Magellan Fund, managed by super money manager Peter Lynch until his retirement in 1990. Magellan's outstanding record of growth for a large fund explains why individual investors are abandoning depository institutions for mutual funds and why the investment-management industry will continue to grow and provide opportunities for small entrepreneurial money-management firms with the right combination of bright people.

From 1977, when Lynch took over management of the Magellan Fund, Fidelity experienced phenomenal growth and returns for its shareholders: $10,000 invested in Magellan Fund shares in 1977 was worth over $200,000 by 1988. Over the same period, Magellan grew from $22 million to become the largest mutual fund in history, with $12 billion in assets at its peak in 1987 and over a million shareholders. This one mutual fund had become a major financial institution: it was larger in asset size than all banks outside the top fifty and all thrifts outside the top ten. It had also generated hundreds of million dollars annually in money-management fees and mutual funds sales commissions (which went directly to Fidelity's management, since salespeople were not employed to sell the fund).

For Lynch's expertise in picking stocks, he was paid several million dollars a year—a bargain for Fidelity, given the revenues generated for the firm by his expertise. A graduate of the Wharton School of Finance, Lynch had the necessary analytical training for the job and capitalized on that training by prodigious research work. He traveled 100,000 miles a year visiting hundreds of companies and looking for investment opportunities. He talked to or received information from dozens of brokers daily and networked routinely with other investment managers and professionals seeking ideas. Lynch's combination of talent, good training, and hard work led to phenomenal financial success—and explains why the money-management business will continue to attract entrepreneurs with limited financial resources but lots of human capital.

Investment Management Creates Successful Niche Players: The Story of Reich & Tang

One of the niche players that have successfully ridden the trends in the money-management field is Reich & Tang (R&T), a Manhattan-based money-management firm that specializes in money-market funds and small growth stocks. R&T was founded in 1970 by Oscar Tang and his partner Joseph Reich and became one of the most successful private investment-management companies on Wall Street, with major activities in institutional equity management and money-market mutual funds. Both founders had previously worked in the investment business as vice presidents and co-heads of research at Donaldson, Lufkin & Jenrette Inc. From its inception, R&T was registered as an investment advisor and was a member firm of the New York Stock Exchange. The firm's original business was the discretionary management of equity portfolios, and in 1974 it created the fourth money-market fund in the United States. These two activities grew considerably and have remained the principal sources of the firm's revenues.

Throughout the 1970s, R&T concentrated its energies on achieving the best possible investment performance record. The core of its capital-management culture was that superior investment performance was the foundation of the business. Marketing was seen as of limited importance; excellent performance would always find clients. During the 1970s, the money-market mutual fund business was considered secondary, a temporary product of legal constraints in the marketplace (Regulation Q of the Federal Reserve Board restricted the ability of banks to pay market rates on many types of deposits) that would probably be eliminated. Management style was that of an informal partnership. The principals devoted most of their time and attention to investment research and selection among smaller companies.

By the early 1980s, it became apparent that R&T could not develop further without a major change of operating style. The mutual fund products flourished because innovation continually outdistanced deregulation. A new management structure was therefore introduced. Within a framework of carefully articulated investment guidelines, the firm's investment professionals were each given a portion of total assets to manage on the basis of their own research.

R&T's investment professionals acted as portfolio managers—there was thus clear accountability and no time lag between research and implementation. This system is significantly different from that used in most other investment-management firms, which separated the research function from portfolio management.

Tang, the chief executive officer, no longer had responsibility for day-to-day investment decisions but concentrated on wider business strategy and, together with his partners, on ensuring that the investment framework within which the firm's professionals worked was adhered to and remained appropriate. The success of this new management structure has been proven by performance: capital management assets under supervision were up from $250 million at the end of 1981 to $1.3 billion currently, and outstanding investment results had been maintained.

In the mutual fund business R&T develop a strategy of serving the needs of the distributor market (such as brokerages or banks). A policy of sharing fees with distributors was linked to aggressive product development and the pursuit of new channels of distribution. The number of funds grew from two to nine, and funds under management increased from $1 billion to over $3 billion in five years. By 1981, R&T had made the transformation from a small partnership of investment managers to a structured financial business with the systems and management necessary for continued growth in its existing and new businesses, and its revenues increased from $8.9 million in 1981 to $22.0 million in 1985.

R&T's Capital Management Group manages fully discretionary U.S. equity accounts. Existing clients provide 75 percent of all asset growth, and R&T has had a relatively long relationship with most of those clients, who are attracted by its performance-driven rather than marketing-driven culture. The large institutions that make up R&T's client list are assigned multiple investment managers, who offer distinctive investment styles. R&T's analysts carry out their own research and evaluate each stock as if they are buying the underlying business entity. They seek companies whose managements emphasize a strong balance sheet, positive cash flow, high return on equity, and growth potential, especially stocks with medium-sized capitalization, above-average prospective earnings gains, and relatively low price-earnings ratios. To be considered for purchase, a company has to have a low market valuation in relation to its value as a business. No attempt is made to "time" the market.

The only real constraint on the expansion of the Capital Management Group's business is its ability to maintain its outstanding investment performance record. Management is determined, therefore, carefully to control the growth both of assets and of staff to ensure consistency of its product and the continuation of its high standard of performance.

OUTSTANDING INVESTMENT PERFORMANCE CREATES WEALTH

Good investment management not only creates wealth for the clients of investment managers but also can create wealth for the investment managers themselves. The classic example of how good investment management creates personal wealth is Warren Buffett, the dean of long-term "value investing."

In 1956, at the age of twenty-five, Buffett started a family partnership with $100,000 in it. After successfully running the partnership over nine years, Buffett took over Berkshire Hathaway, an unprofitable textile manufacturer in New Bedford, Massachusetts, and made it a vehicle to practice his value investing ideas. The results are history.

In September 1990, *Fortune* magazine listed Buffett among the twenty-five wealthiest individuals in the world, with a personal fortune estimated at $3.8 billion, the result of his 44.7 percent ownership of his phenomenally successful investment company Berkshire Hathaway (a share of Berkshire Hathaway purchased for $12 in 1965 was worth over $7,000 in 1990).

At age sixty, Buffett still puts in long hours despite his wealth, saying, "I am doing what I would most like to be doing in the world, and I have been since I was twenty." What keeps him going, he says, is the admiration he holds for his business colleagues: "I choose to work with every single person I work with. That ends up being the most important factor."

R&T entered the mutual fund business in 1974 with the creation of the Daily Income Fund. The Fund was begun to provide equity investors with a cash-management vehicle to complement the management of these longer-term investments. In the late 1970s, with short-term rates rising close to 20 percent, cash management became an important part of any investment program. The money-market fund industry expanded very rapidly, from under $5 billion in assets in 1977 to over $200 billion by late 1982. Throughout the 1970s, the fund was used primarily by a group of dealer distributors for their client accounts. By the early 1980s, this field had become increasingly competitive.

R&T responded by developing new funds and new distribution channels, particularly to regional banks. In 1986, R&T managed nine funds (including the Reich & Tang Equity Fund, for which the Capital Management Group performed investment advisory services) with total assets of approximately $3.2 billion. Within the stated investment objectives of each fund, R&T pursued a policy of maximizing income, but only to an extent that was consistent with the preservation of capital. Its intermediary customers were financial professionals who shared R&T's philosophy that integrity of principal should be the cardinal investment objective of these types of funds.

R&T is a wholesale rather than a retail mutual fund operator. The company does not advertise its products or market "load" funds. It distributes its funds through banks, broker dealers, investment advisors, and other professional investment organizations. The distributors provide the funds in turn to their clients; most of the larger distributors are compensated by continuing payments from R&T under Rule 12B-1. These payments range from ten to forty basis points annually on the average balances maintained in the funds.

R&T has been successful in making its funds attractive to the intermediary market for several reasons:

- The company maintains one of the highest-quality service capabilities in the industry. For example, R&T became one of the first mutual fund organizations to offer its broker-dealer customers the ability automatically to transmit, receive, and include on their customers' statements money-market fund transactions. Since that time, the firm has been in the forefront in the development and use of computer systems, an important competitive advantage.

- R&T is unique in not competing with its intermediary clients for the business of the end customer. It supplies a generic product that an intermediary can package as its own. R&T can be more responsive to the needs of its intermediary clients in creating funds specifically for their markets rather than offering funds developed primarily for its own retail base.

- R&T has been able to offer superior financial incentives. The sophistication and success of its investment management and product design have allowed R&T to achieve, in at least some of its funds, consistently superior investment performance. The Daily Tax Free Income Fund has used Industrial Development Bonds with puts to achieve a higher yield and, arguably, lower risk than competitive funds. This allowed R&T to charge a relatively high management fee, which in turn had made possible 12B-1 payments that were believed to be significantly higher than those paid on competitive products. The Daily Tax Free Income Fund was the firm's largest fund and accounted for most of its business with commercial banks. (Taxable funds competed directly with banks' own money-market and savings accounts.) Overall, distribution payments have grown rapidly from $584,000 in 1982 to $6,400,000 in 1986. They represent both R&T's largest marketing cost and an asset in encouraging distributors to bring business to R&T.

The major distributors of R&T's funds include leading investment banks and brokerage houses and many leading regional banks. Prior to 1983 the company's business depended largely on the broker-dealer market, but since then, R&T has emphasized developing its business with regional banks—a market with great potential as fee-earning business gains importance throughout the banking industry. Even if the banking regulatory hurdle to issuing their own funds were to be removed, small banks are unlikely to have the experience, systems, and resources necessary to design and run a family of competitive funds. In this environment, R&T's funds are expected to continue to be attractive to many banking intermediaries.

In addition to its own family of funds, R&T manages or administers funds for others. There is potential for rapid growth of this area as more banks become intermediaries for R&T's existing products and as new products are developed. So far R&T has designed products to fit no more than a small part of the needs of bank customers. With its broad knowledge of investment markets and its systems capability, this business has significant potential for R&T. The operating leverage of the mutual fund business is high; once a fund is set up and operating, a high proportion of any additional management fees (net of distribution expenses) falls to the bottom line.

In preparation for future growth, R&T went public in 1987, becoming a master limited partnership traded on the New York Stock Exchange. For the next two years, R&T's record was one of continuing growth and profitability. In 1988, the company's first year as a public company, R&T had annual revenues of $36,530,000 and pretax net income of $16,037,000. Its high profitability reflected the fact that many investment management companies have pretax net income that is close to 50 percent of annual revenues. In 1989, R&T's annual revenues grew to $38,333,000, and net income grew to $18,033,000, which was almost double R&T's revenues of $22,071,000 and triple its profits of $6,281,000 of five years earlier (1984). Both figures suffered in 1990, declining to $37,500,000 and $16,100,000, reflecting the poor market that year. As the 1990s progress, R&T should continue to prosper and grow as it serves the growing demand for asset management and mutual fund services.

The Consolidation of the Investment-Management Industry

After a period of dramatic growth, the investment-management industry has begun a period of consolidation as large financial-service companies begin to buy up independent money managers. American Express, for example, has bought over forty independent money managers. This is not surprising given the consolidation trends that other parts of the financial-service industry have experienced. Size can sometimes permit the use of more sophisticated technology and improve service quality.

DAVID DREMAN CASHES IN

David Dreman is the author of three books on investment strategy that champion the selection of stocks with low price/earnings ratios and the president and founder of Dreman Value Management, L.P., a New York money-management firm. His investment philosophy is built on buying stocks when their price/earnings ratios are below the market and selling those same stocks when their price/earnings ratios catch up with the market. Three books—*Psychology and the Stock Market, Contrarian Investment Strategy: The Psychology of Stock Market Success,* and *The New Contrarian Investment Strategy*—developed Dreman's reputation as an expert on contrarian investing, which was reinforced by a regular column in *Forbes* magazine and articles in *Newsweek, Fortune, Barron's,* and the *New York Times.*

But the proof of his expertise and the payoff for it came from Dreman's money-management activity, which manages money for large pension funds. In its first ten years of operation from 1977 to 1987, Dreman's money-management firm grew from a startup operation to over $3.4 billion under management. Most of that growth came after 1984, when the firm's assets under management grew from $400 million to $3.4 billion in 1987 as a result of the increasing reputation of Dreman and the outstanding track record of the firm. The annualized compounded return of 23.8 percent for Dreman's managed accounts put him in the top league of money managers and far above the annualized compounded return of the Standard & Poor's 500. A dollar invested with Dreman in 1977 was worth $7.20 in 1987. This success helped increase not only the value of Dreman's clients but also Dreman's personal net worth. As a result of its growth, by 1987 Dreman Value Management's annual revenues had reached $20 million, up from less than $1 million in 1979. When Dreman sold part of his interest in the firm in 1988, industry sources indicated he made well over $50 million.

This trend is reinforced by the high prices that money-management firms command. Traditionally, money-management firms sell for roughly four times annual revenue. This means that a firm with $100 million under management charging a 1 percent annual fee will sell for approximately $4 million dollars. As the dramatic growth of the money-management business slows in the 1990s, the incentive for many small money managers to sell will grow. Reinforcing this trend will be the fact that many of the entrepreneurs who started these firms are now in their forties and fifties and are looking to diversify the net worth that is generally tied up in their firms. Selling will be particularly attractive to this group because many buy-out arrangements keep the existing management and allow managers to continue to share in the profits of the firm.

The Future of the Investment-Management Industry

In the 1990s, the investment-management industry should continue to grow in importance as more of the assets of the financial system are concentrated in pass-through intermediaries such as pension funds and mutual funds that require the skills of sophisticated investment-management firms. As the industry increasingly consolidates, money managers will be part of large diversified financial-services organizations. However, because investment performance ultimately depends on the quality of the brainpower of the investment-management firm, the small investment-management boutique with sharp analysts will continue to have a role to play.

As the investment-management business continues to grow, it will affect other areas of the financial-services industry. Because using money managers and pass-through intermediaries like pension funds and mutual funds is inherently more efficient than the traditional intermediaries of commercial banks and thrifts, the continued growth of employment in the money-management business will not offset declining employment in the thrift and commercial banking sectors. The growth of securitization of loans will likewise ensure that a few money managers with small staffs will replace many employees in banks and thrifts.

III
THE FUTURE OF THE
FINANCIAL SYSTEM

11

The Driving Forces for Change

Three basic forces will operate to create a significant change in the U.S. financial system over the next fifteen to twenty years. The first two have been at work for the past quarter century, with significant results; the third represents a new development. The forces are

- The attack on the industry structure by those looking for greener pastures;
- The implementation of new computer technology;
- The changing patterns of saving and borrowing by the customers of the financial-services industry.

These changes have had and will continue to have three major effects:

- The consolidation of all aspects of the financial-services industry;
- The blurring of distinctions between different financial institutions, including the advent of nationwide, near-universal banking;
- The elimination of the existing bias in the financial system that rewards borrowing more than saving.

In all probability, as is discussed in the following chapter, this evolution will be slowed and made more costly by the nature of the political process. That has been the experience of the last thirty years, and there is no reason to expect that the future will be different.

Deregulation

Waves of change have been eroding the foundation of the financial-services industry at least since the introduction of the transferable certificate of deposit in 1961. To put this effect into perspective, a brief digression is necessary to distinguish between a "natural" and an "unnatural" or "legal" monopoly.

Natural Monopolies

A natural monopoly is one in which the economies of scale continue to reduce unit costs until the enterprise becomes extremely large: an electric utility and a gas utility are good examples. Running more than one set of parallel electric lines or gas mains is far more expensive per customer served than running only one set, although a few cities have experimented (less than successfully) with mandating two utilities. Power generation and cross-continent gas delivery systems are also efficient in large sizes: a gas pipeline of twice the size can carry more than twice the amount of gas at much less than double the cost of two smaller lines. Left to their own devices, therefore, firms functioning in an environment where great economies of scale exist quickly link up into one large entity. Profits are increased thereby, and market share can more easily be taken from alternative sources (for example, gas from coal) that cannot be or have not been structured in a similarly efficient manner.

From a public-policy standpoint, particularly given the populist heritage in the United States, natural monopolies are distrusted. Once the monopoly is in place, it has the ability to extract profits in excess of the level originally required to attract capital into the business. Government thus enters by providing a mechanism whereby the profits of the natural monopoly can be limited.

The purposes of regulating a natural monopoly are relatively simple. The first purpose is to protect the public from excessive prices by requiring that rates be set as low as possible while still attracting capital to the business. (Contrary to popular belief, however, this commitment does not extend to guaranteeing a return to the lenders or investors in the equity of the monopoly.) Second, the regulation is supposed to encourage efficient operation and ensure that the benefits of efficiency are shared between the providers of capital (debt and equity) and the customer. These principles are simple to state but, as the interminable rate hearings imply, difficult to implement to the satisfaction of all parties.

Unnatural Monopolies

Regulating an unnatural monopoly is an entirely different problem. An unnatural monopoly is a legal grant of monopolistic rights in a situation that does not offer the economies of scale provided by a natural monopoly. A natural monopoly keeps competitors out by the very nature of the production process. An unnatural monopoly is created artificially often by law, and is designed to keep out competition and to provide those players who have an admission ticket with a level of profits to which they would otherwise not be entitled. The unnatural monopoly may be

- Granted by the government to private parties for any of a variety of reasons;
- Created by professional licensing or other controls (such as lawyers and doctors and even the stagehand and tugboat unions in the New York City metropolitan area, which are reputedly closed except to those with family connections);
- Created by the participants themselves, who use threats or violence to discourage competition from entering;
- Created by the government for itself in order to wrest the maximum profits from an enterprise (such as the sale of tobacco or alcoholic products) or to subsidize activities that would otherwise be deemed too costly socially. The U.S. Postal Service is an example of this latter objective: delivery of certain mail costs the USPS much less than the fees,

which are used to underwrite expensive costs such as delivery of mail in out-of-the-way locations.

When an unnatural monopoly is created by law, the government usually (especially in the populist United States) establishes a regulatory body to review and control the profits of the monopoly. This regulatory structure looks on the surface like one established to regulate a natural monopoly. Its function, in fact, is quite different.

Consider the trucking industry, which, until the early 1970s, was operated as an unnatural monopoly under the jurisdiction of the Interstate Commerce Commission. The ICC had originally been established in 1887 to regulate railroads, a natural monopoly (at least in the 1800s). It was given regulation of the trucking industry by the Motor Carrier Act of 1935, when the U.S. government undertook to stem what appeared to be ruinous competition. It handed out franchises to existing trucking businesses and then prohibited others from entering without permission of the ICC. Thus, if your trucking company had been running from Cleveland to Chicago on a given route, you were granted that right in perpetuity.

There are few economies of scale in trucking, which is what caused the severe competition in the first place. Anyone with enough cash to buy, rent, or lease a truck could enter the business. After the unnatural monopoly was created, this market discipline was no longer possible.

The ICC was supposed to set fair rates, which one might incorrectly think would be the rates required to attract capital to the most efficient producer of the service. But to set rates at this level would drive all other competitors out of the business because they were, by definition, less efficient. This outcome would hardly achieve what the unnatural monopoly was intended to provide—a safe haven for less-efficient competitors. Thus, the regulation of unnatural monopolies tends to set prices high enough that the least efficient competitor survives. Under this system, the Teamsters Union extracted high compensation for their members: by granting what the union wanted, management and owners avoided the disruption of a strike, and the unnatural monopoly arrangement allowed companies to pass the increases on to customers.

This is a wonderful arrangement for an efficient competitor.

Once one gets the admission ticket, all benefits of increased efficiency stay with the ticketholder, in contrast to the requirements that a natural monopoly return most of the fruits of its efficiency to its customers. For example, a skilled entrepreneur can buy a poorly run trucking company, turn it around, and sell it for a price based on the higher level of profits.

WHO PAYS THE BILL FOR UNNATURAL MONOPOLIES?

What causes an unnatural monopoly to fail? It appears to be such a wonderful arrangement for all concerned: government gets taxes, and elected officials get votes and financial support from grateful constituents. Government also may tack various social obligations onto the industry (for example, it might require truckers not only to pay for the disposal of their own used tires but tax them to cover the costs of tire disposal in general). The employees obtain above-market compensation. Everyone but the most inept owners makes money. The bill is paid, of course, by the customer.

As the beneficiaries get greedy and extract increasingly greater benefits from the unnatural monopoly, prices must rise to suppport the largess. The customer finally becomes sufficiently discouraged to seek alternatives. If the potential profits are large enough, creative entrepreneurs usually provide alternatives. Because the venture is an unnatural monopoly, there is no economic reason why alternatives are not available. In the case of trucking, manufacturing and distributing firms could set up their own fleets of trucks, even running empty on the return trip, at lower costs than common carriers offered.

Loopholes in the laws are sought. In some cities, taxi licenses are tightly regulated, but private limousine services are allowed to operate at a customer's call. (According to one joke, cruising gypsy taxis carried CB radios so that a prospective customer could comply with the law by radioing in to request a cab.) The laws creating the monopoly also may simply be disobeyed because the penalties are less than the benefits of getting a nose under the unnatural monopoly's tent.

Finally, the situation becomes so extreme that public demand requires adjustment. In the case of the U.S. trucking industry, an unlikely combination—consumer advocates (of a liberal persuasion), opponents of regulation (of a conservative persuasion), the oil crisis (creating a need to have more efficient over-the-road transport, with fewer partly filled trucks), and those who disliked the Teamsters Union—prevailed. The regulation of truck routes, prices, market entries, and profits was dramatically curtailed by the Motor Carrier Act of 1980, and route authorizations, which had been trucking firms' most valuable asset, became worthless overnight.

The splitting up of American Telephone & Telegraph Company was another illustration with two notable aspects. First, the reorganization was motivated by technological advances rather than by excess profitability. Under the old technology, mouthpiece-to-earpiece transmission of electronic impulses over wires was a natural monopoly. The invention of microwave and satellite transmissions, however, dramatically reduced the cost of long-distance telecommunications, thereby undermining the natural monopolistic structure of the industry. Some companies installed private telephone systems. Competitors could offer cut-rate service by leasing lines from AT&T at costs reflecting high-volume use and then reselling telephone service to the public at lower rates than AT&T charged.

Competitors were further aided by AT&T's decision, made in the 1930s, to have the "luxury" long-distance service subsidize local telephone services. Because AT&T set long-distance prices well above costs and local service below full cost, competitors that entered only the long-distance segment of the market could offer tariffs that did not include this subsidy.

The second difference was that AT&T's management decided to jump before it was pushed and attempted to orchestrate the new structure rather than let the company endure the piecemeal buffeting it had been receiving. Management realized that it had lost key regulatory battles and that rulings had knocked holes in the fence protecting its market. AT&T management was also familiar with how the economics of the new technology had changed the fences.

By the early 1980s management concluded that fighting the regulatory trend and public opinion that telephone costs were too high was not a battle the company could win. It therefore proposed splitting AT&T into local telephone companies, where a natural monopoly still appeared to exist, and a long-distance company that would compete with less-regulated new entrants without being saddled with the local-system subsidy. (The development of the cellular telephone raises questions about whether even the local telephone service will remain a natural monopoly.)

Furthermore, legislative bodies have tended to put social costs onto monopolies in order to make the cost of government look less. The assumption is that the monopoly can pass this cost along unnoticed by the consumer. Thus, high long-distance charges subsidized the construction of the local telephone network and its extension to localities that would have balked at paying the full price. This allocation of resources was deemed socially desirable when it was arranged in the 1930s. Because the telephone system was initially a natural monopoly, the consumers grumbled but paid. As the natural monopoly was eroded by technology, the consumers voted with their feet to use alternative, lower-cost services, forcing the end of subsidized local calls.

Financial Markets as Unnatural Monopolies

How does this discussion apply to the financial markets? The evidence can be found in the litter of broken unnatural monopolies that have been destroyed in part by the greed of the players but more generally by the development of new technology that allows new players to enter the market by new means.

For example, the New York Stock Exchange formerly had very strict rules about the commissions that its members had to charge and with whom they could trade. A NYSE member could not offer a discount on commissions to a customer, although the customer was allowed to direct that the commissions be allocated among other NYSE members in addition to the one actually making the trade. This permitted large institutional investors to pay for information provided by security-research boutiques without the boutiques having to invest in a trading function. The firm executing the trade was directed to "give up" some of its commission to another firm. The prohibition of trading NYSE-listed securities with nonmembers helped ensure that the only non-NYSE trading of a listed security took place when both parties to the trade were not members of the Exchange.

This cozy arrangement was initially attacked not by the government but by a private antitrust suit filed by a non-Exchange member who specialized in researching and trading the securities of financial institutions. Most financial institutions had not yet listed their common stock on the NYSE, and even most of the largest bank stocks were traded over-the-counter. Consequently, NYSE members and nonmembers could trade these securities freely with one another. As soon as a major bank announced it intended to obtain a listing on the NYSE, the nonmember firms specializing in bank stocks knew that they either had to join the Exchange or lose most of their business.

One nonmember investment firm, M. A. Schapiro & Co., took umbrage at being forced to make this choice. In 1965, when Chase Manhattan announced its intention to list its common stock on the NYSE, Schapiro announced it would sue the Exchange and its members for violating the antitrust laws. In response, the NYSE modified the rule prohibiting trading in listed securities with nonmembers and began the unraveling of the unnatural monopoly that protected the trading and execution profits of its members.

The process was further hastened by the advent in the early 1960s of the trading of very large blocks of securities (especially compared with the normal round lot of 100 shares traded by auction on the floor of the NYSE) among institutional investors in the "third market," "off the floor" (transactions arranged by an investment banker directly among institutions) at greatly reduced commission charges. The volume was initially low, some ten block-trades a day, but by 1969 it accounted for 14 percent of the Exchange's activity. Although the Exchange attempted to curtail the erosion, competitive and legal challenges by firms such as Weeden & Co. washed away the barriers faster than the NYSE could build them. Volume discounts were under consideration in 1967, and negotiated commissions on large transactions were introduced in 1971. All commissions were made negotiable by 1975.

The savings-and-loan debacle is another problem ultimately caused by the care and feeding of unnatural monopolies. As discussed in detail in Chapter 2, this industry originally was created to provide a service for small savers and to finance owner-occupied residential real estate. Commercial banks were even known to direct small consumer accounts to the nearest S&L. The S&Ls, in turn, kept to their knitting by investing funds in real estate on longer terms than were attractive to banks and by not attempting to enter the banks' territory of short-term consumer and commercial loans and providing demand deposits.

This division of the market worked well as long as the rate the S&Ls paid for short-term deposits was lower than the rate earned on long-term funds invested in mortgages. When the short-term rates rose, passbook savers realized that they were receiving negative yields and thus losing real dollars by leaving their savings on deposit with the S&Ls. The S&Ls, however, had no way of adjusting the earnings they made on the mortgages they owned because most mortgages were contracts for a fixed-interest rate for the duration of the mortgage.

Investors turned their attention to U.S. government securities. In an effort to stop the transfer of deposits out of thrift institutions and into U.S. governments, which would have hastened the failure of many S&Ls, the Treasury announced in September 1974 that the minimum investment allowed in short-term U.S. government debt would be increased from $1,000 to $10,000. In addition, to prevent commercial banks from offering more market-competitive rates to small savers, regulations were promulgated limiting the interest rates banks could pay on savings accounts and on certificates of deposit: the maximum rates for regulated savings deposits rose from 4½ percent to only 5¼ percent over the 1970 to 1981 period.

Innovators began to look for ways around these restrictions to access the profits inherent in borrowing at 5¼ percent and lending at so-called prime rates, which reached as high as 8 percent even before 1970. In 1971, the innovators found a hole in the legal fence: it allowed the establishment of money-market mutual funds whose assets would be invested in very short-term U.S. government debt, short-term debt of corporations (commercial paper), and certificates of deposit of financial institutions. Unlike banks, money funds did not have to maintain reserves with the Federal Reserve, have credit departments, entertain customers, or employ staff to work out troubled loans. They also did not need capital because the investors' purchase of fund shares was legally counted as equity, even though the investors themselves probably thought of shares as akin to deposits at a bank. All that was required of the entrepreneur was a minimal amount of capital in the firm *managing* the fund.

This type of fund was different from the traditional common-stock-investment medium of mutual funds, but it followed the traditional pattern of selling the funds in relatively small dollar amounts and even encouraging small investors to make regular monthly investments. (Chapter 10 discusses mutual funds in detail.) By aggregating deposits, the money-market mutual funds could easily invest in jumbo CDs and in U.S. Treasuries, which the smaller investor could not, and pass along most of the spread.

THE MONEY-MARKET EXPERIMENT

The money-market mutual funds clearly arose because of governmental efforts to protect an unnatural monopoly, the S&Ls, whose foundations had been severely eroded. A developer of an early fund has recalled that he expected the game to last perhaps eighteen months before Federal Reserve regulations were changed; he did not expect the Federal Reserve to allow assets to be drained out of the banking system at the rate they were clearly going. He overestimated the speed with which the government would respond to a change in the system.

Deregulation Commences

At one point, when the money funds were establishing themselves during the 12 percent rate peaks of the 1970s, the Federal Reserve proposed to close the hole in the fence by requiring money-market mutual funds to maintain reserve deposits with the Fed, just as banks were required to do. When the mutual fund shareholders got wind of this idea, they deluged Congress with protests, all telling the government to keep its hands off this new form of investment. The Fed backed off and has never since attempted to change the manner in which the funds work. Rather, it has very slowly allowed the rest of the system to change to become more competitive with the money funds. Even so, the funds totaled about $425 billion at the end of 1990, equivalent to 15 percent of deposits at commercial banks.

Although the Fed's initial effort to bring the money funds under regulatory control was unsuccessful, it was nevertheless increasingly apparent that changes in the system were necessary. The same high interest rates that favored the money funds devastated the thrifts, which had to pay high current rates for deposits but were earning much lower embedded rates on the long-term loans they held. The effort to hold down rates was failing, the thrifts were bankrupt as economic entities, and the commercial banks were coping with a financial system being increasingly distorted as capital flowed around the regulations and structure.

In an effort to strengthen and stabilize the system, Congress enacted two landmark pieces of legislation in 1980 and 1981. They were intended to remove many of the legal restrictions that artificially structured and compartmentalized financial institutions along lines that were increasingly inefficient and ineffective and, hence, costly. The two laws—the Depository Institutions Deregulation and Monetary Control Act of 1980 and the Garn–St. Germain Depository Institutions Act of 1982—contained several key elements:

- Interest-rate ceilings would be phased out by 1986. Regulated financial institutions then could compete at market rates for funds with money funds, which were taking away both the best deposits and the best loans. (No thought appears to have been given to whether adjustments should have been made in the deposit-insurance terms except to increase the amount covered from $40,000 to $100,000 per account. No doubt the thrift industry was in such poor financial shape that any adverse change might have quickly bankrupted it.)

- The differential restrictions between interest rates that savings and loans and banks could pay on passbook and savings accounts and certificates of deposit would end by January 1, 1984.

- Various types of special interest-paying accounts, such as NOW accounts, super-NOW accounts, and money-market accounts, would be available nationwide at the discretion of the institution wishing to issue them.

- Thrift institutions would have expanded powers to offer checking accounts and make farm loans, consumer loans, and commercial real-estate loans. The thrifts could thus have an opportunity to earn their way out of the problems the interest-rate inversion and increase had caused them.
- State restrictions on the enforcement of due-on-sale clauses on home mortgages were overturned for national banks and state savings and loans.
- The national-bank loan limits to any one customer were increased from 10 percent to 15 percent of capital on unsecured loans and 25 percent of capital on secured loans.
- The powers of the Federal Reserve Board to control the money supply and to charge for services rendered, such as operating the check-clearing system, were expanded.

At the time, these two enactments were felt to have adequately restructured the financial system for many congressional sessions to come. In fact, Congress and the administration have been virtually continuously concerned with legislation regulating this industry, partly because of economic developments and partly because of court decisions that the losing parties appealed to Congress to reverse. The details of these efforts have been discussed in the previous chapters relating to the specific industry segments, and their implications for future developments are discussed in Chapter 13.

The Financial System's Technological Revolution

At the same time that the financial system has experienced a rapidly evolving external environment, brought on by the changing economy and society, its internal operating environment has been radically affected by the ongoing technological revolution in computers and communications. Probably no other industry will be more affected by this revolution than the financial-services industry, with the possible exception of military weaponry. The financial-services industry basically deals in the movement and manipulation of information: money is information in motion—who owes and who owns, who is creditworthy and who is not, and what is increasing and decreasing in value.

THE END OF THE TRAIL OF PAPERS

Internal financial-industry operations have historically been a paper factory. The first modern office building, the Old Pension Bureau (now the National Building Museum) in Washington, D.C., was built (1882–1887) to provide space for the efficient processing of pensions due veterans of the Civil War. Processing checks, processing securities, processing claims, and communicating about investments (in the largest sense, including deposits with intermediaries) and all aspects of the financial system that require information and once required massive paper flows.

Because of the computer and communication revolution, however, financial information no longer involves a trail of papers and documents but has become instead little blips of binary code in a computer to which access is available as required. The classic example of this transformation occurred in 1987 when the Treasury Department stopped issuing paper certificates for Treasury securities. After 1987, ownership of Treasury securities was carried in "book-entry" form in the Treasury's computer bank. No actual T-bill or government bond will ever again be issued, putting an end to the largest denomination security ever engraved at the Bureau of Engraving and Printing, the $500 million Treasury note.

The volume of paper used to convey this information led the financial-services companies to be among the earliest and most important users of large mainframe computers. They were also quick to adapt to the micro- and minicomputers, which not only saved time for handling many routine tasks but also made high-priced executives more efficient. Once various financial models were constructed, senior management could quickly test the effects of changing circumstances and revised judgments without having to wait for a manual recomputation of the model. Communication innovations allowed the model and data to be accessed from the executive's home or remote location as well as from the office. The development of inexpensive and accurate facsimile-transmission equipment further enhanced the speed with which information could be moved inexpensively without postal delays or even customs delay at borders, as was discovered during the dissolution of the Russian empire in Eastern Europe.

The impact of computers and communications on the financial-service industry can be expected to accelerate as the technology becomes more powerful and less expensive. Financial-services companies will continue to be in the forefront of using the technology, as it rapidly reshapes the traditionally conservative and static world of financial services. It is irresistible in the sense that it does the same job at a lower cost or a better job at the same cost.

Computerization is occurring in two areas of the financial-services industry. First, internally, new computer technology for office automation continues to reduce the need these companies have for clerical employees and for middle-management personnel to supervise clerical staffs or data flow. Far fewer numbers of skilled computer and data-processing technicians are required. Computer links even are replacing the financial institution's traditional person-to-person method of conducting business with its customer. In some cases, computer links enable two customers to deal directly with one another rather than using the financial intermediary at all.

The most significant example to date of automating the customer relationship is the automated teller machine (ATM); it is activated by special plastic credit cards (or even regular credit cards) and allows the customer to withdraw money from an account, transfer money between accounts, or make deposits to an account without intervention of a human teller. Furthermore, most transactions no longer have to be conducted on the premises of the institution; they can be performed wherever an ATM is hooked into an institution's computer. The Navy Federal Credit Union, located in a suburb of Washington, D.C., operates an ATM network with 100 units around the world.

THE ATM TAKEOVER

Automated teller machines (ATMs) were introduced in the early 1970s to cut transaction costs by eliminating the need for peak-time tellers. Customers were initially given financial incentives to use the machine or, in at least one case, prohibited from using a human teller unless the account balance was above a minimum figure. After a slow start, the ATMs gained rapid consumer acceptance because of the flexibility they allowed. By the mid-1980s, the ATM had become the core of consumer banking systems around the country. From a handful of ATMs in the early 1970s, the number grew to 28,000 by 1982, compared to 40,000 branch offices at that time. Customer acceptance of this arrangement has been so strong that many banks now charge a premium for ATM transactions, compared with the charges for using the tellers in the bank lobby. By the year 2000, the number of branch offices may drop to less than 20,000, but electronic access to the banking system will involve 500,000 formal access points including ATMs, point-of-sale terminals, and other electronic devices.

In the future, other relationships between the financial institution and its customer will become automated, perhaps through home banking that uses microcomputers and the consumer's television set. An additional area of anticipated automation is the point-of-sale terminal, which will allow customers with debit cards to immediately charge their accounts for purchases made from retail establishments.

On the investment-banking side, programmed trading allows transactions to be completed on a massive scale when the computer monitoring the market detects a price imbalance. Before the computer, individuals were on the prowl for pricing aberrations, but a single individual could manage only a small number of analyses.

The second area in which computer technology will be impelling change in the type of job opportunities available in the financial-services industry is the result of the development of technologies such as artificial intelligence and "fuzzy logic." These techniques massively expand the types of uses to which computers can efficiently be put because they are able to handle unstructured analyses rather than being limited to following a predetermined program. Even much of the type of work associated with relatively highly skilled jobs, such as a lending officer or securities trader, will ultimately be done by a computer system with artificial intelligence, expert programming, and expert systems. In fact, prototype expert systems already are being utilized in investment management decisions on Wall Street.

The computer revolution is having a dual effect: it is making obsolete much past investment, technology, systems, and even training currently employed by financial organizations, which marginal institutions may not be able to afford to replace; and it is creating massive overcapacity in the financial-services industry. This overcapacity was illustrated by the merger of Wells Fargo and Crocker National Bank. In 1977, the two institutions combined and employed 35,000 people; by 1987, the merged organization (Wells Fargo) employed only 20,000 but continued to hold the same market share of banking business in California that the two institutions together had held in 1977. Because the market in California had grown substantially over that ten-year period, the absolute volume of business was up significantly.

The lesson from the Wells Fargo–Crocker merger is clear. In 1987, with the aid of new computer technology, which is most visible in areas like automated-teller-machine networks, one person could do the work that had required two people ten years before. A similar experience was reported after the acquisition of Irving Trust Company by The Bank of New York. The total roster was cut by one-third within two years after the merger. Although the recession of 1990 to 1991 may have reduced the business base somewhat at the same time, a one-third staff cut appears to be the accepted objective for enhanced efficiency in a large bank merger.

As deregulation of the financial-services industry continues and mergers of banks across state lines increase, wholesale reduction in banking employment will become the norm. BankAmerica Corporation, for example, estimates that the cost of operating multiple corporations rather than branches across state lines totals $50 million; NCNB Corporation estimates its annual costs for a multiple-corporate structure to be $17 million.

Overall, therefore, the financial-services industry will experience an accelerating rate of change as increasingly powerful and versatile computers contribute to the knowledge and information explosion. For these companies, the acceleration of change will be particularly difficult to manage.

Shifting Patterns of Borrowing and Savings

At the same time that the industry is being transformed by a new legal structure and new technology, it is being confronted with the implications of a secular change in its customers' basic financial needs. First, financial intermediaries, particularly the commercial banks, were buffeted by the shift into and then out of international lending. The shift into international lending occurred when the rise in the price of oil led less developed countries to borrow but led developed countries to reduce borrowing because of the economic recession that the oil-price change induced. Ironically, the shift to sovereign-risk lending was considered as a flight to safety away from the real estate problems of the 1974 recession. Of course, subsequent problems with the LDCs forced the financial industry back to the domestic scene.

Second, and longer lasting, will be the domestic consumer's shift from borrowing to saving. This shift is primarily due to the aging of the U.S. population as the babies born during the 1941 to 1960 period mature. (Figure 11.1 shows how the profile of the population has changed from 1960 to 1990 and how it will look in 2010.) The youngest members of this group are still in the early stages of the family life cycle, but are facing the costs of educating children. As a *Wall Street Journal* article headlined on June 19, 1991, "Turning Conservative, Baby Boomers Reduce

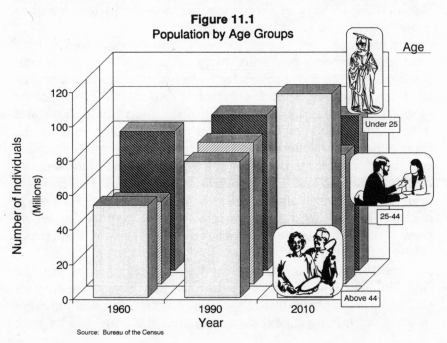

Figure 11.1
Population by Age Groups

Source: Bureau of the Census

Their Frivolous Buying." The older members have completed raising their children and providing them with an education, in total the largest expenditure a family incurs, and many have also made substantial progress toward paying off a mortgage unless they were caught up in the tail end of the real estate euphoria. This demographic group is now entering a savings phase, accumulating assets to be used to support its retirement. This saving will in part come through increased accruals of pension benefits, which begin to compound significantly after twenty to thirty years of employment and to reflect high exit-level salaries. It will be some years, however, before this group begins to draw on its assets to support its retirement. Therefore, by the end of the decade, the savings rate in the United States may rise to an average of 12 percent of GNP, nearly three times the present level.

In addition to these factors, the elimination of artificially low interest rates for savers, which has been reflected in the historically high real-interest rates in the late 1980s, and the perceived need on the part of a younger segment of the consumer population to put aside funds for its children's education, will also boost the savings rate. If real rates of interest fall as a result of the increase in savings, consumers may attempt to save even more of their incomes to compensate.

The result of these two factors—the international-to-domestic shift and the consumer shift away from borrowing to greater savings—will be more funds for investment in domestic industry and businesses. This development also should relieve some of the U.S. government's deficit problems and help state and local governments rebuild the country's infrastructure as the pool of savings becomes available for their use rather than for consumer goods. Furthermore, corporations will undoubtedly be attempting to reduce their reliance on debt and to increase their equity levels back to historic ratios. During this period savers will look to the longer term to build equity for retirement, and they may be more receptive to investment in corporate equities than they have been in recent years.

Nevertheless, these changes will create dislocations for the financial-services industry. For the past generation, the emphasis has been on structures to facilitate the creation and management of debt. For the next decade or two, the emphasis by both the corporation and the consumer will be on debt reduction and saving. It will not be easy to restructure the financial-services industry to run the projector in reverse. After discussing in the next chapter the role of the government in changing the structure of the financial-services industry, the last chapter returns to comment on the implications of these changes and trends for the future of the industry.

12

Government: Guardian of the Status Quo

The relationship between a government and its financial system is a prickly one, as the current controversy about who "caused" the savings and loan crisis illustrates. Elected officials point the finger at the various regulators, who are said not to have been sufficiently vigilant in supervising the behavior of their segment of the market. The regulators, in turn, complain that they were not given adequate staffing to exercise the responsibilities ascribed to them in retrospect. They also point out that elected officials have not responded to the changes in the marketplace with legislation that would rationalize it and facilitate phasing out institutions that no longer efficiently serve a public need. Both parties point to excesses in the industry and to fraudulent activities as though they were typical. The taxpayers evince little confidence in the ability of either the politicians or the regulators to sort out the problems. On the one hand, the public is dismayed at the costs they will have to pay to save their own financial assets. On the other hand, capital, like liberty, does not last long where it is not valued, and the public quickly moves its funds accordingly, regardless of long-established relationships.

FROM GOLD COINS TO COMPUTERS

An effective system of financial institutions, moving funds from surplus segments of society to segments that can invest the funds to generate a positive return commensurate with the risks, is essential to steady per-capita real economic growth. The impossibility today of conducting a large economic system based on barter has been clearly demonstrated in the "guided" economies of Eastern Europe: the central guidance became so out of touch with market realities that even the informal barter system, which had developed to make the economy function, finally collapsed. Imagine attempting to conduct commerce with large stone wheels or bits of colored shells! Not many years ago, financial transactions tended to be conducted in pieces of rare metals, and many families kept a few gold coins in the mattress as protection against the day when the payment system broke down. Today, score is no longer kept in physical units at all, and it is hardly even kept on paper. Financial assets are increasingly represented by bits of binary code in a computer, recording claims and obligations among economic units.

The shift of the financial system from bags of gold to computer printouts demonstrates that financial institutions are increasingly in the information business. They keep track of who owes and who owns and facilitate exchanges of these obligations and assets. Institutions accepting assets from their owners in exchange for claims against the institution, such as banks, mutual funds, and life insurance companies, reissue the assets in exchange for claims on the borrowers. Their information base and skill in using the funds should enable the institutions to make better extension of funds than the original owners of the assets could make, thus cutting losses and increasing the return enough to pay for the operating costs of the intermediation and for whatever equity the institution has to maintain. Finally, security analysts, who may not act as intermediaries in the sense that banks do, are clearly in the business of gathering information about investment opportunities and selling it to those with funds to invest.

Historical and Conceptual Perspective

The financial markets originated in part to facilitate payments (or exchanges of information) among private parties. More important, however, were the requirements of government as a consumer of society's assets. The task was to induce citizens with surplus resources to put them at the disposal of the government to enable it to invest in infrastructure or to fight wars. Infrastructure investments were a value-added expenditure of society's funds, provided they earned enough directly or indirectly (through an increased tax base) to repay the initial providers of the funds. Military expenditures were a less certain investment. Winning territory, treasures, and talents of others, as Suleiman the Magnificent found out, is a wonderful way of enhancing the well-being of one's fellow countrymen. In fact, a significant cause of the decline of the Ottoman Empire was the increasing cost of the marginal conquest relative to the loot and the consequent loss of new resources for the government to reallocate to the citizens.

Governments used extremely creative techniques to obtain funds without using taxes. They held lotteries, issued financial instruments backed by commodities, metal, or land, issued simple IOUs (such as the notorious currency of the Continental Congress, "not worth a Continental"), and tried various special techniques such as bonds with a lottery feature—with temporary success. As each failed, clever minds created new ways to promise something more in the future to compensate for giving up resources to the government today.

Of course, the prudent saver who had loaned the government a claim on the saver's assets sometimes found it necessary to reclaim the value before the contract provided that the government had to repay. Always eager to make a spread, a set of traders developed who matched those who wanted to cash in their investment with those who had spare funds to invest. Sometimes the trader would even purchase an investment for the trader's own account, holding it temporarily while trying to find an investor or in anticipation of enjoying a price increase before selling it again. Nothing prevented a trader from selling short: selling an investment not yet owned and promising delivery later, or borrowing the security from someone who did own it. This allowed a buyer's requirement to be met even if no immediate seller appeared; it also allowed a trader to speculate on the possibility that the price might fall and the borrowed security could be purchased later for less than it had been sold. There was risk in this action, however, for "he who sells what isn't hizzen must buy it back or go to prison."

The tendency is to think of these traders in financial instruments as the men meeting under the buttonwood tree on Wall Street in New York City to trade securities, a group from which the New York Stock Exchange developed. But the analogy in larger terms applies also to staid financial institutions such as banks and insurance companies. Banks started as a place where a saver could leave assets (often coin of the realm but, in the early days, precious metals in other forms such as silverware) for safekeeping. The individuals acting as the depository found that other individuals wanted to borrow the assets for temporary use, such as to buy inventory for sale. The intermediary could not only charge for safekeeping but could also make money by lending out funds. This naturally caused the entrepreneurs to try to attract more funds, requiring them to offer incentives (interest and toasters) to savers to leave resources with the bank, thus sharing the value the borrowers were willing to pay for the use of the funds. The depositors also found that they could exchange the receipts for their assets more easily than going to the trouble to lug along the physical assets themselves.

Insurance companies perform a similar task by taking surplus funds from one sector of the economy that wishes to buy safety and making the funds available to other sectors of the economy that can put the funds to work in ways that create more value than the investment cost. The costs of running the insurance company are the sacrifice that the users and savers make in order to use an intermediary to fund the investments, rather than attempting to find one another directly.

The orderly management of these flows between savers and investors is extraordinarily important to the government. First, these markets enable the government to raise the funds it needs to operate. The government's objective is to use these markets to raise funds as inexpensively as possible so that the drain on the taxpayer to pay for the money is minimized. Second, an efficient movement of funds from those with spare resources to those with opportunities to use resources profitably creates value for the society. Value creation means prosperity, and prosperity tends to mean a relatively easy time for the individuals running the government. Third, the proper system should help protect the saver. Savers who lose their savings to financial institutions are not usually enthusiastic supporters of a government that is seen as having allowed this outcome. Even the special group of savers providing equity capital to the financial institutions may be upset despite their having opted to take higher risks for the chance of higher returns. Fourth, investors seeking funds for projects are upset by problems in the financial system, particularly when the problems occur when a project is in the middle of a developmental phase. Investors turn to the government with loud complaints about inadequate funding and the implications for the future health of the society.

From earliest times, the government has assumed a central role not only in creating the financial system but also in ensuring its smooth operation. This is attempted through the regulation of the financial system—controlling who has access to its benefits, regulating the prices charged, specifying which activities can be undertaken by which institution, and snooping around (prudential supervision) to make sure that the rules are being followed.

A major problem occurs, however, because the interest of some of the beneficiaries runs directly contrary to the interests of others. The sources of capital want high returns; the users of capital (and particularly the government!) want low costs. Furthermore, the historic tendency has been to attempt to control the financial markets as though they were natural monopolies. Because they are legal monopolies, as discussed in the previous chapter, this effort creates very interesting strains.

The Reasons for Slow Governmental Response to Financial Market Changes

The slow response time of the authorities to the development of money funds has been characteristic of the response to the changes in the financial markets throughout the history of the United States. Change has seldom been initiated by the authorities, and the few changes they did initiate prior to the Civil War appear, in retrospect, to have caused damage rather than created benefit. Most of the changes were made in response to a crisis that could no longer be ignored. In that sense, the current S&L crisis and restructuring of the financial system are simply a repetition of past developments.

After all, until the Civil War, there was no uniform currency in the United States. Hard though it is to imagine, coins of various nationalities remained in circulation. Banks issued their own printed notes, which circulated at face value just in the immediate vicinity of the issuing bank. Only when the U.S. government faced the need to finance the Civil War did it establish a national banking system and issue a currency (the "greenbacks") in any quantity. In addition, national banks were allowed to issue bank notes only to the extent that the bank had investments in U.S. government debt. The ability of state-chartered banks, whose investment policies the federal government could not regulate, to issue their own notes was then greatly constrained by taxation originally imposed in 1862 at the rate of 2 percent. In 1866, the tax rate was increased to 10 percent, which made it totally uneconomic for state banks to issue their own notes and left the field to Uncle Sam. The currency-issuing ability of national banks was placed under the supervision of the Comptroller of the Currency, a title that was originally meaningful but that sounds strange to modern ears as the name of one of the major bank-supervisory agencies.

Similarly, the Federal Reserve System was a response to serious problems experienced in the financial panic of 1907. The failure of the Knickerbocker Trust Company, the third-largest trust company in New York City, in October was the immediate cause of the panic. The less immediate causes included the financial problems created for the insurance companies by the great San Francisco fire of 1906, a bountiful crop year that created bottlenecks in the transportation system and thus slowed the velocity of money, and the reliance of the railroads on short-term capital (in the absence of available long-term capital) for investment in plant and equipment. Foreign bankers became concerned about the solvency of U.S. banks, and by the end of 1906 London banks had stopped discounting American finance bills.

The panic was relatively short but quite severe, with many banks in New York City and throughout the country shutting their doors. The U.S. Treasury deposited funds with the New York banks, and J. P. Morgan organized a group of banks and individuals to help provide liquidity and support for the stock market. Restrictions on cash payments were implemented, finally disappearing early in 1908. Commercial failures were up 30 percent in the fall of 1907 over 1906 and 55 percent in the first nine months of 1908 over 1907.

Panics were far from uncommon, but observers commented that each one appeared more severe and that the institutional arrangements appeared increasingly less able to curtail and correct the situation. A National Monetary Commission, significantly consisting of Senators and members of Congress rather than of nonpolitical authorities, was established to review the structure of the financial institutions in the United States. After four years of work, the Commission's report was presented to Congress in March 1912.

The Commission proposed an institutional structure that ultimately became the Federal Reserve System, recommending the establishment of a public institution financed by both state banks and trust companies and by national banks. This institution, a "National Reserve Association" with fifteen branches and directors from all over the country but actually controlled by a Cabinet committee in Washington, D.C., would have the sole authorization to issue bank notes.

As it ultimately developed, the Federal Reserve System attempted to balance the federalist tradition of dual banking and the populist suspicion of central banks against the need to have an effective central bank to assist in managing the money supply and the economy. Individual reserve banks were established in major cities, each with its own board of directors representing financial, business, and public interests. A coordinating body, the Federal Reserve Board, was a government agency located in Washington, close to the Treasury and the Congress, rather than in a mercantile center such as New York City.

Jury-rigged though it was, this complex structure was necessary to secure the congressional support required for the legislation to pass. An interesting speculation is whether this structure contributed to the System's failure to respond as effectively to the financial problems of 1929 and the following years as European banks did. This would help account for why the recession was so prolonged and severe in the United States compared with the European experience.

Further laws regulating and changing the financial scene emerged in the Depression to help prevent a repetition of that event. Three of the most notable changes were included in the (Glass-Steagall) Banking Act of 1933, which prohibited commercial banks from paying interest on funds held in demand deposits. This prohibition was intended to discourage banks from being forced into acquiring risky assets and making risky loans in order to pay for the cost of funds. The act also provided that investment banking and commercial banking would be carried on by separate institutions. Those organizations, such as J. P. Morgan & Co., that were active in both lines of business were forced to dispose of one. Finally, the act created the Federal Deposit Insurance Corporation, funded partly by the U.S. Treasury, partly by an assessment on the commercial banks, and partly by the Federal Reserve banks. The insurance was initially up to the first $2,500 of deposits, but the amount was raised to $5,000 in 1935. This figure covered 98 percent of all individual deposits. The scheme was widely copied, with similar institutions subsequently being created for the savings and loan industry and for credit unions.

A Long, Slow Curve

The revised financial system appeared to work reasonably well for the next thirty years. Intervening years were unusual, however, and the system was not put to the test until the early 1970s or even until 1990.

There were three reasons for this breathing period. First, by the time the Glass-Steagall Act was passed, the worst financial shocks of the Depression were over. Second, the 1939 to 1945 war, coming after an industrial recovery was already underway, boosted the economy of the United States back to a satisfactory level. In order to finance the war effort as inexpensively as possible, the U.S. Treasury soaked up public liquidity by encouraging consumers to invest their savings in government bonds. With funds for plant and equipment investment controlled by a variety of taxes and direct regulations, many companies became extremely liquid. At the end of the war, the commercial-banking system had a ratio of loans to deposits of only 17 percent. These conditions made it easy to keep interest rates relatively low.

Third, the extraordinary liquidity in the system in 1945 combined with reasonable governmental actions permitted a strong postwar economy to develop without straining the financial system. Consumer demands were satisfied, and the damaged economies in Europe and Asia were reconstructed without the problems anticipated by those who had expected a severe postwar depression. Some strains were created by the war in Korea, leading the Federal Reserve in 1951 to cut loose from the arrangements it had used to hold down interest rates in order to reduce the cost of Treasury financing.

By the late 1950s, major banks were finding their ability to raise funds in their local markets was inadequate to supply the demands of their customers. Prohibitions against interstate banking, intended to protect state banks whose legislatures often greatly restricted the ability of state-chartered banks to branch even within a state, prevented the money-center banks from following retail customers to suburbs, especially if they were located across state lines. Prohibitions against paying interest on demand deposits prevented banks from competing for funds against agencies that could pay interest.

The solution was the development of the negotiable certificate of deposit (CD), introduced in 1961 by the First National City Bank of New York (now Citibank) and the Discount Corporation of New York, a securities firm. Federal banking law allowed banks to pay interest on time deposits if the deposit had a contractual maturity date, but the issuer of a certificate was prohibited from buying it back in advance. Until the Citibank innovation, an owner of a certificate of deposit who wished to convert the contract to cash in advance of the maturity date could not do so. By offering to buy the Citibank CDs discounted to the going market rate of interest, the Discount Corporation provided instant liquidity to the CD owner who wished to sell. The Discount Corporation did not plan to hold the CDs itself, however. It would attempt to resell them immediately, making its profit from the spread between the buy and sell price. Thus, although the investor's liquidity could not be provided by the bank, it could be provided by the marketplace. This arrangement had all the characteristics of the typical innovation in the U.S. financial system: economic and financial requirements run up against a structural impediment, which bends or is bypassed in some manner.

The Fast Break Begins

Serious capacity strains on the productive economy began to be evident in the mid-1960s when President Johnson attempted to finance the Southeast Asia military action without a direct increase in taxes. Tax collections were accelerated in 1966, which gave the government a boost in receipts without a change in tax rates but drained resources out of a private sector that needed funds to expand capacity. Simultaneously, in an effort to keep down the cost of money, "jawboning" was used to encourage banks not to raise the rates they were charging borrowers. When the rates the banks were forced to pay for money rose above the rates they could charge, they had little choice but to stop lending. In 1969, for example, the cost to banks for funds in the unregulated European market was 9.48 percent, whereas the prime lending rate in the United States was 7.9 percent. Prospective borrowers were referred to the financial markets in Europe, where similar restrictions did not apply, and the transactions were completed in many cases by the overseas branches of U.S. banks.

These conditions created a level of inflation that caught the attention of the consumer, as did the inflation resulting from the oil crisis and subsequent price and economic dislocations. Despite a wide variety of legislative and regulatory efforts to maintain the status quo of an economic system designed in the depths of a depression, consumers were not interested in the economic sacrifice required to maintain the fences in financial pastures designed to encourage borrowing rather than saving. The fences were undermined, jumped over, and pushed down. The development of new technology, which efficiently handled large quantities of transactions at long distance by telephone, computer, or other electronic means, supported the destruction of the traditional boundaries. Economic battles ended up in the courts and in the regulatory agencies, which were forced to make de facto economic policy in the absence of legislative decisions.

The strains on the existing financial system were further aggravated by the additional social demands being legislatively placed on institutions in the mistaken impression that financial markets were natural, rather than unnatural, legal monopolies and can be used to disguise tax assessments. One instance has been the community-reinvestment requirements—an attempt to retain funds in the area in which they originated. It is not clear, however, that residents of an area in financial difficulty want their savings reinvested in that area in the absence of federal deposit insurance. There is even less logic in demanding that a wholesale bank—raising its funds in the national and international money markets and relending them to global corporations—should be required to invest in consumer mortgages in an urban redevelopment area as a condition of getting approval for establishing a new product line. It is no wonder that money funds and other institutions can run circles about those saddled with the noneconomic demands in an unnatural monopoly such as banking.

The insurance industry has been similarly ladened with legislative enactments and court decisions requiring them to bear environmental burdens for problems that were not anticipated (or even were perfectly respectable) at the time the insurance was written. The effort to force insurers to grant insurance even to very high-risk groups quickly becomes self-defeating. Those who can acquire their insurance elsewhere (via self-insurance for large entities or via an offshore insurance subsidiary) do so, leaving the costs insuperably high for those who cannot.

An illustration of the law of unintended results can be seen in the legislative mandate that universities and colleges offer comprehensive pregnancy health insurance for all students. The introduction of this feature raised insurance costs so much that students not likely to require the benefits seek insurance elsewhere. Those who did need it were then left with such high costs that many take no insurance coverage, defeating the original intention. Legislation to require students to subscribe to the college plans in order to spread out and socialize the costs has not passed so far because of the potential outcry from parents who found themselves being forced to pay again for insurance they already had through their employers.

THE DOUBLE-EDGED COST OF REGULATION

According to one estimate, the cost of regulating the securities markets is $1 billion, approximately $10,000 per stockbroker. The author of this estimate argues that this costly structure was designed to protect small investors, who have been leaving the market in droves despite the protection they enjoy. In these circumstances, the costs of the regulation may far outweigh the benefits derived and should point the way to an alternative, less costly structure. There is evidence, discussed in Chapter 5, that the Securities and Exchange Commission has been moving in that direction with the introduction of regulations such as Rule 144a.

The effort to socialize costs by passing them to private financial institutions operating in unnatural monopolies gradually makes the institutions less competitive. This is not a sudden development. It is similar to the addition of barnacles to the hull of a fast ship, which gradually slow down the ship until it is seriously threatened by competition that once would have been left in its wake. Ultimately, overburdened and inefficient, it is scrapped, leaving the barnacles wondering what happened to their free lunch.

Sources of Inactivity

The inability of Congress and state legislatures to act results from a combination of populist tradition, federalist structure, and political-pressure groups. Both early efforts to operate a national bank were terminated, with much of the opposition coming from state interests that feared the power potentially accruing to such an institution. Those of the populist tradition wished to keep financial decisions close to the borrower rather than in a distant city, an approach that was congenial to local politicians, who drew financial support from the business community and wished to maintain their influence and their patronage, in the form of bank supervisory positions.

National banking was also feared by local, state-chartered bankers, who appreciated the ability of a large institution to diversify, to be more efficient, and perhaps to indulge in predatory pricing practices. It took the financial crises of the Civil War for the federal government to enter the banking business. Even then, its entrance was by way of chartering individual banks more or less equal in powers to state banks but regulated in a way to inspire confidence among depositors. Eventually, the Federal Reserve System established a national central bank, but the System represented a compromise among the competing pressures—twelve banks and a coordinating body rather than a single bank.

The financial crisis of the 1929 Depression put the federal government into the business of regulating the raising of funds and trading of investments by investment banks, adding the Securities and Exchange Commission to the state securities regulatory bodies, because the problems were perceived as finally having extended beyond the ability of individual states to control them. In addition, the federal government assumed responsibility for regulating the securities exchanges. This function has now proliferated into several competing bodies controlling stock, options, and commodities exchanges.

Of the major financial segments, only the insurance industry has remained relatively untouched by federal regulation and structure. The indirect influence on the industry increased, however, with the establishment of a federally sponsored agency, Pension Benefit Guaranty Corp., to insure employee pensions. In response to a perceived crisis in that area, this institution was hastily approved and founded on the basis of a number of assumptions that are now proving to have been unsound, with extremely costly results. In addition, the efforts of state legislatures and the courts to impose on insurance companies the responsibility for curing various social ills may force further national structure in order to save the industry from impossible demands.

The competing pressures of federalism, localism, popularism, and economic efficiency have—not surprisingly—resulted in a

Figure 12.1
Federal Bank Regulatory Agency Relationships

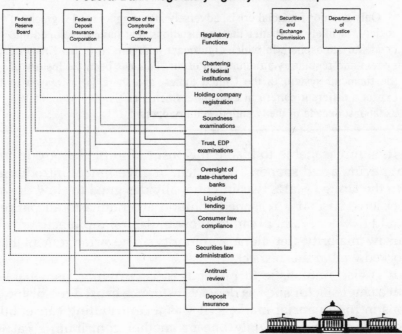

regulatory system of great complexity, further adding to the inertia that faces the government when changes are required. Figure 12.1 shows the structure of federal regulation of national banks as it existed in early 1991: five regulatory bodies supervise ten different functions. In addition, a state regulatory layer interacts with four of these bodies to supervise state-chartered institutions.

Given the tendency of organizations to defend and expand their responsibilities rather than contract them, reform efforts that modify structure to meet the new demands of the economy have been notoriously unsuccessful. If anything, the pressures of populism, federalism, and dual banking systems have led to further complexities, with the addition of more levels and organizations rather than fewer. For instance, instead of consolidating agencies or functions, coordinating committees are established in areas such as examination (to try to ensure that credits are evaluated comparably regardless of examining authority) and assessment of international country risk.

MAJOR CRISES PRODUCE MAJOR CHANGES

Only a major financial crisis, adversely affecting a broad segment of society, is likely to shatter the encrustations that have developed and create an atmosphere in which significant realignment of the financial system and regulatory structure can occur. This has been the history of the financial system in the United States, and there is no reason to expect a different pattern in the future. Such a crisis may have arrived as the last decade of the twentieth century opened.

It is unreasonable to blame this institution or that group for not having acted sooner. The system of government introduced into the United States was intentionally designed to slow down decisions, so that a reasoned solution acceptable to all parties would develop, rather than to allow unilateral rapid action by a narrow majority (let alone a minority). The arrangement has worked well in this respect.

It is also unrealistic to pretend, as is currently fashionable, that a single factor such as deposit insurance caused the dislocations in the financial markets. It was a contributing cause, but focusing attention on only one or another contributing cause will obscure the true, underlying nature of the problem.

Furthermore, in many instances, each straw added to the camel's burden was judged to be such a little straw, that more and more demands were placed on entities whose market position would not allow them to bear the ultimate burden. Does the first straw or the last one break the camel's back, when all straws are socially meritorious?

The questions that now should be asked are, What are the underlying structural issues, and how should the reorganization of the financial system and its regulation be undertaken to make the next sixty years as stable and prosperous as the last sixty have been? If the risks to the financial system are seen as serious enough to require a realistic assessment of what the system can do and how it should do it, the multitude of players may be willing to make the necessary changes to bring the system into harmony with underlying economic, social, and technological factors. The final chapter discusses these issues.

13

The Financial System and Its Future

As 1991 began, the future of the financial system and the role of federal and state governments in that system were subjects of intense national debate. During the 1980s, Congress passed a series of laws and changes in laws addressing the financial system. The first in the series was the Depository Institutions Deregulation and Monetary Control Act of 1980, which dealt with the losses incurred by the savings and loans as a result of record high interest rates in 1979 and 1980. The series ended the decade with the Financial Institution Recovery and Reform Act of 1989, which yet again dealt with the growing crisis of the savings and loan industry.

Like a financial Vietnam, each major new piece of legislation was alleged to solve the problem of the financial system. But the problems weren't solved. As 1991 started, fears were growing about the potential insolvency of the Federal Deposit Insurance Corporation, even though less than two years earlier the FDIC had been expected to be the savior of the savings and loan industry.

In addition to the problems and issues confronting Congress (and the public) about the banking system, questions were also being raised about the solvency of the insurance industry and the Pension Benefit Guaranty Corporation. Major investment banks were escaping failure courtesy of deep-pocket parents, a number of which drew their strength from positions in nonfinancial industries. Even a couple of money-market mutual funds had experienced close calls. In sum, by early 1991 virtually every aspect of the U.S. financial system was having difficulty despite a decade of legislative and administrative tinkering that, in retrospect, dealt with the symptoms rather than addressing the systemic causes of the problems.

This final chapter begins with a brief outline of the comprehensive proposals that the Bush administration made in the spring of 1991 to address these systemic difficulties. The proposals were nominally concerned with the FDIC and the place of commercial banks in the financial system, but in fact they were substantially more comprehensive. The administration presented a chart of the rocks and shoals and suggested a channel leading to a safe harbor. The congressional sailors have the challenge of finding a better course for the boat.

At the time of this writing, the discussion of the proposals in subcommittees of the House is under way. To judge from the daily press reports, the preliminary decisions are veering wildly back and forth, like a sailboat compensating for dramatic changes in a strong wind as it dashes for sheltered waters. Nevertheless, the direction and dangers are now clear enough that it is appropriate to analyze the administration's proposals. These proposals will be the framework within which debate continues. Thus, even though substantial progress may be made before this book is published, an understanding of the administration's original ideas should help the reader interpret what has happened and what continues to be happening.

The second part of the chapter reviews the positions that have been taken on the administration proposals by the various segments of the financial industry. It will come as no surprise that almost everyone is in favor of change as long as it is at someone else's expense. This section of the chapter is designed to help the reader keep track of the players and their positions.

In the concluding section, we speculate about the future structure of the financial industry based on technological and demographic trends that affect the system regardless of legislative fiat. Some of these speculations have been advanced in earlier chapters, but these concluding pages draw together the ideas and raise a series of questions about institutional change. Many of these suggestions have not yet been widely circulated. The comments are intended to be provocative and to stimulate the reader to further reflect on the financial restructuring with which U.S. citizens must contend.

The Treasury Proposals

Because earlier legislation failed to solve the problems of the financial system, and the government was incurring growing losses resulting from failed savings and loans institutions (and, increasingly from failed banks), the Bush administration at the beginning of 1991 prepared comprehensive legislation that would overhaul the structure of the financial system. The Administration's proposals were expected to have four goals:

- Draw more capital investment into the banking system,
- Impose more discipline on the operations of banks,
- Limit the subsidy that banks (and ultimately borrowers from banks) received by being able to attract federally insured deposits, and
- Protect deposit insurance for savers.

The Bush administration released in February, 1991 the results of a three-year Treasury study on the financial system, a report titled *Modernizing the Financial System: Recommendations for Safer, More Competitive Banks*. This report contained the key recommendations for changes in the legal and regulatory structure of financial system that the administration would be incorporating in its proposed legislation, along with the administration's economic justification for those proposals. The Treasury argued that the package of recommendations was a balanced, integrated one—no single recommendation would be effective by itself, and indeed, could be counterproductive if adopted in isolation.

Although the proposals were interrelated, they fell into four general groups:

- The role of capital in strengthening the responsibility of bank performance,
- The return of deposit insurance to its function as a protection for the small, uninformed depositor,
- The restructure and strengthening of the commercial banking system,
- The simplification of the regulatory system in order to improve efficiency and to make the regulatory structural process more effective in addressing problems before they become as serious as they became during the 1980s.

Enhance the Role of Capital

The basic Treasury position with respect to capital adequacy was that capital standards need not be raised but that the role of capital to protect bank depositors should be strengthened. Specifically, the Treasury proposed that bank regulation should move further toward a system of *capital-based supervision,* providing rewards (carrots) and penalties (sticks) that would encourage banks to hold adequate capital.

Well-capitalized banks would receive greater regulatory freedom. Banks with capital in excess in minimum requirements would be eligible to engage in a broad new range of new financial services. The lot of those banks whose capital levels were weak would be stricter supervision requiring "prompt corrective acts" to address problems well in advance of insolvency. As capital levels declined below the minimum acceptable levels, banks would be subject to increasingly stringent corrective action—including dividend cuts or even forced sale of the bank—aimed at preventing failure. Banks with low capital levels would be limited to core banking business.

A further carrot called for deposit-insurance rates to vary inversely with a bank's capital position: the higher the capital, the lower the rate. The Treasury argued that flat-rate premiums subsidized high-risk, poorly run institutions at the expense of well-run institutions and taxpayers. In addition, without a cost to offset the upside potential of high-risk gambling with the insured deposits, there is a perverse incentive for managers to take risks. Interest-rate risk (the degree to which to maturity of the institution's sources does not match the maturity of its investments) as well as the credit risk of the portfolio would be considered in setting premiums.

In the short term, the Treasury would use premiums based on capital levels to reward institutions that build capital to act as a buffer ahead of the insurance fund. Looking to the long term, the Treasury would use a demonstration project to test the setting of premiums by private insurance.

Squaring this insurance circle with the dual banking system presented some problems because the state legislatures and regulatory authorities wished themselves to control the policies of state-chartered banks. The Treasury, while admitting that state regulatory responsibilities are important, argued it was essential to protect federal taxpayers from potentially risky activities by banks regardless of the source of the bank's charter. Therefore, state-chartered banks with federal deposit insurance should not be allowed by their state charter to engage in transactions that are precluded for national banks and therefore would not be allowed to engage in direct investment activities.

Reform of Deposit Insurance

The basic Treasury proposal was to return deposit insurance to its original purpose—the protection of small investors who cannot protect themselves. The Treasury therefore recommended that after a two-year phase-in period insurance coverage for individuals be limited to $100,000 per institution plus another $100,000 per institution for a retirement account. Many types of pass-through coverage, whereby large deposits are split into many accounts in different names, would be eliminated, thus reducing government protection for large, sophisticated institutional investors. Insurance of brokered deposits would also be eliminated.

Because the administration, not so secretly, would prefer even more restricted deposit and insurance coverage, the Federal Deposit Insurance Coporation (FDIC) would be required to conduct an eighteenth-month study of the costs and benefits of moving toward a systemwide $100,000 per-person insurance limitation. This plan would not be implemented until it could be shown that the benefits would outweigh the potentially large administrative costs, which have been estimated as high as $5 billion annually. Costs of this magnitude would clearly be damaging to the banking system unless they could be offset by substantial savings.

In order to limit de facto (and thus uncompensated) coverage of uninsured depositors, the FDIC would be allowed to reimburse uninsured depositors of a failed institution only if that would be the least costly approach. To protect the financial system in those (hopefully) rare instances in which an institution's failure might be a potential systemic risk, the Treasury and Federal Reserve could order that uninsured deposits be covered. (This policy would be implemented after three years to allow for an appropriate transition.) Coverage of nondeposit creditors would be eliminated entirely.

To ensure adequate capitalization of the separate credit union insurance fund, the double counting of certain assets by both the fund and the insured credit unions would be eliminated over a twelve-year period.

Restructure of the Banking System

The Treasury report maintained that nationwide branch banking would lead to safer, more efficient, and more competitive banks, decreasing taxpayer exposure to losses. Banks are less protected from competition and less steadily profitable than they were in the past. Because interest-rate controls have been eliminated, banks no longer enjoy protected access to low-cost funds. Given the cost savings of interstate branching, the advantages to consumers and taxpayers are significant. As a result, the Treasury argued that out-of-date laws restricting interstate branching must be adapted to give well-capitalized banks the opportunity to reclaim the competitive position they have lost to other institutions as the result of changing markets in which they have not been allowed to participate.

The Treasury noted that nationwide banking was a reality, with thirty-three states already permitting nationwide banking, thirteen permitting regional banking, and only four prohibiting all interstate banking. The trend was clearly toward interstate banking activities, but there was almost no authority for interstate *branching* as a medium to conduct the transactions. Thus,

banks were forced to set up multitudes of separate, incorporated subsidiaries in each jurisdiction they wished to enter at a
cost of hundreds of millions of dollars the financial institutions
could ill afford.

To deal with this set of problems, the Treasury recommended
that interstate branching should be authorized immediately for
qualified national banks in any state in which the bank's holding company could presently acquire a bank. After a three-year
delay, bank holding companies would be permitted to engage
in full nationwide banking.

Well-capitalized banks would be allowed to enter new types
of financial markets on a national basis through a financial-services holding company, a new type of holding-company structure. The financial-services holding company could own
separately capitalized affilitates engaging in banking, securities,
mutual funds, and insurance. The new rules would allow commercial firms to own these financial services holding companies, but only the bank subsidiary would have access to deposit
insurance. The bank would be subject to strict regulation. The
reason this aspect of the proposals appeared to be contrary to
the nationwide-banking proposals was the need to protect the
deposit insurance system from financial problems in the nonbank affiliates.

Revising the Regulatory Structure

The Treasury emphasized that the existing regulatory structure
for banks was complicated, overlapping, and confusing.
Individual institutions are often supervised by several regulators, and bank holding companies rarely have the same regulator that their subsidiary banks have. The redesigned structure
would reduce duplication, improve consistency, accountability,
and efficiency, and separate the insurer from the regulator.

The existing four regulatory agencies (the Federal Reserve,
Office of the Comptroller of the Currency, Federal Deposit
Insurance Corporation, and Office of Thrift Supervision) would
be reduced to two: the Federal Reserve and a new Federal
Banking Agency, to be assigned to the Treasury Department.
The Federal Reserve would supervise all state-chartered banks
and their holding companies. The Federal Banking Agency

would supervise all national banks and their holding companies. The same regulator would be responsible for a bank holding company and for its subsidiary bank. Thus a holding company that owned both state-chartered and national banks would be, in its entirety, under the jurisdiction of the agency responsible for the largest subsidiary bank.

The Federal Banking Agency would take over Office of Thrift Supervision responsibilities on the date it completed assigning thrifts to the Resolution Trust Corporation. The FDIC would be solely responsible for insurance and the resolution of failed institutions. To provide accountability to the administration for credit-union regulation, the federal banking regulator would serve on the National Credit Union Administration board of directors.

The Treasury did not ignore the problem that had galvanized Congress, the possible elimination of the Bank Insurance Fund's (BIF) net worth: under the most pessimistic assumptions, the FDIC estimated this could happen over the next two years. The Treasury report stated that the FDIC must exercise the authority given to it by the FDIC Assessment Rate Act of 1990 to recapitalize the BIF in the near term. Because industry participation would be essential, the Treasury called for the recapitalization to be worked out with the industry by the FDIC. But the restructure had to provide sufficient resources to avoid subsequent restructuring and should rely on industry funds, had to take into account any impact on the health of the banking system, and had to use generally accepted accounting principles.

Response of the Financial-Services Industry

The comprehensiveness of the Treasury's proposals has ensured that virtually all elements of the financial-services industry will be affected by the restructuring. Because of their substantial economic impact, these proposals have engendered significant debate and opposition in Congress, inflamed further by intensive lobbying on the part of the multitude of industry associations. Various parts of the industry have advanced their own proposals for restructuring the financial system, and some of these suggestions will undoubtedly be incorporated in the final legislation. To understand the debate as it unfolds, it is useful to be familiar with the conflicting positions and desires of various segments of the financial-services industry.

Most segments of the financial-services industry say that their overriding concern is to safeguard the health of the financial system and the U.S. economy and to promote the public interest. Realistically, all segments of the financial industry are seeking to protect the benefits their members receive under the current regulatory structure and to expand them under the new structure, safeguarding and promoting their own self-interests. Ultimately, the reshaping of the financial system will be dictated not only by what is best for the country but also by the relative effectiveness of the lobbying efforts of different industry groups.

For example, consider the proposals made by the *Securities Industry Association* (SIA), an organization vehemently opposed over the years to expansion of bank power, which purported to be particularly concerned about international competitiveness:

- Create a type of bank-holding company that could establish nonfederally insured national banks known as "investment banking financing companies" (IBFCs) that could own "securities subsidiaries." These IBFC securities groups could have no direct or indirect contact with or support from any affiliated federally insured bank or thrift.

- Establish a private mechanism to supplement or replace the Federal Reserve System's large dollar payment system. SEC-registered broker-dealers as well as banks would have direct access to such a system, allowing the broker-dealers to bypass the banks in making these payments.

- Allow commercial banking organizations to carry out wholesale securities and securities-related activities without government support, provided these businesses remain separate from the organizations' federally insured banks: federal deposit insurance would not support or be at risk from these activities. This will reduce the risks for other federally insured banks, the Bank Insurance Fund, and taxpayers.

- Permit securities firms to own federally insured retail banks; these banks could in turn establish SEC-registered broker-dealers to carry on detail securities brokerage activities on an agency basis (but not for their own account). New management and new capital would be attracted to the banking industry as a result of securities firms owning banks.

The SIA proposed that the securities subsidiaries of banks be required to register their brokers-dealers with the Securities and Exchange Commission (SEC) and that the SEC have jurisdiction over the securities activities of commercial-banking organizations. The Comptroller of the Currency (or FDIC if state-chartered) would control the activities of a federally insured bank subsidiary of the registered broker-dealer of a securities firm. The Comptroller would regulate an IBFC regardless of whether its parent was a banking organization or a securities firm. During a liquidity crisis, as acknowledged by the SEC, the SIA proposed allowing prequalified SEC-registered broker-dealers to have access, on a fully collateralized and nondiscount basis, to the Federal Reserve discount window. With this arrangement in place, securities firms would not be at the mercy of commercial banks in a stock market crisis, as they felt they were during the October 1987 market disruption.

The American Bankers Association (ABA) took a different position from that of the SIA. It focused on deposit insurance reform as it related to the well-being of the U.S. economy and to the health and vitality of the financial system. The most important objectives of the legislation should be to assure the safety, soundness, and stable operation of the U.S. financial system, to increase the competitiveness of U.S. banks relative to domestic nonbank and international financial service entities, to maintain the private-enterprise character of banking, to treat all banks fairly and equally, to protect "depositors" (those protected by the $100,000 level of insurance) not investors (in uninsured deposits) and unsecured creditors, and to minimize the cost of deposit insurance. In order to accomplish these objectives, the legislation should address the problems of how to eliminate the "too big to fail" doctrine while treating all banks equally and preserving liquidity in the system; how to create a stronger and more sound deposit insurance system; how to raise regulatory attentiveness and effectiveness; and how to impose market discipline onto the banking system. Yet the roles of separate federal and state regulation in the dual banking system should be respected.

Specific recommendations that the ABA made included: maintain the current $100,000 level of coverage, reject the idea of 100 percent protection of all deposits, treat foreign deposits in U.S. banks as though they were domestic deposits over $100,000, restrict the ability of brokered deposits to abuse deposit insurance, and let investors in uninsured deposits share in the risk that the institutions to which they commit their funds might fail. Insurance costs for a bank should be paid by that bank, regardless of whether the costs were based on domestic or foreign deposits.

The *Independent Bankers Association of America* (IBAA, representing small bankers) sees the problem of the financial system as stemming from government's modification of the original intent of deposit insurance and protection of all the deposit liabilities of major banks in the United States but not all the deposits of smaller banks. It sees a need to increase objectivity and equality within the banking system. The IBAA would grant full deposit-insurance coverage to all liabilities of depository institutions and assess all liabilities, including foreign and nondeposit liabilities (such as promissory notes, bankers acceptances, and bank notes) in calculating a bank's insurance premium to the BIF. The BIF would be maintained at 1.25 percent of all its contingent liabilities, including all domestic deposits, foreign deposits, and nondeposit liabilities, but it would not be used to bail out the savings and loan industry. The IBAA proposals would not require depositors to impose "market discipline" by monitoring the health of the banks where they invest because this would shift the risk of loss to depositors. It would also increase the level of bank primary (Tier 1) capital over time from 3 percent to 4 percent in order to shift a portion of the risk from the insurance fund to banks' shareholders.

In the regulatory area, IBAA would correct the disparity between regulations for banks and credit unions (which are greater competitors for smaller banks than for large ones). Credit unions have many powers that banks have, but they are not regulated in a comparable manner. For example, credit unions are allowed to deposit 1 percent of their shares with the

National Credit Union Share Insurance Fund (NCUSIF) but also to count that deposit as an asset. This helps to overstate the solvency of the credit-union industry by inflating its capital strength. Those shares are at risk and could be used by NCUSIF in an emergency. The 1 percent should be expensed. Credit unions also do not pay income taxes, but this dispute was left to future tax legislation.

The *Investment Companies Institute* (ICI, which represents mutual funds) saw a danger if banks are allowed to sponsor and underwrite mutual funds. It argued that reform legislation should protect mutual funds and their shareholders by providing for "functional regulation." Under this concept, similar products would be subject to the same regulatory controls regardless of the type of financial institution offering the product.

The ICI also wanted to create a "two-way street" among banks, securities firms, and other members of the financial-service industry. If banks could enter the securities business, then the Bank Holding Company Act should be amended to permit securities firms to carry out banking activities. If geographical restrictions on banks were eliminated, which would allow larger banks to distribute securities nationally through a system of local branches, the branch offices of securities firms should be permitted to engage in banking.

To ensure the safety of federal deposit insurance, the firewalls previously proposed by the Federal Reserve to insulate the commercial bank deposit-acceptance function from other financial functions of a holding company should be strengthened by restricting the types of assets that can be held by a federally insured bank affiliated with a securities firm. For example, by limiting their investments to safe, highly liquid securities, bank affiliates would not have an incentive to engage in a broad range of risky activities. Securities firms affiliated with banks would also not have an unfair competitive advantage due to an ability to finance their activities with lower-cost, insured funds.

If banks were allowed to sponsor and underwrite mutual funds, the ICI wanted to strengthen the firewalls designed to protect a fund and its shareholders from the unique conflicts of interest arising from commercial-bank mutual fund activities:

- Mutual funds could not have the same (or similar) name as the sponsoring bank.

- Bank-sponsored mutual funds could not invest in securities of their debtor companies in order to bolster the financial condition of the borrower.

Finally, the ICI thought that banks should be made subject to the same regulatory controls as other providers of financial services. Banks were currently exempt from registration and regulation as broker-dealers under the Securities Exchange Act of 1934 and as investment advisers under the Investment Advisors Act of 1940. Yet banks were permitted to engage in brokerage activities and to serve as investment advisors to mutual funds and others. The SEC should be given the same jurisdiction over banks it had over other financial institutions with comparable powers.

The *American Council of Life Insurers* saw no benefit in expanding bank powers, particularly in allowing them to underwrite insurance. Expanding bank powers so that risk can be diversified in an economic downturn is unreasonable, it argued, proven by the fact that both banks and insurance companies have been adversely affected by the current economic downturn, and the competitive gap between smaller and larger banks would widen because only a limited number of money center banks would utilize these powers.

The Future of the Financial System

As is undoubtedly evident to those who have read the first twelve chapters of this book, our sympathies lie with the direction taken by the Treasury Report. By concentrating on the banking system, the Report probably does not go far enough in addressing the changes that are occurring in the financial-service industry. It may not be politically feasible to go further at this time without risking even these relatively modest efforts to bring the official financial system into congruence with the real world of practice. We are not sympathetic with many of those resisting the changes, although we certainly appreciate their efforts to defend their constituencies. The problems arise when this defense creates costs that are paid by those not benefitting from what is probably a respite in an inexorable technological, economic, and social process.

In the remainder of this final chapter we draw together our ideas about where the financial system is going and raise some questions we think should be asked about how to get there. Some of these thoughts may appear a bit extreme compared with the discussions currently taking place in Congress, but Keynes once remarked to the effect that one generation's economic heresy is the next generation's orthodoxy.

Over the decade 1990 to 2000, the changes in the financial-services industry will continue to be great. Specific changes that are forecast by industry experts include implementing national electronic-funds-transfer systems utilizing smart cards with a built-in computer chip to link clearing houses, shared ATM systems, and point-of-sale networks; merging all federal financial regulatory agencies into a single agency; issuing general characters for financial institutions that allow them to participate in the full range of financial services; and enacting legislation permitting full interstate financial services. Most of these developments are clear outgrowths of the various trends discussed in this book—consolidation, universality, rate deregulation, and niche-players.

Consolidation

The consolidation of the banking industry with the advent of nationwide banking is being monitored by consulting firms with banking practices. For example, Edward Carpenter & Associates, which specializes in commercial banking, has predicted that by the year 2000, the number of commercial banks in the United States will dwindle to 1,500. (Others, using California and North Carolina as models, forecast between 3,000 and 4,000 banks.) However, it also forecasts that there will be 500,000 formal access-points to those financial institutions versus the 68,000 branches and 28,000 ATMs that existed in 1982.

To support its projections, Carpenter & Associates points out that between 1940 and 1980, the number of banks worldwide declined from 150,000 to 35,000. This is ample evidence of the fundamental economic pressures that encourage consolidation of banking and financial systems. The United States is the only major country that has not yet gone through this consolidation. Over this same forty-year period, the number of U.S. banks actually increased slightly from 14,500 to 14,700. The United

States has not followed the worldwide patterns mainly because of regulatory restraints, which have limited the ability of the financial-services system to consolidate. As a result the United States has excess capacity in the banking industry with 33 percent more banks and branches than fast food outlets. It is no wonder that the banking system has had profitability problems.

There is ample evidence, however, that a consolidation is already strongly underway. For example, the numbers of savings and loans in the United States declined from 4,240 in 1980 to approximately 2,700 in 1991, an overall decline of more than one-third. By 1991, the number of banks had declined to about 12,000, although this figure counts banks individually that belong to the same holding company. It has been suggested that the number of independent commercial banking groups may now be less than 9,400. Nationwide banking is becoming a reality.

The structure is in place for many organizations rapidly to develop multistate or interstate banking and financial operations as soon as the laws permit them. Specific examples of major financial institutions with multistate banking or thrift operations include Citicorp, First Interstate, Norwest, NCNB Bank, Chemical Bank, First Nationwide Savings, and BancOne. This list does not include the major banks that have interstate commercial-finance, consumer-finance, and mortgage-banking subsidiaries, creating, in effect, nationwide financial-services organizations. Nationwide ATM networks, nationwide issuing of credit cards, loan-production offices for corporate and commercial banking, Edge Acts for international banking, and banking-holding company subsidiaries in consumer finance, commercial finance, and mortgage banking provide most major commercial-banking institutions with some form of interstate presence.

In the future, ATM networks and the availability of electronic, nationwide banking will grow even more dramatically. Fueling this growth will be the debit card; the economic advantages to the financial institutions should lead to steadily increased use of these cards over the coming decade.

A Two-Tier System

Accompanying the automation of the financial system will be its consolidation into a two-tier financial system, the components of which are already evident. The first tier will consist of between ten and twenty giant national institutions (popularly known as *megabanks*) that will handle most consumer financial services and the majority of large corporate banking. Many of these institutions will be part of global networks of financial-services companies. The second tier will be composed of a range of specialized financial-services organizations primarily oriented to small- and medium-sized businesses. The development of this two-tier system will cause a merger movement that will extinguish thousands of financial-services companies. The commercial-banking system currently has approximately 9,400 individual companies nationwide, and it is estimated that these may shrink to between 1,500 and 4,000 by the year 2000 as individual banks fail or are swallowed up in a nationwide consolidation and merger process.

McKinsey & Company, a major consultant to the financial-services industry, has developed a model for the financial firm of the future that organizes it around major functional areas. Expounded in the book *Breaking Up the Bank*, by Lowell Bryan, this model is more elaborate than the Treasury plan. Both models show, however, that we are moving toward a structure in which the dominant financial-services organizations are universal in their activities, providing all the major financial services.

The consolidation of the banking industry and the advent of nationwide banking will blur distinctions between different types of tier-one financial institutions as each presently specialized financial-services institution diversifies into other fields. The most prominent current example is Merrill Lynch, which in four years with its Cash Management Account took in more deposits, over $50 billion, than Citibank had acquired in over 117 years. These brokerage customers not only represent a large source of funds but also are a component of the affluent market that most banks are seeking. Adding to the free-for-all that is developing in the commercial-banking and financial-services arena is the entry of nonbanking financial-services companies into investment banking and commercial banking and of nonfinancial institutions into financial services. Some of the most prominent examples include American Express, Prudential Insurance Company, Sears Roebuck, and AT&T.

No Interest-Rate Controls

The third major effect of the forces working on the financial-services industry is the elimination of interest-rate controls and the consequent elimination of the savers' subsidy of the borrowers that was implicit in these controls. One clear result of the liberation of interest rates from legislative controls has been the emergence of *true-cost banking*. With true-cost banking, customers pay the actual cost of individual services performed by the bank rather than pay more than true cost for some services (such as checking, which historically was very profitable for the bank due to the free funds it provided) and less than true-cost for others that were subsidized by checking. The end result of true-cost banking is that all financial transactions will be priced and charged for explicitly or offered in packages that in sum cover the costs of the components. True-cost banking results in higher interest rates paid on checking and savings accounts because the rates have to be competitive rather than protected by unnatural-monopolistic regulation. Of course, this also results in higher borrowing costs to consumers and corporations, including higher costs for mortgages, because the legally enforced subsidy is gone.

In this new environment, there will be a changing role for niche players such as the small commercial bank. Small banks will suffer from the loss of free funds, which historically has been one of their major competitive advantages. However, they will have an opportunity to succeed and survive the forecasted consolidation of the industry if they take advantage of their local-service orientation and effectively fill specific market niches.

Job content will change dramatically. The lender's role, for example, will change from that of a credit-allocation expert to an originator of loans that are packaged and sold as securities. This change will put increasing premium on sales and marketing skills and take away the requirement for credit expertise, which will increasingly reside in "expert system" computer programs. Narrowing spreads, with the phasing out of free deposits, will further alter the lending officer's role from an order taker for money to consultant-seller, utilizing the bank's products to solve customers problems. The role of a job such as a teller will shift from operations to customer services.

The key to profitable lending in this new environment will be the ability to tailor the specific loan to the customer's needs and to price that loan accurately to reflect the institution's true cost. This new role will require more sophisticated lending officers who will be motivated by incentive systems tailored to their performance. These changes will present a challenge for smaller, niche-market institutions.

In the investment-banking area, premiums will be placed on creativity as the traditional number-crunching is carried out by machine. Similar demands will be placed on insurance company investment officers, faced with a myriad of new techniques to enhance return rather than only the buy-and-hold strategy.

Financial-services companies will experience the impact of the same trends that are reshaping other types of businesses. Companies will restructure to facilitate the flow of information and knowledge and to promote entrepreneurship by

- Smashing the managerial hierarchy or pyramid that impedes the flow of information and decision-making,
- Restructuring business into smaller organizational units that facilitate the flow of information, and
- Developing incentive systems for information sharing (networks).

Successful financial-services organizations will institutionalize an entrepreneurial philosophy and develop a new, more flexible type of organization that systematically innovates with new services that are responsive to changing markets.

Of all the trends affecting the future of financial services, the most significant is the continued growth of the new-age financial institutions. The growing dominance of pension funds and mutual funds in the institutional structure of the financial system will have a range of effects that are not yet fully understood. For example, the instruments used by the Federal Reserve for implementing economic and monetary policy may have to be modified as more and more financial assets are outside the banking system.

Unasked Questions and Creative Alternatives

As we approach the twenty-first century, many of the issues that have surrounded the financial system in the United States for over 200 years remain unresolved. Issues such as centralized power versus decentralized power and special interests versus the general-public interest will continue to shape the financial system over the next ten years. Just as the Founding Fathers debated whether we should have a strong central bank, we continue to debate how much the financial system should be centralized and consolidated with its implications for economic and political power. Beyond the unresolved issues that have been debated for 200 years, there are questions that when asked generate some creative alternatives to be considered in the ongoing debate.

Why Not a Third Bank of the United States?

A Congress that was interested only in improving the efficiency and safety of the U.S. financial system would replace deposit insurance with the Third Bank of the United States (TBank). The Federal Reserve already allows individuals to establish accounts with a Federal Reserve Bank through which they may purchase T-bills, although this process is intentionally made difficult for small investors. It would be a modest additional conceptual step to authorize the establishment of TBank by the Federal Reserve to provide individual checking and savings accounts in much the same way that postal savings systems operate in other countries. These deposits would be required to be invested in federal government debt. There would be no need for deposit insurance for TBank's liabilities because the deposits would be invested in a direct liability of the federal government. With modern computer technology, it would be easy and efficient to establish such a system, and the Postal Service could provide a branch offices necessary for over-the-counter transactions. (Given the problems of post office profitability and loss of volume to new methods of information transmission, it could only benefit from having another service to offer.)

Deposit insurance could be phased out for other banks

because it would not be economically appropriate to maintain it. Depositors wanting absolute safety and willing to accept commensurately low rates on their savings would use the TBank. Depositors willing to take risks in exchange for higher returns could use any of the variety of depository vehicles with which the marketplace abounds.

The Federal Reserve would be responsible, as under the administration's proposal, for intervening in the event of a systemic threat to the financial system. But it should be authorized to step in to protect the system from the failure of any type of financial institution, including money-market funds, insurance companies, and investment banks. The idea that firewalls will insulate the components of an institution from one another has been shown repeatedly to be invalid. It is unrealistic to expect the concept of work in the future.

It is unlikely, however, Congress will adopt such a system as a solution to the current depository-system crisis and the losses with depository insurance. For one thing, the Federal Reserve and TBank cannot contribute to political campaigns, which reduces congressional enthusiasm for such a scheme. Even though TBank would be a much more efficient way to provide safe savings for all the ballyhooed small saver than the current system of regulating and insuring thousands of individual banks, its very efficiency means the loss of jobs in the private sector. As Congress is generally more concerned with social harmony and growth in employment than it is productivity and growth in wealth, the TBank scheme has several marks against it.

And TBank would not provide a satisfactory solution to many of the social and emotional issues that shape congressional thinking. Many people have an image of a small bank as run by a friendly, elderly, white-haired gentleman, eager to make loans at low rates but not anxious to collect them. The public equates the small bank with the small town of an earlier, simpler America just as it equates the family farm with that same America. In today's increasingly complex and fast-paced life, where tasks that once took days or even weeks can be accomplished in minutes or hours, the small bank has the same emotional pull that the family farm has. Even if it no longer makes economic sense, there is a strong desire to protect these institutions out a nostalgic yearning for an earlier America.

In addition, TBank would eliminate the hidden role of deposit insurance, which many deposit-insurance advocates want both to keep and to keep hidden. Deposit insurance is a massive subsidy by the taxpayer that is growing more massive as losses increase in the depository system. But it is far from exclusively a subsidy of savers, as many presently argue. Without deposit insurance, savers would take their money wherever they had to in order to protect it. That is what used to cause consumer runs on banks. Deposit insurance is also a subsidy for the employees of the depository system, many of whom would have to find other jobs if consolidation was allowed to occur, improving efficiency in the system. And deposit insurance is a subsidy for the allocation of capital, attracting it where it otherwise would not go. Sometimes this subsidy is intended, as in the Community Reinvestment Act, which forces banks to lend money where they might not in a purely free market. Sometimes this subsidy is unintended, as when it contributed to the massive overbuilding of the real estate markets in the 1980s. Sometimes it is partly intended, as it attracts capital to support a financial system that is inefficient and overcapitalized.

As the complexities surrounding the idea of TBank show, although demographics and technology will be the driving forces in reshaping the financial system in the 1990s, the ultimate shape the system takes will be determined by political issues such as centralization and decentralization of power, growth in employment versus productivity increases, and allocation of capital to socially desired uses. An increasingly important issue will be that of technology and power as the issue of ownership of data and information flows begins to enter the debate.

Why not Let the Dying Die in Peace?

As we have discussed throughout this book, the demise of the thrift industry and the consolidation of the commercial-banking system is an adjustment to changing economic condition. It is inevitable that thousands of thrifts and commercial banks will go out of business just as it in inevitable that a patient with a terminal illness will ultimately die. No amount of protestation will change this outcome. The demise of major portions of the depository system follows Schumpeter's economic doctrine of creative destruction: newer, more efficient ways of doing business replace older, less efficient ways of doing business. However, just as with any terminal illness, we must go through a period of emotional adjustment, mourning, before we accept this reality.

As the distinguished therapist Kübler-Ross discovered in her landmark study, *On Death and Dying*, people go through the five stages in dealing with change—denial, anger, bargaining, depression, and acceptance. Only when the fifth stage is reached can the terminal patient die in peace. The longer the patient remains in the first or second stage, the more difficult the adjustment becomes.

In dealing with the crisis of the depository system, the American people and Congress have to make the same types of adjustments to change that the terminal patient and the patient's family must make. We have to accept that many banks and most thrifts will cease to exist over the next decade; no amount of denial or anger will change that ultimate event. Righteous speeches in Congress will not change the reality that many banks and thrifts are going to pass out of existence. The longer we deny that reality and avoid taking the necessary steps to make that change as painless as possible, the greater the cost to us all as taxpayers as well as to the very institutions and employees we are trying to protect. This is evident in the thrift institutions, which could have been helped to slip quietly away fifteen or twenty years ago with far less cost to the public and far less dislocation to the employees than the effort to keep the industry alive.

Why Not Make the Whole Financial System Pay?

Currently, there is strong pressure in Congress to put as much as possible of the burden of restructuring the financial system on the depository system by raising the premiums for deposit insurance and by assessing a one-time charge on banks to recapitalize the Bank Insurance Fund. This is intended to spare the taxpayer the direct cost of the rescue effort and to punish the depository system for its wrong-doing.

The effort has two unfortunate side effects, however. The first is to speed the demise of much of the banking system because the cost of deposits is increased and the competitive position of the banks vis-à-vis the money-market funds is eroded. The second effect is to compound the difficulties of the insurance funds as fewer and fewer institutions, holding a smaller portion of total financial-system assets, are required to pay for the adjustment.

A better solution might be to require all financial intermediaries, including insurance companies, pension funds, and mutual funds, to contribute to the bank insurance fund as a way of spreading the burden of the adjustment to the beneficiaries of the changes in the financial system as well as to the losers. Such a shift would more than double the financial base to contribute to the insurance funds. It might be implemented in conjunction with a reform of the government's protection of financial assets so that bank and thrift deposits, money-market fund shares, life insurance, annuities, and pensions could all be covered in a single, integrated and comprehensive scheme. (We have already suggested it would be wise to broaden the Federal Reserve's ability to handle system threats to the financial system.)

The "share-the-bill" approach would have two benefits. First, it would prevent the piecemeal extension of financial-asset protection in response to a crisis in a particular financial sector, as was the case with banks in the 1930s, pension funds in the 1970s (with the PBGC), and may be the case with insurance companies in the 1990s. Second, it would shift the burden of the changes in the financial system from the general taxpayer (as is currently the case) to the holders of financial assets. This would serve to allocate the costs to those who benefit from the system.

Why Not Regulate the Financial System by Function?

Currently, the financial system is regulated along industry lines and segmented within industry. The thrift industry has its own system of regulation, as do the banking industry, the insurance industry, the securities industry, the mutual-fund industry, the farm-finance industry, credit unions, and the pension system (among others). Regulation by industry and subindustry produces many jobs for regulators and lawyers, a morass of conflicting laws and regulations for the regulated industries, and an inability of the political system to respond to changing social and economic needs in ways that minimize the misallocation of resources.

Regulating by function would have a variety of benefits. *Asset supervision* would be responsible for ensuring that the asset quality matched the published institutional objectives. *Disclosure supervision* would verify that accurate and appropriate information was being provided to the public about an institution's risks and returns so that investors could make intelligent decisions about placing their funds. A *fair-play board* (on the order of a utility regulator) would supervise the emerging information monopoly to ensure equitable access at nonmonopolistic costs. *Prudential supervision* would regulate capital structure on behalf of whatever insurance arrangements were provided. *Damage control* would be provided by the lender-of-last-resort, supporting any financial sector whose problems threatened the financial system.

In Conclusion

As the financial-services industry continues to experience massive change over the next decade, it will evolve into a new system. It will remain in the headlines, and we hope that the reader of this book will be better able to understand the news relating to the financial system. Even more important, we hope we have assisted you in appraising the multitude of ideas for changing the system and its institutions that you will encounter.

Index

191; junk, 3, 74, 75, 76, 79-80,
95-96, 98, 133; municipal, 110,
127; price of, 93; revenue, 91;
trading and markets, 92, 111
Booz Allen Hamilton, 61
Brady, Nicholas, 6, 65
Breaking Up the Bank (Bryan),
268
British Petroleum Company, 111
brokerage industry, 84, 854, 86;
commissions and fees, 85, 86,
92, 93, 158, 225; institutional,
92; real estate activities, 111
Brumbaugh, R. Dan, 22
Bryan, Lowell, 132-33, 268
Bryan, William Jennings, 40
Buchanan, Peter, 106-107, 109
Buffett, Warren, 210-11
Burke, James, 181
Burnham and company, 95, 177
Bush, George, 6, 186, 254, 255
Bush, Neil, 18

California insurance industry,
65
calls, 158-59, 160-61, 162, 164,
169
Canadian banking industry, 54,
94
capital-asset pricing model
(CAPM), 206
capital markets, 11, 13-14
Carnegie, Andrew, 113, 122
Carpenter, Michael, 103, 104
Carter, John B., 75-76, 77
cash-management accounts, 127
Castro, Fidel, 189
Cathcart, Silas S., 103
CBS common stock (in hedging
example), 158-62, 164
certificates of deposit (CDs), 48,
118-119; jumbo, 228; transferable, 220, 246
Chapman, Max, 103

Charles D. Barney & co., 177
Charter Company, 71
Chase Manhattan Bank, 63, 177,
226
Chase Manhattan Corporation,
128
checking accounts, 40, 61
Chemical Bank, 267
Chemical Bankcorp, 51
Chicago Board of Trade, 150,
168
Chicago Board Options
Exchange, 150, 168
Chrysler Coporation, 45
Chrysler Finance company, 137
Citibank, 138-41, 268
Citicorp, 74, 105, 140, 141; consumer banking services, 26-
27, 29, 267; credit cards, 45;
international activities, 193;
mortgage loans, 19, 26, 27-32
Clariden Bank, 195
Clayton & Dubilier, 97
Coldwell Banker, 41, 42
commercial paper, 47-48, 55,
133; competition for financial
services and, 59, 90, 91;
money-market investments
in, 127; yields, 119
commissions on securities trading, 85, 86, 92, 93, 158, 225
commodities
markets/exchanges, 111, 149,
169
Common market countries, 55
communications technology, 13,
230-32
community-reinvestment
requirements, 248, 273
competition, 12, 13, 82. See also
specific types of institutions
computerized loan origination
systems (CLOs), 31-32
computer (s): expert system,

new-product cycles, 82, 83, 90, 92

New York City securities firms, 108

New York Stock Exchange, 192, 225-26, 241; investment bank trading, 90; price of seats, 85-86

nonfinancial institutions, 8; commercial paper debt, 48; competition with commercial banks, 41-46, 62; mortgage markets and, 25;new business financing, 60

Norwest Bank, 129, 267

NOW accounts, 229

October 1987 crash, 4, 94, 99, 103, 110-11, 167

Office of Thrift supervision, 259, 260

Ogden, William, 50 ,51,

oil prices, See petroleum industry/petrodollars

option(s), 167; agricultural, 149, 155-58; call, 158-59, 160-61, 162, 164, 169; on common stocks, 149-50; contracts, 150-52, 164; financial example, 158-62; in/out of the money, 170; put, 159-61, 162, 164, 170; value, 150-51, 170; writing of, 171

Oxford Provident Building Association, 19

PaineWebber Inc., 100

PASS, Inc. 146

passive indexing, 206

Peabody, George, 176

Penn Square Bank, 50

Pension Benefit Guaranty Corporation (PBGC), 5, 120, 124, 250, 254, 275

pension funds, 8, 92, 147, 275; commercial paper debt, 48; corporate, 118; growth of, 118, 120, 122, 123-24, 130-31, 133; historical perspective, 119-20; industrial holdings of, 121-23; investment levels, 204; junk bonds holdings of, 96; management, 203, 204, 215; mortgage holdings of, 121; nonprofit institution, 118; role of, 121-23; tax status, 121, 131

Perella, Joseph, 108, 109, 112, 195

petroleum industry/petrodollars, 180, 188, 235, 247

Pickens, T. Boone, 97

point-of sale networks, 233, 266

Polaris Aircraft Leasing, 104

Pool mortgages, 136, 238, 139, 141, 142-43

populism, 249-51

portfolio theory, 206

Posner, Victor, 98

Power without Property (Berle/Means), 96

prepaid debit cards, 12, 233, 267

Presbyterian Minister funds, 67

prices: exercise, 158-159; hedging schemes and, 149-50; spot market, 152, 153-55; strike, 158-59

"Pricing of Options and Corporate Liabilities, The" (Black/Scholes), 150

Primerica, 105, 177

private sector, 186-194

Prodigy network, 12

Prudential-Bache Securities, 73, 82

Prudential Insurance company and subsidiaries, 32, 72-74, 77, 97, 98, 105, 268; securi-